HISTORY OF THE GERMAN ARMY

HISTORY OF THE GERMAN ARMY

KEITH SIMPSON

THE MILITARY PRESS

A BISON BOOK

Published 1985 by
The Military Press, distributed by
Crown Publishers Inc.

Produced by Bison Books Corp.
17 Sherwood Place
Greenwich, CT 06830, USA

Printed in Hong Kong

Library of Congress Cataloging in Publication Data

Simpson, Keith.
The history of the German army.

"A Bison book."
1. Germany. Heer-History. 2. Prussia. Armeee-History. 3. Germany (West). Heer-History. 4. Germany (West) Nationale Volksarmee-History. 5. Germany-History, Military. I. Title.
UA712.S66 1985 355.3'0943 85-4907
ISBN 0-517-45138-7

hgfedcba

Page 1: A panzer column pauses for regrouping during the invasion of Russia in 1941.
Page 2-3: Prussian troops storm a street barricade in Le Bourget during the Franco-Prussian War in 1870.
This page: Parade in Potsdam in January 1912 celebrating the 200th anniversary of the birth of Frederick the Great. The 1st Guard Regiment marches past.

Contents

Introduction 6

1 The Origins of the Prussian Army 8

2 The Age of Frederick the Great 22

3 Defeat and Reform 36

4 The Prussian General Staff 50

5 The Kaiser's Army 70

6 War and Revolution 88

7 The *Reichsheer* and Politics 112

8 Preparing for Blitzkrieg 126

9 Hitler's Army at War 140

10 The *Bundeswehr* and the *Nationale Volksarmee* 176

Index 190

Acknowledgments 192

Above: Blücher meets Wellington at Waterloo.
Below: *Afrika Korps* infantry advancing in 1942.

Introduction

The image of the German army provokes violently different reactions from total abhorrence of an institution epitomizing 'militarism,' through professional admiration of a technically superb fighting machine, to an emotional fascination. Symbolized by such powerful images as the *Stahlhelm*, or German steel helmet of two World wars, the 'goose-step,' or parade march, and the evocative sound of a German military band noisily playing such marches as 'Fredericus Rex' or 'Preussens Gloria.' It is claimed that the German army created the general staff system, produced the greatest military thinker, Karl von Clausewitz, and established a formidable fighting power which was only defeated after two world wars. It is sometimes forgotten, however, that there was a German military tradition before 1871, and indeed one if not two after 1945.

Before 1871 there was no such thing as a German army, and strictly speaking, even during the *Kaiserreich* of 1871-1918 there were several state contingents which made up the *Kaiserheer*. This absence of a unified German military tradition was the direct consequence of a lack of political cohesion which was rectified only in the second half of the nineteenth century by the driving force of the political, economic and military leadership of Prussia. The German military tradition before 1871 was divided between many individual German states, including the largest such as Prussia and Bavaria, and the smallest such as Jülich-Berg and Mainz. Although the history of the German army is closely identified with the history of the Prussian army, it should be remembered that other German states contributed to the German military experience.

The history of the German army did not take place in isolation, and it is possible to detect the influence of foreign armies, particularly the Austrian, Russian and French, on questions of organization, weapons and uniforms. In turn the German army has influenced many other armies and also the conduct of war.

Top: T-72 tank of the *Nationale Volksarmee* seen during a parade in East Berlin. The equipment of the NVA is in many respects the most modern of any of the Warsaw Pact countries apart from the USSR.
Above: Bundeswehr troops examine a 0.5-inch machine gun during a NATO exercise.

The Origins of the Prussian Army

History of The German Army

In the seventeenth century, 'Germany' was a geographical expression covering a bewildering array of some two thousand principalities, cities and independent duchies who came collectively under the nominal authority of the Holy Roman Emperor, who was usually the reigning head of the Austrian house of Hapsburg. The problem for these German states was their geographical position bordered by powerful neighbors – France in the west, Sweden in the north, Poland and Russia in the east and Austria in the south. Germany was devastated by the Thirty Years' War 1618-1648, which owed its origins to dynastic and religious conflicts. Powerful French, Swedish and Austrian armies fought over German territory, and the majority of German states followed the changing fortunes of war by moving from one alliance to another.

The larger German states raised their own armies usually by hiring mercenaries while the majority of petty principalities had ludicrously small armies or none at all. The important military characteristic of European armies before and during the Thirty Years' War was the fact that they were based on the mercenary band. Few European monarchs could afford to maintain any standing army and to fight wars had to rely upon the recruitment of mercenaries who were managed by leaders who were the commercial proprietors of such bands. These mercenary bands took service in one army or another as a result of financial rather than political or national considerations.

The most powerful and successful mercenary leader of the age, until he was murdered in 1634, was Albrecht von Wallenstein, an ambitious Czech adventurer who became a freebooting Imperial general. Superficially, raising armies by hiring mercenary bands appeared attractive to both princes and their people. Armies in peacetime were expensive to maintain and required billets and food. Mercenaries could be hired for a fixed contract and paid off when no longer required. Unfortunately, in practice, such a simple arrangement rarely worked. Mercenaries were difficult to control, motivated almost entirely by monetary considerations, and regarded the territory they were occupying as a legitimate source for looting and foraging, regardless of the fact that it might belong to the prince for whom they were nominally soldiering. At the conclusion of the Thirty Years' War the princes and estates of Germany were desperate to disband their mercenary armies and expel them from their territories.

After the Thirty Years' War the characteristics of armies gradually changed with the development of the 'standing army,' a force of soldiers kept in being in time of peace as well as war,

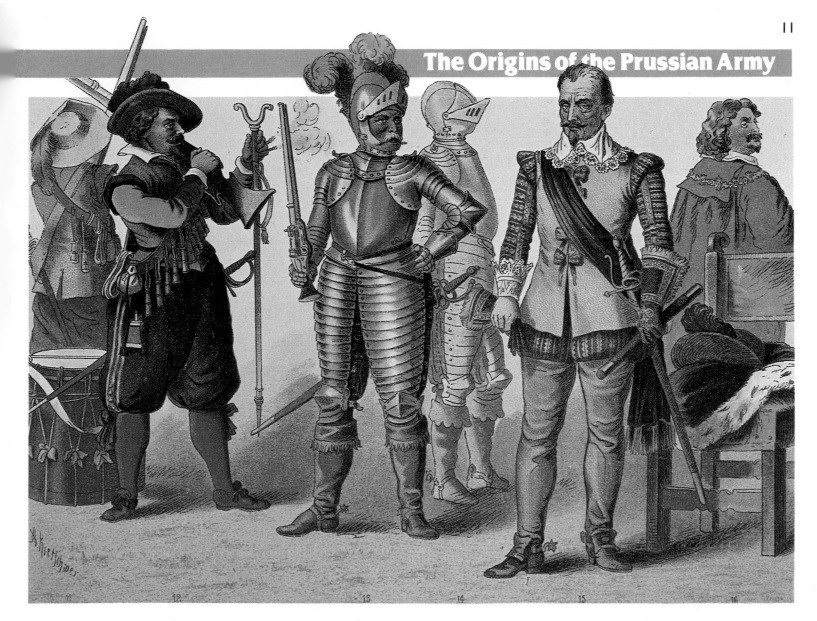

Page 8-9: Field Marshal von Derfflinger, commander of the Brandenburg-Prussian army at the battle of Fehrbellin, 28 June 1675.
Above: Albrecht von Wallenstein, second from right, with Cuirassiers and Musketeers during the Thirty Years War.
Left: George William, Elector of Brandenburg 1595-1640, father of Frederick William, the 'Great Elector.'
Below left: German states' soldiers during the Thirty Years War.

controlled and recruited by absolute monarchs who could use them as a coercive political force at home as well as an instrument of foreign policy. The transition from a mercenary to a professional standing army in most European states took place over some fifty years, and even in the largest standing armies, such as those of France and Austria, there was always a mercenary element. Louis XIV of France symbolized the absolute monarch with a centralized government under royal control which directed national policy. The French army gradually evolved from a variety of mercenary bands controlled by independent leaders into a disciplined force whose officers gave obedience and loyalty to the monarch in return for royal pay and privileges.

The need to secure national defense, the problems of European insecurity and the desire to imitate the absolutism of France encouraged the larger European states to establish standing armies. One of the larger German states which had fought in the Thirty Years' War was Bavaria. After 1648 the Bavarian army of 20,000 soldiers was disbanded at the request of the estates, and only a few essential troops were retained. The Elector of Bavaria slowly acquired a small standing army of nearly 2000 troops by 1674. During the War of the Bavarian Succession the small Bavarian army did not perform well. Despite having a relatively large territory and population, Bavaria was to maintain an insignificant army which made only a small contribution to state defense other than providing the Elector with a useful force to intimidate his subjects.

By 1675, the Elector of Saxony had raised a small standing army of some 8000 soldiers which by the turn of the century numbered 20,000. Such a significant military force was regarded by the Elector as a necessity to counter the growing power of neighboring Prussia. Unfortunately, maintaining a relatively large army tempted the Electors of Saxony to participate in an extravagant and ambitious way in European affairs. The result was defeat and occupation by the Swedes in the Great Northern War.

Smaller German states such as Württemberg, Jülich-Berg and Weimar, frequently maintained ludicrously large standing armies in relation to the size of their population and economic strength. Faced by the formidable French army they were easily brushed aside, but such defeats failed to deter their royal masters who firmly believed that a standing army symbolized the ultimate physical power and authority of an absolute monarch.

The majority of German princes found that they could not afford to maintain a standing army after the Thirty Years' War. To ease their financial burden, they hired out their armies or just individual regiments to larger states. This hiring out of armies differed from the old mercenary tradition because governments contracted with each other and not with mercenary leaders, and because the hiring states placed the rented soldiers within their own standing armies. The Dukes of Hesse-Cassel and Württemberg hired out regiments from their own armies to other princes, and whilst those of Hesse-Cassel enjoyed a high reputation for military efficiency and bravery, those of Württemberg did not.

Among the main exponents of the use of foreign troops were the rulers of Brandenburg-Prussia, who were forced to man their armies with whatever was available. When Frederick William became Elector of Brandenburg in 1640 he found himself the ruler of five separate territories — Brandenburg, the counties of Mark and Ravensburg, the Duchy of Cleves, and Prussia. These territories were spread across northern Germany and separated by

Above: Messenger bringing news of the peace concluding the Thirty Years War in 1648.
Left: Musketeers and pikemen repel a cavalry charge during the Thirty Years War.
Below left: Brandenburg-Prussian soldiers engaging the Swedish rearguard after the battle of Fehrbellin.

other states. During the Thirty Years' War Brandenburg was totally ravaged, and Frederick William found his inheritance threatened by the rivalry of France, Sweden, Poland and Austria. He was determined to unite his territories and establish political independence from his powerful neighbors.

Following the signing of the Treaty of Westphalia which concluded the Thirty Years' War in 1648, Frederick William and his advisers proceeded with caution in establishing a standing army. The first requirement was to organize all the finances and resources of the state toward this objective, and to that end, Frederick William broke the power of the noble assemblies and began to colonize and reclaim vast tracts of land in Prussia. Having allowed his old army to be reduced to a cadre after 1648, Frederick William carefully established the beginnings of a small standing army, garrisoned on the lower Rhine, recruited mainly from Dutchmen and Prussians.

Frederick William had been influenced as a young man through serving with Dutch forces, and he combined this military knowledge with lessons drawn from the reform of the French army by Louis XIV. Frederick William created new regiments and appointed their colonels, and although he was unable to eradicate the practice of regimental officers then being appointed by those very colonels, he began the process of binding the officers of his army to the person of the sovereign. This was inevitably a slow and uneven business as the majority of officers and men making up the Elector's army were recruited on the open market, and at first the local nobility were hostile to Frederick William's policies. His most effective military commander, Field Marshal von Derfflinger, was an Austrian of humble birth, who had served as a mercenary during the Thirty Years' War before joining the service of the Elector. Within certain constraints, Frederick William was very successful ultimately in maintaining a peacetime army of 7000 troops and in war of 15,000 troops. Eventually, the strength of the army stood at 30,000 troops.

Despite Frederick William's introduction of a uniform system of taxation, and equally importantly, an effective method of collection, he never had sufficient revenue to maintain a real standing army. Thus he was forced to resort, like other German princes, to foreign subsidies, which by their very nature, involved intricate maneuvering in foreign policy, and frequently disastrous consequences as alliances changed. In 1674 Brandenburg-Prussia had been a frustrated member of a Great Coalition against France. While the bulk of the Elector's army was in winter quarters in Franconia, the Swedes joined the French and invaded Brandenburg. It was the 70 year old Derfflinger who took command of the Elector's army and moved it north into Brandenburg by a series of forced marches, having first divided the army into small units.

Above: German officer and drummer, early seventeenth century.

The Elector's army surprised the Swedes who were unaware of their own numerical superiority, and they evacuated the fortress of Rathenow and began to retreat. Derfflinger pursued the Swedes and attacked their encampment at Fehrbellin on 28 June 1675. Although outnumbered and weak in artillery, Derfflinger's cavalry and infantry defeated the Swedes, pursued them further and inflicted another defeat on them at Tilsit. By the standards of the time the battle of Fehrbellin was a small affair, and the ultimate political consequences were not particularly favorable to the Elector. But the victory indicated to other states that Frederick William's army was to be taken seriously, and Fehrbellin became the first battle honor of the Prussian army.

Frederick William died in 1688. Although he had failed to achieve all his political ambitions – the unification of his separate territories; independence from foreign subsidies and security against invasion – he did leave behind him an army of 30,000 men and the nucleus of a centralized military bureaucracy which were to become the basis of the future Prussian state. Frederick William became known as the 'Great' Elector.

His successor, Frederick III, was quite unlike his father. Determined to follow the baroque traditions of the French monarchy, Frederick III nearly bankrupted his territories in providing a magnificent court. This extravagance combined with the cost of maintaining a standing army of 30,000 troops, necessitated the continuation of foreign subsidies and the hiring out of soldiers to other monarchs. And yet Frederick III did achieve some important successes relevant to the development of the Prussian army. In 1701 he persuaded the emperor to raise him to the authority of king in Prussia and thus became King Frederick I. He was also astute enough to encourage the able Prince Leopold of Anhalt-Dessau, later known as *der Alte Dessauer*, to reform the army along modern lines, including the introduction of the flintlock musket and new infantry drills.

During the War of the Spanish Succession 1701-1713, Frederick I was obliged to support the emperor with 8000 troops

Above: '*Der alte Dessauer*' at the battle of Hochstadt, 13 August 1704.
Left: The Great Elector at the battle of Fehrbellin.
Bottom far left: Parade of the Guard in Berlin during the reign of the Great Elector.
Bottom left: Prussian army discipline in the eighteenth century.

against the French. Prussian troops were deployed piecemeal during this war and saw action at the battles of Blenheim, Turin, Cassano and Ramillies. The Duke of Marlborough and Prince Eugene both praised the military skill of *der Alte Dessauer*, and Prussian troops were noted for their bravery and discipline, unlike many of the troops from other German states. But the Prussian contribution to the allied war effort was small, and in political terms, Frederick I gained few territorial advantages. In 1713 Frederick I died and was buried amidst scenes of baroque splendor, leaving his son an army of 39,000 troops and considerable debts.

The new king of Brandenburg-Prussia, Frederick William I, was totally different in character and style from his father. His strong Lutheran beliefs and natural piety soon made him reject the ostentatious trappings of his father's court and he based his life and

Above: Frederick William, the Great Elector of Brandenburg-Prussia, 1640-88.
Below: Prussian Dragoons of the Great Elector's army formed up for a formal parade.

History of The German Army

Far left: King Frederick William I of Prussia with pressed recruits for his '*lange Kerls.*'
Left: Prussian edict stating the consequences for desertion and for helping deserters from the army in 1726.
Bottom left: 'Running the gauntlet' in the army of Frederick the Great.

policies on austerity and sobriety. However, Frederick William was determined to continue his father's and grandfather's policy of making their territories politically and militarily independent of foreign powers. By a series of drastic economy measures Frederick William saved enough money to increase the size of his army within a few years from 39,000 to 45,000 troops, and at the same time maintain them without foreign subsidies. He continued to develop a centralized administration for royal government, and ultimately created a General Directory responsible for the entire internal and financial administration of the state, including army supplies and military finance.

In breaking with the baroque life style of his father's court, Frederick William was rejecting also the influence and outlook of France. This became formalized in 1718 with the *Stillbruch*, or break in style, when Frederick William adopted a plain and sober military uniform for his personal dress. This combined with his interest in military matters earned him the nickname of '*le roi sergent.*' Frederick William also began to organize the army so that it would become an effective military force which would obey its royal master without question.

Recruitment was a major problem for the Prussian army as with most other European armies, and soldiers were usually recruited by force. The harshness of Prussian military service meant that desertion was endemic. During Frederick William's reign some 31,000 men fled from the army. To prevent desertion, Frederick William resorted to the use of the death penalty in addition to the punishment of flogging, and for a brief period even offered a general pardon in the hope of enticing deserters back into the army. Prussian recruiting officers were the scourge of their own lands as well as those of other German states. A combination of

Above: 'Der alte Dessauer.' Field Marshal Leopold zu Anhalt-Dessau, a loyal officer and servant of the kings of Brandenburg-Prussia.
Below: The Expansion of Brandenburg-Prussia, 1713-95 showing the gains made in war and by diplomacy.

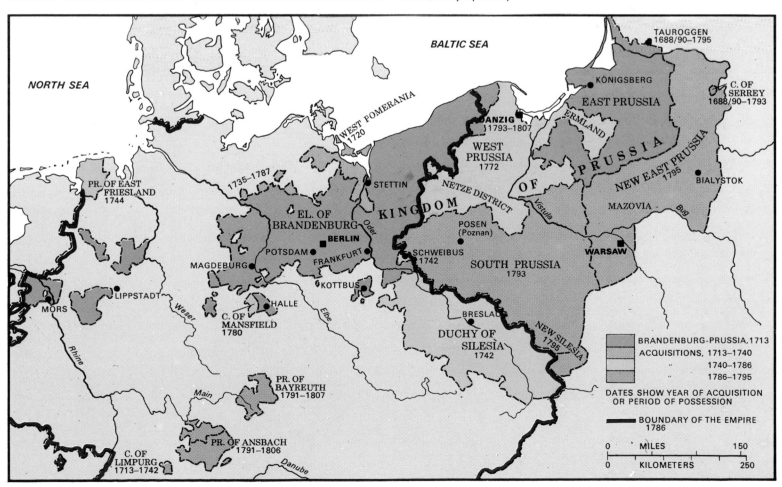

History of The German Army

Main picture: Frederick William I casting a discerning eye over new recruits for his '*lange Kerls*.'
Bottom left: Frederick William I and his cronies enjoying some rough humor in the 'Tobacco Council.'

external and internal pressures forced Frederick William to find a new method of recruitment. The external pressure came from the rulers of foreign states who protested about the activities of Prussian recruiting officers in their territories. The internal pressure was created by the agrarian population fleeing the land to escape enlistment. This population movement damaged Prussia's economy and therefore the financial foundations of the royal state.

Frederick William's *Cantonal Règlement* of 1733 divided the country into regimental cantons and recruiting districts. In each cantonment there was a compulsory enlistment of the youth, who after basic training did three months military service per year, and were then placed 'on leave,' which enabled them to return to work. It was possible to purchase a substitute and the bourgeoisie were excluded from service. By this method, Frederick William was able to man his army without disturbing the Prussian agrarian economy. At the same time the recruitment of foreigners remained an important method of filling the ranks of the Prussian army where they were regarded as 'cannon-fodder.'

Frederick William began to integrate the *Junker* class into his officer corps and thus bind them to his state. Many unsavory characters and foreign adventurers were weeded out of the officer corps, and replaced by the Prussian nobility who at first were forced to serve as an expression of their vassalage to the king. By wearing a simple uniform himself, Frederick William identified service in the officer corps of the Prussian army with nobility and honor. After the *Cantonal Règlement* of 1733, the bond between the king and his officers and in turn their authority over locally recruited soldiers was enhanced by the fact that it perpetuated the feudal relationship, as officers and men from the same regimental cantonment were at the same time landowners and peasants.

Frederick William and his adviser, *der Alte Dessauer*, also turned their attention to the more practical aspects of military reform. The royal parks of Berlin and Potsdam were turned into parade grounds and Berlin began to take on the atmosphere of a

Above left: Musketeer (1682) and drummer (1700) of the Bavarian army.
Below left: Officer and Grenadiers of the *Potsdamer Riesengarde* of Frederick William I's Prussian army.
Below: Frederick the Great, while Crown Prince, watching a battalion drilling.
Above: Grenadier, Cuirassier and General of the Württemberg army, 1730.

giant barracks. The first Prussian hussars were recruited, the nucleus of a Prussian armaments industry was created, the iron ramrod was introduced, and new patterns of muskets and swords established that were to serve the Prussian army for the rest of the century. During this period there were also significant developments in the uniform of the Brandenburg-Prussian soldier. The uniform consisted of coat, waistcoat, breeches, stockings, shoes, and hat or coat. Although there was a variety of colors for coats, generally the dominant color became blue, and this was to remain the historic color of the Prussian soldier until 1914.

One eccentric element of Frederick William's military activities was his grotesque obsession with the physical size of soldiers. He tended to equate military prowess with stature, and he recruited a 3000 strong regiment of giant grenadiers, his '*lange Kerle*,' from all over Europe, some came voluntarily, others were kidnapped, and some were given as gifts to him by other princes. The shortest was over six feet in height, whilst the tallest was nearly eight feet.

Despite all his warlike preparations, Frederick William was extremely reluctant to use his army in battle. He achieved a major dynastic aim, the possession of Stettin and control of the River Oder, by diplomacy and intrigue. In 1734 he did send a contingent of troops to support the emperor against the French on the Rhine, but this was an insignificant campaign.

When he died in 1740, Frederick William left his son a formidable legacy. He had consolidated his territories and strengthened the institutions of the Prussian state, expanded the economy, militarized agrarian society, introduced a successful system of recruitment, reformed and expanded the army and forged the link between the Prussian nobility and service to the king through membership of the officer corps. Finally, he had established a particular Prussian style of behavior and attitude of mind which encompassed piety, duty, obedience and endurance.

In 1740 the Prussian army of 83,000 men consumed 80 percent of the total state budget and was maintained without foreign subsidies. It was the largest individual German state army and the best disciplined, but as yet without any real military experience.

The Age of
Frederick the Great

History of The German Army

Eighteenth century warfare was largely defensive, because all states, large or small, were concerned primarily with the maintenance of the status quo, which was a result of the experience of the Thirty Years' War. Military commanders wanted to fight at an advantage and subsist off their opponent. The most important aim in war was to maintain an army intact as long as possible and avoid battle. This was achieved usually by maneuvering behind lines of defensive fortifications and strong-points waiting for an opportunity to strike at the enemy's lines of communication and thus cut him off from his base and supplies. Only if a commander enjoyed superiority of numbers and an advantageous position would he knowingly risk battle.

Once armies became locked in battle the outcome became a very uncertain business. The main element of battle was usually the direct exchange of musket volleys between opposing infantry at point-blank range with the supplement of cannon fire from artillery. Such confrontations were to be avoided because of the inevitable casualties for both sides, and each casualty represented a loss of investment. The eighteenth century was a period of Enlightened Absolutism and Limited War – that is until Frederick II succeeded his father as king of Brandenburg-Prussia in 1740.

Frederick had had a difficult relationship with his bad tempered father, and for many years had been the subject of insults, and at one point was nearly executed. However, as Crown Prince he learned the rudiments of soldiering and delighted in the company of such veteran officers as Leopold of Anhalt-Dessau and General

Schwerin. Frederick was to follow the policy of his father with regard to internal affairs, but in foreign affairs he was determined to seize opportunities for territorial aggrandisement.

The Prussian army was to fight four wars during the twenty-six year reign of Frederick II – the First Silesian War 1740-42; the Second Silesian War 1744-45; the Seven Years' War 1756-63 and the War of the Bavarian Succession 1778-79. This collective military experience was to give the Prussian army a formidable reputation and earn Frederick II the title of 'Great.' But this was achieved at some cost, as the Prussian army lost 180,000 men during the Seven Years' War alone. It is estimated that many Prussian regiments had a manpower turnover of four or five times during the reign of Frederick the Great.

Above: General Hans Joachim von Zieten, 'The Hussar King,' who was one of Frederick the Greats notable cavalry generals.
Left: Seydlitz at the battle of Rossbach, 5 November 1757.
Below: Frederick the Great, 1712-86.
Pages 22-23: Frederick the Great watches the Prussian infantry repel a cavalry advance at the battle of Kunersdorf, 12 August 1759.

Above: Parade of a Prussian Guard battalion inspected by Frederick the Great.
Left: Hussar officer, Cuirassier and Mounted Grenadier of the Prussian army, in uniforms of the Seven Years' War.

Unlike his contemporaries, Frederick was unable to fight limited wars. He miscalculated badly the reaction of the Austrians when he seized the province of Silesia in 1740, and in later years he found himself at a disadvantage fighting wars against powerful coalitions. This forced Frederick to take the offensive to prevent his enemies from bringing their superior forces to bear, and thus he sought quick, decisive battles. And yet the military reputation gained by Frederick and the Prussian army was based on some uneven results. At times both Frederick's strategic and tactical judgement were flawed and at times the performance of the Prussian army was indifferent. Frederick suffered a number of major defeats, and during the Seven Years' War came close to disaster, but time and time again he was saved by his own genius, the harsh but effective discipline of his soldiers and the confusion of his enemies.

Within a year of becoming king, Frederick had increased the strength of his army to 100,000 men, a figure that was to rise to 143,000 in 1756, 160,000 in 1768 and 190,000 in 1786. But this was not a continuous natural increase in strength, because during each major war the greater part of the Prussian army was burnt out. At any given moment half the Prussian army was recruited from foreigners who were regarded by Frederick as being totally expendable. At times he resorted to the mass impressment of captured soldiers to augment his army, something he did with captured Saxon troops in 1756. The result was disastrous as the Saxons deserted at the earliest opportunity.

Frederick relied heavily upon the total commitment and loyalty of his officers who faced the prospect of an early and painful death or an impoverished old age. In exchange, the Prussian officer

Above: Death of Field Marshal von Schwerin at the battle of Prague, 6 May 1757, whilst rallying his regiment.

enjoyed a greater prestige in society than any other contemporary officer. Frederick continued his father's policy of identifying totally the officers with the monarch, and the fact that he wore a simple blue uniform enabled all officers to say that they carried the *Königs Rock*, 'the King's coat.' In theory, the Prussian officer corps was a closed circle of nobles, but Frederick was never able or willing to operate the system with complete rigidity. Basically, he decided whether an individual candidate met with the necessary criteria, and during his later wars he was reduced to commissioning many bourgeois officers to fill the depleted ranks of the officer corps. But at the end of the Seven Years' War Frederick purged his officer corps of bourgeois members. Social exclusiveness, whilst never quite as absurd as that pertaining to the French officer corps of the *ancien régime*, however, did become a characteristic of the Prussian officer corps.

Frederick was very much the head of state, commander-in-chief of the army and chief of staff all in one. This was because he wanted to retain ultimate power and because he never had sufficient faith in his senior commanders ever to let them exercise really independent command. Leopold of Anhalt-Dessau, Schwerin and Keith were considered efficient, but Frederick did not encourage a great deal of initiative amongst his senior officers.

Frederick awarded successful or deserving officers with land and money, and bestowed in considerable profusion the Order *Pour le Mérite*, which he founded in 1740. There was no specific criteria for the award, which could be given for bravery, a useful memorandum or merely having a smartly turned out company. Frederick was just as quick to punish officers who displeased him by imprisonment, cashiering and ultimately execution. Although there were a number of officers, like Ewald von Kleist, Prince Henry and General von Retzow, who were genuinely interested in their profession and intellectual pursuits, the majority of officers were boorish and narrow-minded. Frederick's officers

were not motivated by patriotism, and whether Prussian or foreign they were bound by loyalty and duty to the person of the king.

For the rank and file of the Prussian army, Frederick still relied upon foreign mercenaries to make up half the strength, and the rest were provided from the cantonal system. Frederick made sure that this drain on manpower caused the least possible inconvenience to the Prussian economy, and there was a growing list of exemptions. Whilst Frederick believed that some of his subjects, like the Pomeranians, made excellent soldiers, others, like the East Prussians, had little to recommend them. Frederick required blind obedience from his soldiers, and 'in general the common soldier must fear his officer more than the enemy.' Officers and NCOs frequently beat their soldiers with swords, sticks, spontoons and fists. Apart from imprisonment and flogging and branding, the Prussian authorities were most fond of imposing the running of the gauntlet, particularly for desertion. Although virtually every other European army, and for that matter navy, maintained a similar disciplinary code the Prussian one was noted for its harshness. Discipline and order among the rank and file was also maintained by a large and diligent body of NCOs. Frederick selected many of his NCOs in person from among long service soldiers who had an air of authority, and he raised their status by giving them a distinctive uniform and additional pay. Frederick's reliance on NCOs did not extend to commissioning many of them, but it began a tradition for which future German armies were to be noted.

The basic organization of the Prussian army at this time was roughly similar to other eighteenth century armies, with a division between infantry, cavalry and artillery. The infantry regiment

consisted of about 1700 men, and was split into two battalions. There were distinctions between reliable and aggressive troops like the Grenadier battalions and the Garde, the basic Fusilier regiments who varied in quality, down to rather shabby garrison troops. Unlike the Austrians, Frederick never really established a force of light infantry beyond a few Jäger and some Free battalions. This was to place his army at a disadvantage when it attempted to discover the movements of the Austrians who screened their main force with light infantry and irregular troops like the Croats who also posed a continual threat to Frederick's lines of communication.

Frederick dressed his infantry in fairly skimpy uniforms and armed them with a clumsy and inaccurate musket. But Frederick was not concerned with accuracy of fire, but rather with the volume of fire, and certainly in his first campaign wanted his infantry to close with the enemy as quickly as possible using the bayonet. Frederick was experimenting continually with infantry drill and tactics, and in the 'oblique order of battle' he believed he had found the answer to the problem of having sufficient superiority at the decisive point on one or other wing of an infantry line. Any complex movement on the battlefield such as one calling for a sudden wheeling turn required considerable march discipline. Frederick taught his soldiers to march at different rates and to keep in step, only changing the rate of march at the word of command of an officer or NCO. This gave the Prussian army a degree of mobility and flexibility over many of its opponents. These tactics and drills were only slowly developed by Frederick through his military campaigning and by repetitive practice through drill and on maneuvers. Faced with an enemy who was not thrown by such tactics, or a breakdown of discipline among

Left: Officer and Grenadier of a Prussian Guard battalion, 1760.
Below: A romanticized nineteenth century print of the charge of the Prussian Cuirassiers during the battle of Freiburg, 29 October 1762.

his own troops, or unfavorable terrain, then the whole exercise could end in failure. Frederick's tactics were not new, he had learned a lot from studying military history and by observing other military commanders, but he did put the sum total of this into action. Combined with the speed with which Prussian infantry delivered their fire, this tactic appeared to many foreign observers to indicate that the Prussian army was the main innovator in the art of war in Europe in the middle of the eighteenth century.

Frederick's reorganization and expansion of his cavalry was a decisive improvement in the fighting capability of the Prussian army. There were broadly three types of cavalry, the cuirassiers who with their powerful horses and iron breastplates were the heavy cavalry whose tasks were to crush the enemy cavalry and the flanks of the infantry; the dragoons, who combined firepower with mobility; and the hussars, who formed a category of light cavalry. During the First Silesian War, Frederick had been horrified to see how the Austrian cavalry ran rings round the Prussian cavalry. Over the next twenty years Frederick and his advisers reorganized the cavalry and worked to teach a charge which combined speed and weight. Frederick was fortunate to command a number of brilliant cavalry officers who trained and led his cavalry, including Hans Joachim von Zieten, 'The Hussar King,' and Friedrich Wilhelm von Seydlitz. The Prussian cavalry not only

Above: The battle of Rossbach, 5 November 1757, a spectacular Prussian victory over the French and Imperial armies which were routed at a cost of a few hundred Prussian casualties.

became effective in battle but were used as 'whippers in' for the army, dealing with stragglers and deserters.

Frederick took only a limited interest in artillery and engineers, mainly because their occupation was unglamorous and their officers bourgeois. Although he was to make brilliant use of his fortresses, Frederick did not show the same attention to artillery development, and this was a major area of weakness in the Prussian army.

Frederick controlled everything to do with staff work just as he did with finance. The responsibility for what would later be called general staff work was divided between two departments, those of the *Generalquartiermeister* and those of the *Generaladjutant.* The post of *Generalquartiermeister* had been established in 1657 by the Great Elector who had copied the Swedish model of having one officer and a staff to plan the movements of the army. Under Frederick the *Generalquartiermeister* and his staff were concerned with intelligence, quartering and devising orders of battle. The staff of the *Generaladjutant* managed the army as an institution, dealing with reviews and maneuvers, pensions and records. Despite the expansion of work caused by the growth of the army

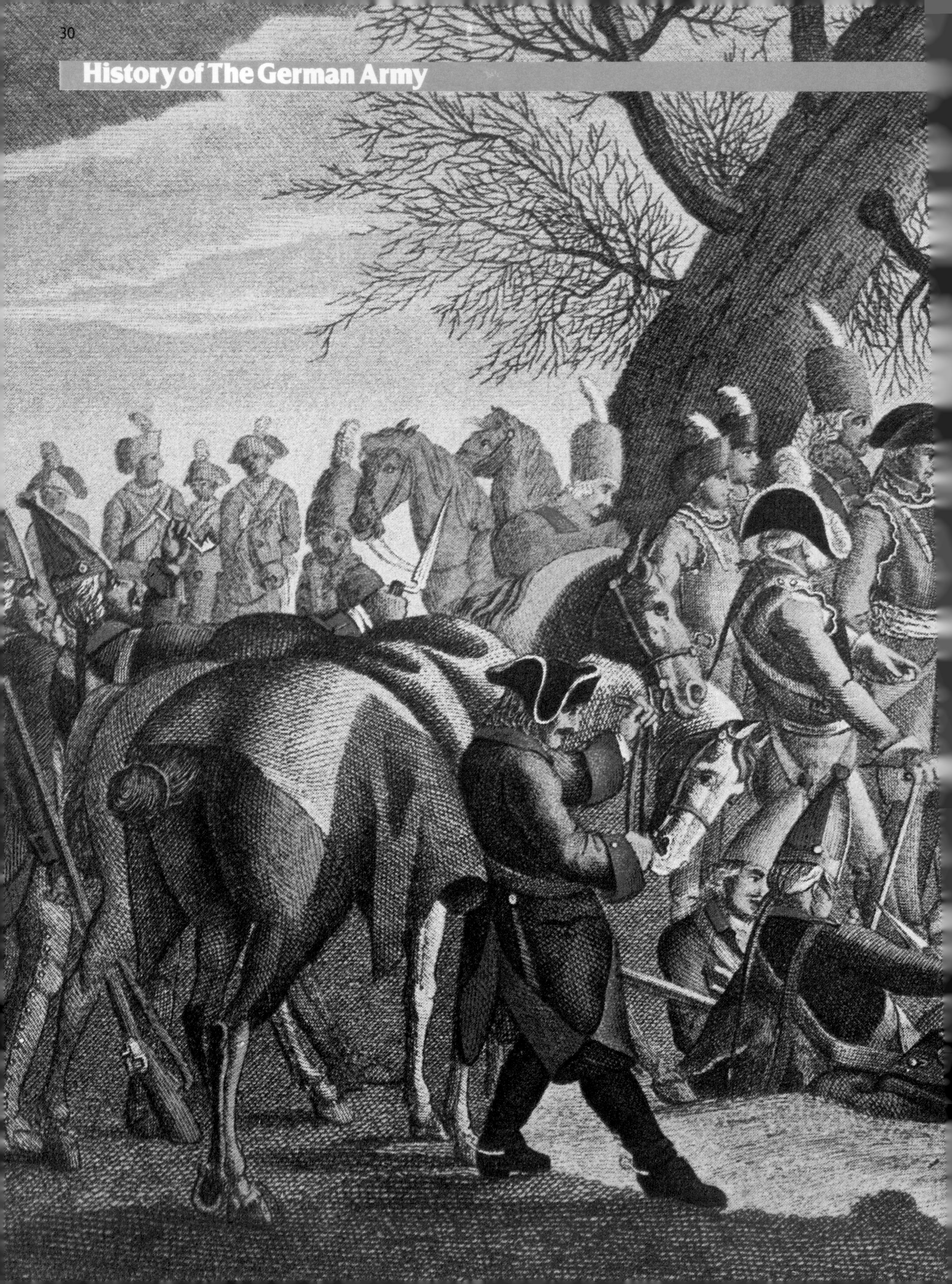

The Age of Frederick the Great

Frederick the Great at the battle of Torgau, 3 November 1760.

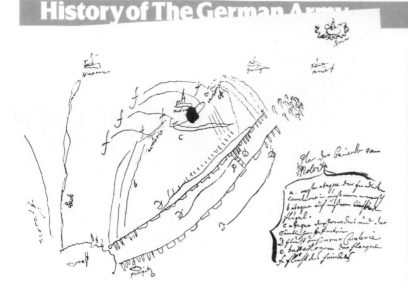

Above: Frederick the Great's own sketch map of his plan for the battle of Mollwitz, 10 April 1741.
Right: Von Zieten reporting to Frederick at Bunzelwitz, September 1761.
Far right: Battle of Hohenfriedberg, 5 June 1745.

and the course of the war, Frederick attempted personally to control every detail.

The military reputation of the Prussian army hung in the balance during the first major engagement of the First Silesian War. After Frederick's troops had occupied Silesia against light Austrian resistance, they were surprised near the village of Mollwitz in April 1741. Frederick attacked the Austrians early in the morning, but the Austrian cavalry soon overwhelmed the slow-moving Prussian cavalry, and it was only the discipline of the Prussian infantry which broke the Austrian attack and forced them to retreat. Frederick had retired from the battle somewhat hurriedly following the defeat of his cavalry. After the battle Frederick immediately began to attend to the weaknesses revealed.

During the Second Silesian War Frederick and his army achieved a decisive victory over an Austrian and Saxon army at the

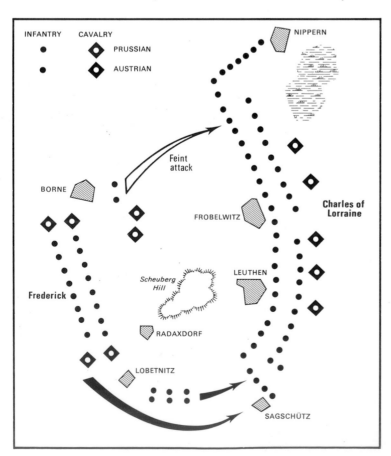

Right: Field Marshal Herzog Ferdinand of Brunswick, 1721-92.
Left: The Prussian attack at Leuthen, 7 December 1757.

battle of Hohenfriedberg on 5 June 1745. Frederick surprised the Saxons after a night march which took his troops past the Austrian camp. The Saxons were beaten by the Prussian infantry, while on their right flank the Austrian line was broken by Prussian cavalry in an action which included a magnificent charge by the Bayreuth Dragoons. The success of the Prussian infantry attack against the Saxons confirmed Frederick in his mistaken tactical belief that an enemy position could be taken by an infantry charge with fixed bayonets without opening fire or checking the march. This ignored the fact that in this battle the supporting fire had come from the battalions on either flank.

During the Seven Years' War the fortunes of Frederick and the Prussian army ebbed and flowed with the tide of politics and battles. Frederick was forced continually to attack his enemies before they combined and annihilated his army. He won significant victories at Prague, Rossbach and Leuthen in 1757, but at Kolin in the same year, and at Zorndorf and Hochkirch in 1758 his army suffered defeat or heavy losses in attritional battles.

When Frederick the Great died in 1786 he left an impressive legacy to his nephew. In territorial terms, Prussia had expanded with the acquisition of Silesia and West Prussia as a result of

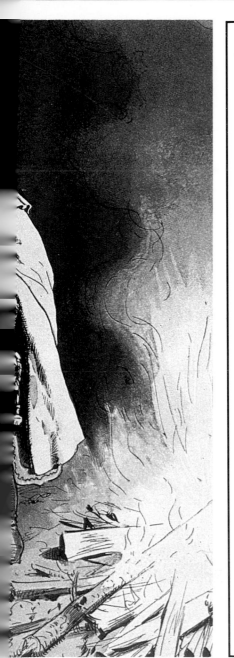

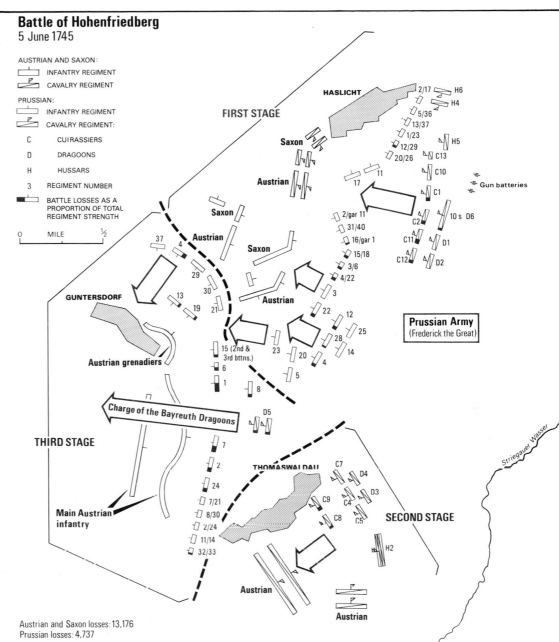

Battle of Hohenfriedberg
5 June 1745

AUSTRIAN AND SAXON:

INFANTRY REGIMENT

CAVALRY REGIMENT

PRUSSIAN:

INFANTRY REGIMENT

CAVALRY REGIMENT:

C   CUIRASSIERS

D   DRAGOONS

H   HUSSARS

3   REGIMENT NUMBER

BATTLE LOSSES AS A PROPORTION OF TOTAL REGIMENT STRENGTH

0   MILE   ½

HASLICHT

FIRST STAGE

Saxon

Austrian

Saxon

Austrian

Saxon

Austrian

GUNTERSDORF

Austrian grenadiers

THIRD STAGE

Charge of the Bayreuth Dragoons

Main Austrian infantry

THOMASWALDAU

SECOND STAGE

Gun batteries

Prussian Army
(Frederick the Great)

Striegauer Wasser

Austrian

Austrian

Austrian and Saxon losses: 13,176
Prussian losses: 4,737

military conquest. The Prussian army of 190,000 troops was regarded by most contemporaries to be the finest of its kind in Europe. Other monarchs copied Prussian discipline, drill, tactics and read the military writing of Frederick the Great. The victories of the Prussian army at Rossbach and Leuthen were to inspire many Germans who were beginning to think in terms of national consciousness. Frederick became a legend in his own lifetime. The military reputation acquired by Frederick the Great and his army was important in influencing the French army of the *ancien régime* to adopt Prussian drill and tactics just before the revolution. Mad Tsar Peter III of Russia became so besotted with Frederician influences that he dressed his army in Prussian uniforms.

And yet the Frederician legacy was flawed. In the aftermath of the Seven Years' War Frederick had attempted to make good the numerical losses in his army and to instill the old traditions of discipline, loyalty and obedience. Instead of creating an army which reflected the lessons of war, Frederick became obsessed totally with instilling a code of unthinking inflexible discipline. The Prussian officer corps, inculcated with an intense personal loyalty towards Frederick and almost unquestioning obedience was content to ossify having survived the bloody business of war. The army which Frederick bequeathed to his successor was a conservative and inward looking institution.

Although Frederick the Great and the Prussian army symbol-

ized German military experience in the eighteenth century, there were other traditions. Apart from the fact that Frederick's recruiting officers filled the Prussian army with thousands of recruits from other German states, many Germans fought against Frederick either in Austrian or French service, hired out for dynastic or financial considerations. Some of Frederick's victories were due to the unimpressive performance of German state armies, such as the Saxons at Hohenfriedberg and the Württembergers at Rossbach and Leuthen.

The British also had an interest in hiring German mercenaries, not least because of the dynastic links with Hanover. The British had soon realized that it was more economical to hire German troops for war either in Europe or overseas than maintain a large standing army.

An Anglo-Hanoverian army fought in Europe during the Seven Years' War, and during the course of the American War of Independence, the British hired over 32,000 German mercenaries. British troops in Minorca and Gibraltar were relieved by 2400 Hanoverians, whilst 17,000 troops from Hesse-Cassel, 6000 troops from Brunswick, 2500 from Ansbach-Bayreuth, 1200 from Waldeck and 1100 from Anhalt-Zerbst were to serve in America. A large number of individual Germans were to fight on the side of the rebels, and Washington was grateful to have the advice of Friedrich Wilhelm von Steuben, who had served in the Prussian army during the Seven Years' War. Steuben was to write his famous *Regulations for the Order and Discipline of the Troops of the United States Army* in 1778-9 based upon the memory of Frederick the Great's Prussian Infantry Field Manual.

Above: View of a Prussian army encampment, 1741.
Above right: Frederick the Great at the bloody battle of Zorndorf, 25 August 1758, a costly victory over the Russians.
Right: The Prussian Grenadiers at the battle of Leuthen, perhaps the best example of Frederick's theory of the 'oblique order' in action.
Below: Frederick the Great on the night before the battle of Lobositz, 1 October 1756.

History of The German Army

There is a common belief that the most radical changes in strategy and tactics and the involvement of the masses in war came about as a result of the French Revolution and the influence of Napoleon Bonaparte. But in the decade before the French Revolution attempts were made to change the accepted formal discipline of war as perfected by Frederick the Great. Unfortunately, Frederick's successor, his nephew who became King Frederick William II, did not have the ruthless determination of his uncle with regard to military matters. His attempts to modify the highly conservative and rigid system inherited from Frederick the Great were not very successful in the face of complacency and reaction amongst the Frederician officer corps. Nonetheless, during the reign of Frederick William II a number of fusilier regiments were converted into light infantry and a few limited administrative reforms were passed. The king established a reform commission in 1788 under Field Marshal von Mollendorf which was concerned with the disruptive effect on the economy of the recruiting system. Although the principle of universal service was propounded, nothing was achieved, and the officer corps remained a preserve of the nobility while the rank and file were recruited from foreign mercenaries and rural recruits were provided by the cantonal system.

The French Revolution in 1789 shocked the monarchical system of Europe with its attack on the principle of monarchy, the collapse of order and the unleashing of popular and nationalistic passions. In 1791, the Austrians, Prussians and Saxons decided to join forces and intervene against the revolution. The campaign began in 1792 with the allied army under the Duke of Brunswick arrogantly confident that its discipline and experience would triumph over the revolutionary rabble which purported to represent the army of France. However, at the battle of Valmy on 20 September 1792, the Prussian army suffered a nasty shock when the French revolutionary army not only withstood a heavy artillery bombardment but successfully launched a counter-attack, forcing the allies back across the Rhine. The Prussians conducted a lackluster campaign along the Rhine in 1793, and then concluded a peace treaty with the French in 1794 so they could concentrate on partitioning Poland.

Neither Frederick William II, nor his successor Frederick William III who became king in 1797, were prepared to correct the deficiencies revealed as a result of the battle of Valmy. The majority of Prussian officers preferred to think of the defeat in terms of failure by individual commanders or as a consequence of allied squabbles, rather than face the need for major reforms in the army. After defeating the Polish Uprising in 1795 they were convinced of the superiority of the Prussian army, despite the fact that to suppress the Poles it had taken a considerable effort. Neither the Prussians, nor the Austrians and their allies amongst the German states, were willing to study the organization, strategy and tactics of the French revolutionary armies. Indeed, the French decision to mobilize the population, select officers by merit, motivate soldiers by appealing to their patriotism was the last thing the absolute monarchs and the majority of their officers sought. Only political reform could bring about substantial military reform, and it took military defeat to force the old regimes to face the inevitable. Ironically, Napoleon was to stimulate German unification and nationalist feeling when in 1805, after defeating the Austrians and their German allies at the battle of Austerlitz, he created the Confederation of the Rhine, reducing the number of German states to a mere thirty under French supervision.

The Prussian army was not entirely indifferent to reform, and before the disaster of 1806 a number of attempts were made to remedy some of its obvious weaknesses. In his *Observations on the Art of War* published in 1799, Georg Heinrich von Behrenhorst attacked the Frederician tradition of turning soldiers into unthinking machines suitable only for the parade ground. Behrenhorst argued that the soldier needed to be given better treatment and encouraged to show enthusiasm and individuality. Another

Pages 36-37: French pursuit of the Prussians after the battle of Valmy, 20 September 1792.
Above: Marshal Murat leads the French cavalry at Jena.
Right: Prussians retreating after the battle of Jena.
Below: The blinded General Ferdinand of Brunswick being led away after the battle of Auerstadt.

military thinker, Baron Friedrich Wilhelm von Bülow argued for the mobilization of the masses and the development of tactics based upon *tirailleurs* (light infantry).

In 1802, Gerhard von Scharnhorst, an officer serving in the Hanoverian army, was persuaded to transfer to Prussian service. Scharnhorst was the son of a farmer who had served as an NCO in the Hanoverian army. Despite his humble origins, Scharnhorst had been commissioned and had seen service against the French. He was convinced that the French Revolution had been a profound political, social and military upheaval, and he expressed his opinions in a number of pamphlets.

Scharnhorst was appointed a lieutenant colonel in the Prussian Field Artillery Corps, and was soon principal military staff assistant to Frederick William III. He reorganized the Officers' Military Institute in Berlin and transformed it into the Academy for Young Officers in 1804. Scharnhorst established a military discussion society in Berlin, and he stimulated an interest in organizational and doctrinal reform amongst many young Prussian officers who were also influenced by the philosophical ideas of Kant and Hegel. One such young officer was Karl von Clausewitz.

The reformers in the Prussian army also pressed for improved officer training. In 1803 the training of staff officers was made more professional, with officers being selected by examination and then given a basic course in theory combined with frequent visits to regiments. Most senior army officers, however, were highly suspicious of the staff and were contemptuous of the concept that education should be one of the criteria for deciding whether an officer made a good field commander. Scharnhorst and Karl von Knesebeck argued for universal military service and the establishment of a permanent militia. As late as April 1806,

Scharnhorst had submitted a memorandum on army reform. He proposed the mobilization of the entire people for war, arguing that the army should be motivated by bravery and a sense of honor, and that rewards should go to the brave whatever their social background. He urged the army to abolish all the draconian and humiliating punishments which were inflicted on the ordinary soldier and which made service in the army so degrading.

Frederick William and his military advisers regarded such proposals as 'jacobin,' and rejected outright any reforms which touched at the heart of absolute monarchy and the rights and privileges of the officer corps. Scharnhorst was regarded as a social leper by many conservative officers who could not imagine an army beyond one composed of unthinking soldiers bound together by drill and discipline and trained in Frederician traditions.

Above: The Hanoverian-born General Gerhard von Scharnhorst, 1755-1813, was wounded at Auerstadt in 1806 but played a leading role in the revival of the Prussian army in 1812-13.
Left: Contemporary print of the battle of Jena.

In October 1806 the Prussians were confident and arrogant enough to issue Napoleon with an ultimatum. Prussia had occupied Hanover with French permission, but when during the course of peace negotiations, Napoleon offered to return it to Britain, Prussia decided to resist. The Prussians mobilized an army of 200,000, which was hopelessly divided among different field commanders. Frederick William was ignorant of military affairs and took with him into the field his military cabinet and the 82-year-old Field Marshal von Mollendorf. The Prussian commander, the Duke of Brunswick, failed to move the Prussian and Saxon armies with any degree of haste. The French mobilized an army of 186,000, and quickly advanced against the blundering Prussians. In battle the Prussian army still marched at 75 paces a minute loaded down with all kinds of impedimenta, as in the time of Frederick the Great, while the French stepped out at 120 paces a minute.

On 16 October 1806, Napoleon trapped two Prussian corps at Jena, and outmaneuvering them, he attacked with infantry and artillery before Murat's cavalry swept the Prussians from the field. Although an important victory, the main battle against the Prussians was fought on the same day at Auerstadt a few miles to the north. The Prussians outnumbered the French by 35,000 to 28,750, but despite desperate infantry assaults they failed to break the French, and after six hours the Prussians began to retreat. As the fugitives from Jena joined those from Auerstadt, the retreat became a rout, and the Prussian governmental system collapsed. Many Prussian fortresses surrendered without firing a shot and whole regiments were captured by the French in the course of their energetic pursuit.

One of the few Prussian units which maintained its cohesion was the division commanded by General Gebhard von Blücher, a pugnacious, aggressive and eccentric old soldier. Remnants of the Prussian army retreated to East Prussia accompanied by Frederick William, where they were belatedly joined by a Russian army. But following the failure of the Prussian campaign against the French in

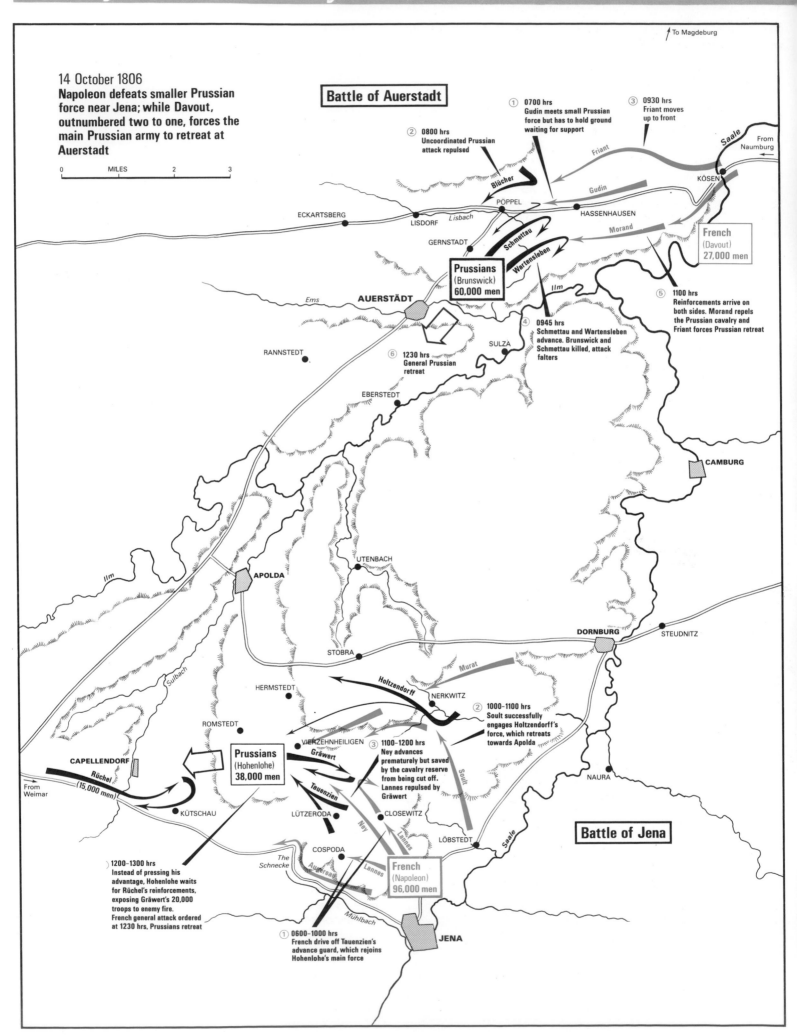

↗ To Magdeburg

14 October 1806

Napoleon defeats smaller Prussian force near Jena; while Davout, outnumbered two to one, forces the main Prussian army to retreat at Auerstadt

0   MILES   2   3

Battle of Auerstadt

① 0700 hrs
Gudin meets small Prussian force but has to hold ground waiting for support

② 0800 hrs
Uncoordinated Prussian attack repulsed

③ 0930 hrs
Friant moves up to front

Saale

From Naumburg ←

Friant

Gudin

KÖSEN

Blücher

POPPEL

HASSENHAUSEN

Morand

French (Davout) 27,000 men

ECKARTSBERG

LISDORF   Lisbach

GERNSTADT

Schmettau

Wartensleben

Prussians (Brunswick) 60,000 men

⑤ 1100 hrs
Reinforcements arrive on both sides. Morand repels the Prussian cavalry and Friant forces Prussian retreat

Ems

AUERSTÄDT

Ilm

④ 0945 hrs
Schmettau and Wartensleben advance. Brunswick and Schmettau killed, attack falters

RANNSTEDT

⑥ 1230 hrs
General Prussian retreat

SULZA

EBERSTEDT

CAMBURG

Ilm

APOLDA

DORNBURG

STEUDNITZ

STOBRA

Sulbach

HERMSTEDT

Holtzendorff

NERKWITZ

Murat

② 1000-1100 hrs
Soult successfully engages Holtzendorff's force, which retreats towards Apolda

ROMSTEDT

VIERZEHNHEILIGEN

Gräwert

③ 1100-1200 hrs
Ney advances prematurely but saved by the cavalry reserve from being cut off. Lannes repulsed by Gräwert

CAPELLENDORF

Rüchel

Prussians (Hohenlohe) 38,000 men

Tauenzien

Soult

NAURA

From Weimar

Rüchel (15,000 men)

KÜTSCHAU

LÜTZERODA

Ney

CLOSEWITZ

LÖBSTEDT

Saale

Battle of Jena

1200-1300 hrs
Instead of pressing his advantage, Hohenlohe waits for Rüchel's reinforcements, exposing Gräwert's 20,000 troops to enemy fire. French general attack ordered at 1230 hrs, Prussians retreat

COSPODA

The Schnecke

Auergraben

Lannes

Lannes

French (Napoleon) 96,000 men

Mühlbach

JENA

① 0600-1000 hrs
French drive off Tauenzien's advance guard, which rejoins Hohenlohe's main force

East Prussia, Frederick William accepted a humiliating agreement with Napoleon at the Peace of Tilsit on 25 July 1807. Prussia was forced to surrender all her territories west of the Elbe, renounce all her Polish territories, and pay an enormous indemnity to France.

Among the chapter of disasters suffered by the Prussian army in the ten months between Jena and Tilsit there were a few hopeful signs. Some Prussian units fought against the French with dogged determination, and the defense of the Baltic port of Kolberg by August von Gneisenau, a passed-over major who had transferred from Austrian service, became a symbol of Prussian resistance. Serving as the chief of staff to an army corps in East Prussia, Scharnhorst was largely responsible for the arrival of Prussian troops at the battle of Preussich-Eylau in 1807, transforming a likely Russian defeat into a drawn battle against the French.

Following the Peace of Tilsit, Frederick William could no longer prevaricate over political and military reform. The demonstrable failure of the Prussian army combined with the successes achieved by the advocates of reform such as Scharnhorst and Gneisenau, forced the king to establish a Military Reorganization Commission in 1807. Scharnhorst, promoted to major general, was appointed to head the commission, and was supported by such military reformers as Gneisenau, Grolman and Boyen, as well as two civilian members, Stein, the Prime Minister of Prussia, and Könen the auditor-general. Although the reformers had a clear majority on the commission, conservative opposition was represented, and their access to the king was guaranteed through one member, Karl von Lottum, the king's adjutant.

The Military Reorganization Commission was instructed to examine all aspects of military policy, but in particular to punish

Above right: Uniforms of Prussian *Landwehr* infantry, 1813-14.
Left: The battles of Jena and Auerstadt. The French forces at Auerstadt held out against superior numbers while Napoleon won the crushing victory at Jena. The rapid French pursuit gave the Prussians no chance to recover from the defeat.
Below: The Convention at Tauroggen, 30 December 1812, General Yorck agrees to the neutrality of the Prussian Corps.

those officers who were found guilty of cowardice or incompetence during the war; to investigate the feasibility of allowing the bourgeoisie to enter the officer corps; to examine the problems of recruitment, and, finally, to reform military law and punishments.

The investigation of the conduct of officers during the war took place over several years, and was mainly the work of regimental tribunals. By 1809, of the 142 generals in 1806, 17 had been cashiered, 86 honorably dismissed and 22 remained on active duty, and only two of those, Blücher and Tanentzien held command in 1813. Similar statistics applied to junior officers, and there is no doubt that the commission was able to remove many old or incompetent officers.

To replace those officers removed from the army and to open up officer selection and promotion to ability rather than privilege or length of service, the reformers on the commission struck at the heart of Prussian absolutism. In August 1808, Grolman drafted a law which stated that anyone with the right education and qualities could become an officer. In November of the same year, the promotion of officers in senior ranks only according to their length of service was abolished. It became a requirement for all officers due for promotion to sit examinations which tested not only their military knowledge but also their general education. In theory these measures should have opened up the officer corps to the bourgeoisie and established a system of promotion based upon merit. In practice, regiments selected potential officers and thus became self-perpetuating élites, the educational requirements effectively denied large numbers of able men the opportunity to be considered, and the old cadet schools only admitted the sons of officers. The reactionary element within the officer corps thus diluted these reforms effectively and the nobility retained its privileged position.

Perhaps the most important part in Scharnhorst's military thinking was the idea of universal service. Scharnhorst believed that universal service was necessary in military terms to provide Prussia with a large enough army to fight one day a new war with France. But he was also convinced that it was a citizen's obligation to defend the state, and that if he was motivated by patriotism he would be a better soldier. Universal service struck at the roots of the old Prussian order, because it meant the abolition of the cantonal system which relied on the peasants and mercenaries to provide recruits. Scharnhorst and the reformers proposed dividing military service between a standing army and a militia. Those without means of providing for a uniform and equipment would serve in the standing army, whilst those who had such means would serve in a militia. Although not a perfect system, it was the cheapest way of expanding the army. Frederick William's doubts and the opposition of reactionary officers to this proposal were settled by Napoleon at the Convention of Paris in 1808. Hearing that Prussia was reforming her army and fearing a revival of military strength, Napoleon limited the Prussian army to 42,000 long service volunteers, and forbade a national militia or reserve force.

An attempt to get round this restriction was created through the *Krümper* system. One way to increase the reserves was to make sure that as many as possible of those on the cantonal rolls were trained. Under the *Krümper* system, every month three to five men were sent on leave from each company and their places taken by recruits. Thus it was hoped to build up a substantial reserve of trained men. In reality, it was far less successful than the planners had imagined, and by 1813 the Prussian army's reserves amounted to 65,675 compared to 53,523 in 1807.

The defeat in 1806 had also stimulated a vigorous debate over training and tactics. Scharnhorst and his reformers slowly moved the army away from an emphasis on constant drill toward field exercises and target shooting, placing more emphasis on the individual soldier. A commission consisting of Scharnhorst,

Below: Prussian *Landwehr* in action at the battle of Grossbeeren, 1813.

Clausewitz and General Hans Yorck von Wartenburg was responsible for the new training regulations published in 1812. Although Yorck was a reactionary officer who opposed reform of officer selection, he was a specialist in light infantry tactics and a competent field commander. The new regulations combined an amalgam of eighteenth century experience, Napoleonic tactics and lessons from the defeat of 1806. Prussian tactics were to be a mixture of linear formation, battalion columns and the tirailleurs, thus combining effective firepower, mobility and shock action. The cavalry was made more clearly subordinate to the infantry and restricted in its independent role, whilst the artillery was trained to provide the infantry with maximum fire support following the example set by the French.

It is impossible to exaggerate the influence Napoleon had on the Prussian army reformers. Not only were they fascinated by his political and military reforms and his brilliance as a field commander, but in the case of Clausewitz, for example, he nurtured an intense hatred of Napoleon and all things French, a legacy which would bedevil Franco-German relations for the next 150 years. The French victory in 1806 also had an impact on the uniform and equipment of the Prussian soldier. The plait was abolished, the coat became a tailcoat, and the shako replaced the cap. The Prussian soldier now wore lace-up boots, with knee breeches, and officers and men were given precise rank distinctions.

Scharnhorst and the reformers were aware that the Prussian army lacked a military structure which could administer the army effectively and prepare strategic and operational plans. Not only was there an inadequate central organization, but staff work in the field was frequently poor or non-existent. There was a requirement for commanders to be advised by a staff who not only had professional ability but also considerable initiative,

something which was anathema to reactionary officers who had been raised on Frederician traditions. In 1810 the Military School for Officers was established in Berlin where civilian as well as military instructors taught. Eventually this school was to become the *Kriegsakademie*.

The reformers were not concerned solely with a narrow military professionalism, but also with the important question of where ultimate political and military authority should lie within the state, and the relationship between the civil and military authorities. This touched on the sensitive question of the authority of the king, who saw the army very much as his personal possession. In March 1809, Frederick William reluctantly agreed to establish a Council of Ministers, and with it a Ministry of War. The king refused to appoint a Minister of War, but made Scharnhorst head of the General Department, and thus effectively chief of the general staff. But to balance Scharnhorst's influence, the king appointed the conservative Karl Heinrich von Wylich und Lottum as head of the Administrative Department.

The final area of work of the Military Commission was the reform of military law and punishments. The reformers were ardent supporters of a new system of punishments believing that to attract a better type of recruit into the army needed a change in discipline. In 1808 the practice of running the gauntlet was abolished, and beatings were allowed only by special disciplinary units. Deserters were no longer shot but were liable to heavy prison sentences. Although the new articles of war represented a major reform, in practice the ill-treatment of soldiers continued by officers who feared little in the way of official disapproval.

A law of 1809 attempted to restrict the application of military law against civilians. But the officer corps was still able to protect its members against civil proceedings, or for that matter discipline a dissenter in its own ranks through the system of honor courts.

Above: Field Marshal Gebhard von Blücher, in private life a highly-eccentric individual but a most effective leader.
Below: Prussian staff officers at the decisive battle of Leipzig in 1813. A large part of the retreating French force was cut off when a bridge over the Elster river was prematurely destroyed.

Above: Soldiers of the King's German Legion, 1812, who served in the Peninsula and at Waterloo.

While Scharnhorst and the reformers were reorganizing the Prussian army, Napoleon's fortunes had not singularly prospered. French setbacks in Spain encouraged the Austrians to invade French dominated Bavaria in 1809 and to appeal to Prussia and Russia for assistance. The Prussian reformers urged Frederick William to declare war, but he refused. Napoleon defeated the Austrians at Ratisbon and Wagram, and apart from the independent action of Major Ferdinand von Schill who took his Hussar regiment to Westphalia to harass the French, the Prussians remained aloof from the hostilities.

Napoleon placed considerable pressure on Frederick William to dismiss Scharnhorst and other reformers, and although the king did remove some from office and change certain appointments, he still relied on their advice. In 1811 Napoleon began to prepare for war against Russia, and Frederick William reaffirmed his allegiance to France and agreed to contribute to the *Grande Armée* assembling for the invasion. Out of the total of 600,000 troops in the *Grande Armée*, some 180,000 were supplied from the German states. Many of the reformers resigned in disgust at what they believed was the craven action of their king. Some thirty of them, including Clausewitz, went to Russia and took service in the Tsar's army. The Prussian Corps in the *Grande Armée* was eventually commanded by General von Yorck, and spent most of the campaign engaged in limited operations along the Baltic coast. Napoleon's failure decisively to defeat the Russians and the onset of winter saw the *Grande Armée* withdrawing in disorder. In the Baltic the Prussians under Yorck agreed to a truce with the Russians. Clausewitz played a significant part in the negotiations which resulted on 30 December 1812 in Yorck signing the Convention of Tauroggen which declared the neutrality of the Prussian corps.

Yorck's action forced Frederick William's hand and he reluctantly denounced the alliance with France, moved his capital to Breslau, and appointed Scharnhorst as Quartermaster General. Frederick William and his reactionary advisers were forced into these actions by a tremendous wave of national and patriotic sentiment. The East Prussian *Landtag* had enthusiastically welcomed the Russian army and raised a *Landwehr*, or militia, without royal assent. Although Frederick William wanted to see the French defeated he was unenthusiastic at the prospect of it being achieved at the expense of the traditional Prussian political and military institutions.

Following the break with France, the reformers were in a position to implement many of the ideas they had been propounding since 1806. In February 1813, Scharnhorst established the principle of universal military service, firstly by establishing voluntary Jäger detachments, and secondly by organising the *Landwehr*, in which all men between the ages of seventeen and forty who were physically fit were required to enrole for duty. Although neither the Jäger units nor the *Landwehr* were quite the democratic military forces popularized in history, their recruitment and selection of officers was sufficiently democratic seriously to alarm reactionary officers. The military effectiveness of the *Landwehr* was to be limited, but it was to make an important contribution to the 'War of Liberation' and became an important symbol in Prussian history. In 1813 the *Landsturm*, or Home Guard was raised, with the idea of utilizing those citizens not enrolled in either the regular army or the *Landwehr*, to act as irregular forces against the French. In the event, the *Landsturm* was never properly organized, but the very notion of irregular warfare and the possibility of arming the people against Napoleon horrified the reactionaries who feared that such an organization would end by having revolutionary consequences for the Prussian state.

On 11 March 1813 Frederick William introduced the award of the Iron Cross, and in the public decree it stated, 'In the present great catastrophe in which everything is at stake for the Nation, the vigorous spirit which elevates the nation so high deserves to be honored and perpetuated by quite peculiar monuments. That the perseverance by which the Nation endured the irresistible evils of an iron age did not shrink to timidity is proved by the high courage which now animates every breast and which could survive only because it was based on religion and true loyalty to King and Country.' The Iron Cross represented endurance and toughness, and there were then three grades of award, which could be made either to soldiers or civilians who distinguished themselves in the forthcoming struggle. Rank or privilege would have nothing to do with its award.

On 16 March 1813, Frederick William issued his famous proclamation, *An Mein Volk*, 'To My People,' which was enthusiastically received throughout Germany. Over the next year the Prussian army received more than 50,000 volunteers from all over Germany. As the Prussians and their Russian ally worked to organize their military forces, Napoleon cobbled together a new army from the remnants of the *Grand Armée*, along with raw French recruits and contingents from his reluctant German allies in the Confederation of the Rhine.

In the spring of 1813, a Prussian corps under Field Marshal Blücher took the field as part of the main Russian army. Scharnhorst, who was Blücher's chief of staff, had persuaded the king to appoint the old man as effectively commander of the Prussian army, despite his great age and idiosyncracies. The first encounters between the Prussians and the French at Grossgörschen and Bautzen were won by the French, but at considerable cost. Despite the fact that Prussians were inexperienced, compared to the troops of 1806, they were motivated by patriotism and fanaticism. One unfortunate consequence of the battle of Grossgörschen was that Scharnhorst was wounded, and eventually died of blood poisoning on 28 June 1813.

Napoleon agreed to an armistice in the summer of 1813 to rest his army and train recruits. During the armistice, the Prussians and Russians were joined by the Swedes and the Austrians. When the armistice expired on 26 August, the allies had a combined army of 480,000 troops, whilst Napoleon had 450,000. The ensuing campaign became known to the Prussians as the 'War of Liberation.'

The allied command structure and the organization of the armies rested upon the various national contingents. There were four principal allied armies; the Austrian under Schwarzenberg,

Above right: Death of the Duke of Brunswick at the battle of Quatre Bras 1815. Brunswick had led his duchy's forces against the French in 1809 and had later fought, in exile, with the British in Spain.
Right: The march of the Prussian forces to join the fighting at Waterloo.

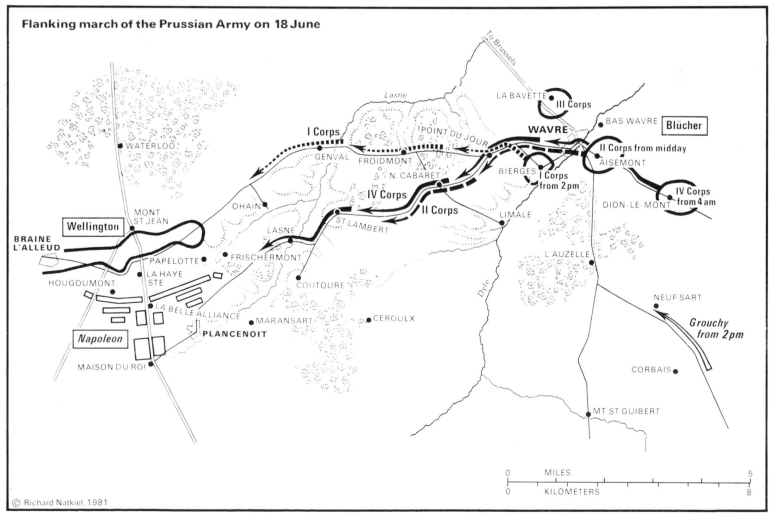

Flanking march of the Prussian Army on 18 June

© Richard Natkiel, 1981

the Prussians under Blücher, the Russians under Bennigsen and the Swedes under Bernadotte. The Prussian army was divided into separate corps, one attached to each of the allied armies. Much of the successful coordination between the allied armies resulted from the work of the Prussian reformers such as Gneisenau, Boyen, Grolman and Clausewitz, who were appointed chiefs of staff at corps level. Gneisenau, who succeeded Scharnhorst as chief of staff to Blücher, was to formulate a very important principle for the Prussian army, that the chief of staff of a major command was to share responsibility with the commander.

The aim of the allied autumn campaign in 1813 was to encircle Napoleon's army at Dresden. Although Napoleon attempted to defeat his enemies in sequence, he failed, and the allies moved to encircle him at Leipzig. The battle of Leipzig lasted from 16-19 October 1813 with fierce fighting taking place in the city itself. The allies were unable to envelop Napoleon's army, but effectively destroyed it, capturing many guns and prisoners, including the majority of Napoleon's German allies. The Prussians were jubilant, and believed that the victory at Leipzig avenged the defeats of 1806.

Following a period of rest and recuperation, the allies advanced into France, meeting comparatively little resistance, and with Wellington's army advancing in the south from Spain, the allies entered Paris on 31 March 1814 and Napoleon abdicated. The War of Liberation appeared to have reached a successful con-

Below: Napoleon's flight after the battle for Belle Alliance, Waterloo, 18 June 1815. The confusion of the retreat was so great that Napoleon had to abandon his coach because of the crowd of fugitives. The Prussian cavalry led the pursuit of the beaten army.

clusion. In Prussia, Boyen was appointed Minister of War with Grolman as chief of the General Department. After the defeat of Napoleon, Boyen was determined to implement Scharnhorst's plan for a new system of national mobilization. The Army Law of 3 September 1814 established the principle of universal service in Prussia, even in peacetime, with the possibility of exemptions or the purchase of substitutes. Recruits were selected by lots, and were to serve three years with the regular army and then two years in the active reserve, before transferring to the *Landwehr*. However, young men from the educated classes who could pay for their own equipment served only one year, and then went straight to the *Landwehr*, where the majority became officers. Boyen regarded the *Landwehr* as an essential link between civil society and the army. But its bourgeois officers and part-time soldiers aroused the reactionary prejudices and contempt of many Prussian officers.

This reorganization of the army was still in progress when Napoleon escaped from Elba, returned to France, and was joined by most of his old army. Among the allies, only the British and the Prussians were on a war footing, with the British in the Netherlands and the Prussians under Blücher in the Rhenish provinces. The reformers were well represented on Blücher's staff, with Gneisenau as his chief of staff, Grolman as Quartermaster General and Clausewitz as chief of staff to Thielmann's III Corps. The Prussians advanced to join the British, but Napoleon moved with even greater speed to prevent such a union, hoping to beat the allies separately. On 16 June 1815, Napoleon attacked the Prussians at Ligny and later the British at Quatre Bras. The French captured the town of Ligny at the end of a hard day's fighting

which saw the Prussians badly pressed and Blücher wounded and nearly captured. Napoleon was confident that the Prussians had been defeated and would retreat to their base on the Rhine. Marshal Grouchy was despatched to harass the Prussians in the direction of Liège whilst Napoleon concentrated on Wellington's army at Waterloo.

Gneisenau was responsible for persuading Blücher to abandon his main base and instead march towards Waterloo to join Wellington. It was this action on 18 June which came as a complete surprise to Napoleon. The Prussian army evaded Grouchy and reached the field of Waterloo at a critical moment for Napoleon and Wellington. The Prussians reformed for an attack from their marching columns and struck at the French right wing and flank. The French army collapsed and began a headlong retreat. With the British exhausted, the Prussians undertook to harass the French, but the pursuit was a desultory affair. Napoleon, however, was finished, and the Bourbons finally restored to power. For the Prussians and other Germans, Blücher's army had played a significant part in the overthrow of 'the French tyrant.'

The French revolutionary and Napoleonic wars had been a traumatic experience for the German states. Politically, the French had smashed the old Holy Roman Empire and shaken Austria's authority to influence German affairs. Napoleon had reduced and reorganized the number of German states and created a French grouping with the Confederation of the Rhine. After 1805 the majority of German states modelled their armies on the French example, and when the *Grande Armée* invaded Russia in 1812, it included German state contingents from Bavaria, Saxony, Westphalia and Kleve-Berg. Although the battle of Leipzig in 1813 was called 'the battle of the nations' and was seen as the culmination of a German 'people's war' against the French, it should be remembered that a sizeable proportion of Napoleon's army were troops from his German allies.

Troops from German states had also fought in the British army during these wars. Following the French occupation of Hanover in 1803, the Hanoverian army had been disbanded. But many Hanoverian soldiers went to Britain where a King's German Regiment was raised, later to form the basis of the King's German Legion. Of the 15,000 troops who served with the King's German Legion until 1816, some 75 percent were Hanoverians, 17 percent from other German states, and 7 percent from other countries. The King's German Legion served with distinction in Wellington's army in the Peninsula and then at Waterloo, and was generally considered one of the most reliable and effective formations in the British army. After Waterloo, the King's German Legion was disbanded and its soldiers absorbed into a reformed Hanoverian army.

The German military experience had been diverse in the French revolutionary and Napoleonic wars, but the awakening of nationalism and reform, particularly in Prussia, was something which alarmed the German princes who had fought to preserve the old order and defeat 'jacobinism.'

Below: Prussian dead being dragged away and wounded being treated after the battle of Waterloo. Many of the casualties at Waterloo were robbed as they waited for help. As in most battles of the period several days elapsed before all the wounded were collected.

The Prussian General Staff

History of The German Army

Following Napoleon's defeat, the Prussians acquired territory at the expense of France along the Rhine and in the Saar. So by 1816, the kingdom of Prussia consisted of two separate groups of territories, the eastern, predominantly Protestant, and the western, predominantly Catholic, divided by the states of Hesse and Hanover. At the Congress of Vienna in 1815, the German princes agreed to unite in a confederation, and a permanent diet of plenipotentiaries from 34 dynasties and four free city states met at Frankfurt-on-Main under the presidency of Austria. The diet's main objective was to secure the principle of monarchic legitimacy and oppose the forces in favor of German unity. Frederick William and many Prussian reactionaries feared the liberal democratic movement behind German unity and allied themselves with the reactionary powers of Austria and Russia.

Reactionary Prussian officers were determined to reverse the reforms brought about by the impact of the Napoleonic war. Frederick William had always been a reluctant reformer and had been antagonized by Scharnhorst's and Gneisenau's attempts to limit his royal prerogatives. Many Prussian officers wanted to restrict the process of democratization, particularly with regard to the officer corps, and to take control of the hated *Landwehr*, which was seen as a military joke and a hotbed of revolutionaries. Although the *Landwehr* was dismissed as an effective military force, nevertheless it numbered 163,000, and was seen as a potential threat to the 136,000-strong regular army.

The leading military reformers, Gneisenau, Boyen and Grolman, were sharply critical of the Congress of Vienna which had established the post-Napoleonic boundaries and looked beyond

Previous page: Prussian artillery in action during the War with Denmark, 1864.
Above: General August von Gneisenau who succeeded Scharnhorst after 1813 as the leading Prussian military reformer.
Left: General Hermann von Boyen, Prussian Minister of War, 1814-19 and 1841-47.
Right: Soldiers of the Kaiser Franz Regiment of Guard Grenadiers c. 1835.

the limits of Prussian sovereignty to a vision of a reformed and united Germany, eventually based upon a liberal constitution. Gneisenau felt so strongly about the need for political reform in Prussia, that when Frederick William failed to promulgate a constitution, he resigned from active service and went into premature retirement.

Boyen remained as Minister of War and appointed Grolman as head of the Second Department, or general staff. In the four years that Grolman was effectively chief of the general staff, he carried out a series of organizational changes and established procedures to translate concepts into operational reality. In 1816 he re-organized the general staff into three principal divisions, one for each potential theater of war. The staff in each of these three divisions studied the countries concerned and prepared strategic plans and looked at problems of mobilization and deployment.

In 1817, Grolman established a fourth division of the general staff responsible for studying military history, and a fifth division called the *Truppengeneralstab*, or Troop General Staff, with officers from the central organization in Berlin being rotated for duty with corps and divisional staffs. To prevent the general staff from getting out of touch with the rest of the army, Grolman insisted upon frequent rotation of officers between the line regiments and the general staff.

Against fierce opposition from reactionary officers, Grolman insisted on continuing to improve officer education, with particular emphasis on scientific education. Finally, Grolman was concerned to improve military communications within Prussia to overcome the strategic problems, and to that end supported the building of an adequate road network, the establishment of magazines and the development of an army mechanical telegraph system.

While Grolman worked to improve the technical efficiency of the general staff, Boyen struggled against Frederick William and his reactionary advisers. Boyen and the reformers were shocked

Above: Officer and standard bearer of the 6th (Tsar Nicholas') Regiment of cuirassiers, a Brandenburg regiment, in the uniforms of 1840.
Below: General Wrangel's troops disarming a motley group of volunteers of the *Bürgerwehr* in Berlin following Wrangel's occupation of the city in the aftermath of the revolutionary crisis of 1848.

by the Carlsbad Decrees of August 1819, whereby the German states agreed to take coordinated and drastic action to halt the spread of liberal and nationalist concepts among the youth of Germany. After the autumn maneuvers of 1819, the performance of the *Landwehr* was severely criticized by many army officers. Frederick William decided to accept the advice of those who opposed the *Landwehr*, and ordered that in future it would come under direct army supervision. Boyen and Grolman in consequence resigned, so that the Carlsbad Decrees and the *Landwehr*'s loss of independence in 1819 can be seen as the political triumph of reaction over reform in Prussia. But although the movement to turn the Prussian army into 'a nation in arms' had been defeated, the purely technical military reforms had not.

Another reformer was also a casualty of the triumph of reaction in 1819. Clausewitz had been appointed by Grolman in 1818 as Director of the General War School as part of the efforts to strengthen the army's education system. Boyen's replacement as Minister of War restricted Clausewitz's role to that of administrator, and he was to have little influence over the curriculum of the War School or the appointment of staff.

As early as 1816 Clausewitz had begun work on a comprehensive analysis of war. For the next fourteen years he compiled studies of Napoleonic campaigns and draft chapters for his proposed book. But in 1831 Clausewitz died of cholera in Silesia with his book incomplete. However, his widow acted as editor, and she presided over the publication of his writings in the volumes *Vom Kriege* (On War) published in 1832-34. Clausewitz had rejected a lot of past military writing as having failed to discover any real theory of war. Clausewitz analyzed the theory and practice of war, the importance of moral factors, ends and means in war and the difference between limited and absolute war. Clausewitz believed that the outcome in war was frequently determined by 'friction,' which consisted of tangible elements such as terrain and climate and intangible elements such as the morale of troops and chance. Military leaders overcame 'friction' through 'genius,'

something which could be acquired through study and experience. Clausewitz believed that war was a political act, and that since 'War is the continuation of policy by other means,' then decisions relating to national policy, including military ones, ultimately had to be determined by statesmen.

Vom Kriege had only a limited impact on the contemporary Prussian army, and was hardly noted outside the country. It was really as a result of Helmuth von Moltke's influence as chief of the general staff some thirty years later, that Clausewitz became required reading for Prussian officers. Moltke had read Clausewitz and was convinced that he had provided an intellectual framework for soldiers. *Vom Kriege* also became required reading in foreign armies, particularly after Prussia's successes in the Wars of Unification. But many of Clausewitz's careful arguments and Hegelian dialectic became simplified and distorted beyond recognition. A new emphasis on 'the decisive battle' and absolute victory made Clausewitz into the symbol of Prussian militarism.

In the 1820s control of the War Ministry and the general staff passed into the hands of reactionaries, who continued to improve, nevertheless, the technical efficiency of the system. In the War Ministry the department of Personnel Affairs was established, initially only responsible for officers' personal records. The head of this department was Major General von Witzleben, who was also Adjutant General and a personal friend of Frederick William. This close relationship between Witzleben and the king meant that although the department of Personnel Affairs was part of the War Ministry, in fact it served the King. This was an attempt to recreate the Military Cabinet, something which Scharnhorst had abolished in 1807. When eventually the Military Cabinet was re-established, it became the center of military reaction, since by keeping a firm control over officer appointments, undesirable elements could be prevented from reaching any positions of power and influence in the army.

For most of the decade, General von Müffling was chief of the

Above: General Karl von Clausewitz, 1780-1831, Prussian military thinker and author of *Vom Kriege.* Clausewitz's description of the relationship between warfare and political objectives remains a vital part of contemporary military theory.
Below: Federal troops of the German states in action against the Danes in 1848.

History of The German Army

Above: The Prussian 1st Guard Infantry Regiment advancing during the battle of Königgrätz, 1866.
Below: Prussian artillary engaging the Austrians at Königgrätz.

general staff, and he made a number of changes in organization and procedures. He re-established the annual general staff rides which had been begun by Scharnhorst. The aim of the staff ride was to familiarize the entire staff with one of the potential operational areas by examining the terrain, preparing maps and marking out areas for the deployment of troops. Müffling abandoned Grolman's geographical breakdown of the general staff and assigned responsibilities on a topical basis. Despite the fact that Müffling was a political reactionary, he continued the reformers' efforts to establish promotion by merit in the general staff. He was concerned to assure consistency and thoroughness in general staff work, and under his direction the first staff manual was compiled. Work was begun on a detailed history of Prussian operations in the final campaigns against Napoleon in 1813-15. But the work was highly selective in that the aim of Scharnhorst and Gneisenau to create a 'People's Army' and the role of the *Landwehr* were largely omitted.

Müffling also adopted an idea developed by a young Guards artillery officer in 1820 for planning battles and campaigns by using maps and diagrams. In 1824 the first manual for the *Kriegsspiel*, or War Game, was published, and under Müffling and his successor it was adopted for use throughout the army. As developed by the general staff, the *Kriegsspiel* enabled officers to operate as teams of commanders and their staffs to simulate realistic combat situations on maps. At another level, the *Kriegsspiel* was used as a method of instruction for NCOs.

Above: General Albrecht von Roon, Prussian Minister of War, 1859-73.

In 1829, Müffling was succeeded as chief of the general staff by Major General von Krauseneck, a commoner who had been enobled for his service during the Napoleonic wars. Krauseneck had assisted Scharnhorst in preparing the training regulations for the reformed Prussian army after 1806. Krauseneck was a quiet, professional soldier, who in his nineteen year tenure as chief of the general staff, continued the work of his predecessors. Under his direction, the general staff responded positively to the technological developments of the period which were to have a profound impact upon the conduct of war.

The improvement in Prussia's economic position after 1815 was reflected in the growth of the road building program. In 1816, Prussia had a total of 3162 kilometers (1965 miles) of state owned roads which by 1848 had become 11,852 kilometers (7364 miles). The general staff had a particular interest in road building as the planning of new routes could dramatically influence the strategic mobility of the army. With Prussian territory spread across northern Germany, and since Prussia faced potentially powerful adversaries to the west, south and east, it was important that the army had good internal communications to deploy rapidly. The general staff were very interested in the development of railroads. The first railroad in Germany was a short line outside Prussia, between Nürnberg and Furth, built in 1835. Almost at once, the general staff initiated a study on the potential of railroads for accelerating army mobilization. In 1848, Prussia was to possess 2363 kilometers (1469 miles) of railroads, and the general staff was to determine the extent and route of future railroad construction.

This period was also notable for Prussia's industrial expansion, especially the heavy industry of the Ruhr. In 1829, Nikolaus von Dreyse invented a breech-loading rifle, or 'needle-gun,' with three times the rate of fire of the muzzle-loader and with a narrower bore. In the Dreyse needle-gun, the bolt closing the breech contained a needle which, on a spring being released, pierced the paper cartridge case striking the detonating composition and igniting the charge. At first, Dreyse had technical problems on how to mass produce the rifle and faced opposition from reactionary officers who defended the muzzle-loader. It was not until the 1860s that the needle-gun replaced the bronze muzzle-loader in the Prussian army.

The general staff continued to modify the visual telegraph system to assure the rapid transmission and reception of information to and from subordinate commands and frontier posts. Soon the Prussian army was experimenting with the new electric telegraph invented by Samuel Morse in 1844.

In the early 1830s the general staff proposed that the period of active military service be reduced from three years to two, and the period of service with the *Landwehr* be increased by one year. This was because more young men were reaching military age each year than could be trained within the existing manning levels. By the proposed method the nation's potential mobilized strength would be expanded by nearly fifty percent. Despite the fears of some officers that by reducing the period of active service there would be a corresponding reduction in the quality of training, the measure received royal assent in 1833.

In the thirty years following the end of the Napoleonic war the main concern of the Prussian officer corps was to combat reformist and revolutionary movements within the state, and also in other German states. The commanding generals of the nine army corps were directly responsible to the king and took precedence over the civil authorities. After 1820 they were able to intervene in civil strife without first receiving a request by the civil or police authorities. Draconian sentences were given to civilians who refused to obey military orders or who were insubordinate.

Above left: 'The sinews of war' – a Prussian army supply column during the 1866 campaign.
Left: Prussian infantry in a fire-fight at Königgrätz. Despite the introduction of more modern rifles and artillery weapons, the close-order firing line remained a feature of infantry tactics.

Apart from dealing with Polish unrest in 1830, the experience of the Prussian army during this period was almost exclusively concerned with civil unrest. The Prussian army intervened in 1830 when there was widespread political unrest throughout Germany as a result of the revolution in France. It was also deployed in some of the smaller German states to crush protest movements against absolutism and the lack of political freedom.

Frederick William III of Prussia died in 1840 and was succeeded by his son, Frederick William IV. The new king had a reputation for sympathizing with liberal ideas, but despite his outspoken comments, he was firmly opposed to the two basic aims of Prussian liberals, a Prussian constitution and German national unity. Frederick William IV was an emotionally unbalanced man who was to disappoint the liberals and arouse the suspicions of reactionaries, particularly those in the army.

The new king hoped to appease the Prussian reformers by re-appointing the elderly Boyen as Minister of War. Although Boyen was able to carry through a number of technical reforms, including the adoption of the Dreyse needle gun, an increase in army pay and rations, and a more liberal code of military justice, he found he was politically unable to influence the king. Boyen resigned from office in frustration in 1847.

In February 1848, Louis Philippe of France was forced into exile and a republican government seized power in Paris. Revolutionary activities began to spread across Europe, and there were disturbances in the Rhineland and Berlin. Frederick William dithered between the contradictory demands of the liberals for reform and the reactionaries for oppression. In an attempt to prevent bloodshed, the king promised a constitution in March, but this failed to prevent bitter street fighting between liberal mobs and the army.

Over the next ten months the German states, including Prussia and Austria, were swept by revolutionary violence. Reactionary Prussian officers were horrified by what they saw as the king's weakness, and even contemplated a coup d'état. In March, the army was deployed in Poland putting down an uprising by the national liberation movement, and in contrast, also in Schleswig-Holstein supporting local Germans against Danish attempts at annexation. In Schleswig-Holstein the Prussian army appeared to be executing the orders of the diet of the German Confederation. In August 1848 an armistice was agreed between the German states and Denmark.

Despite the hopes of the Prussian liberals, they were unable to maintain the revolutionary momentum, and in November 1848, General von Wrangel marched 40,000 troops into Berlin and established martial law. On 5 December, Frederick William magnanimously proclaimed a constitution as a sop to the liberals. In practice, the constitution changed nothing, and as far as the army was concerned it left the king with an unrestricted power of command and the sole right to declare war and conclude peace. The army remained outside the constitution owing direct loyalty to the king whose power of command was subject to no constraints.

In Frankfurt, the diet had continued to debate the issue of German unity and in March 1849 proposed a German constitution. The governments of the German states rejected the constitution, and in May fighting broke out in Dresden and spread throughout Germany. Prussian and Austrian troops were called in to crush the revolutionaries. In the German confederation there were some thirty different armies, the majority of which were militarily ineffectual and politically unreliable. The federal army consisted of three Austrian, three Prussian, one Bavarian and three mixed corps, the latter manned by troops from eighteen separate states. As revolutionary violence spread throughout Germany, units of the Prussian army assisted local troops, particularly in Saxony and Baden, to crush the uprisings. Despite the fact that the Prussian army frequently faced enthusiastic *Landwehr* formations, the Prussians triumphed because they were better armed, equipped and supplied and commanded by ruthless

Above: General Helmuth von Moltke, Chief of the Great General Staff, 1857-88.
Top right: Tattered glory – French prisoners in 1870.
Bottom right: The Franco-Prussian War, 1870-71.

leaders. By the summer of 1849 the revolutionary movement in Germany had been broken.

The experience of 1848-49 revealed the deep hostility of the Prussian officer corps to the idea of political reform. This hostility meant that ultimately some officers were prepared to overthrow the king if he had given way to the reformists. These events had influenced also the political thinking of both Karl Marx and Friedrich Engels. Marx was already known as a revolutionary thinker, but Engels, who fought the Prussians in the defense of Elberfeld, was to develop as a perceptive analyst of military affairs and an acute observer of Prussian military power. Marx and Engels represented a completely different political and military intellectual tradition from that of the Prussian officer corps, but their influence was considerable, and eventually was to challenge and triumph over that of the German military establishment.

The diet at Frankfurt offered Frederick William the crown of the proposed German empire, which would exclude Austria, in April 1849. For a few months it appeared that there would be a direct confrontation between Austria and Prussia, and Prussia came close to mobilization. But Frederick William withdrew from direct confrontation with Austria and signed the Convention of Olmütz on 29 November 1849, whereby the concept of a German empire without Austria was abandoned. German nationalists were disgusted by this act, and even Prussian reactionaries were outraged by what became known as the 'humiliation of Olmütz.' The Convention of Olmütz stimulated anew Prussian antagonism toward Austria. Just to complete Prussia's embarrassment, it was agreed that a joint Austrian-Prussian army would intervene in Schleswig-Holstein and restore Danish royal authority, a complete reversal of previous policy. One result of this insignificant campaign was to impress upon Austrian officers the efficiency of the Prussian army.

Between 1848 and 1857 the chief of the general staff was General von Reyher, an intelligent, competent and unswervingly loyal officer. He continued the professional improvement of the

army in a decade of reaction in which the king was increasingly influenced by his aide-de-camp, the conservative, aggressive and highly ambitious Major Edwin von Manteuffeul. In October 1857, Reyher died, and before Frederick William could fill the vacant post, he himself suffered a severe stroke. Frederick William's younger brother, Prince William, was appointed first as deputy to the king, and then as Regent. Prince William had been an officer since seventeen, and was by temperament a reactionary. One of his first appointments was that of Major General Helmuth von Moltke as acting chief of the general staff.

Moltke's appointment surprised many officers because he was hardly known and only had a limited reputation as a military historian. He had never commanded a unit as large as a company, and had spent most of his military career with the general staff. Moltke was the son of an impoverished Mecklenburg nobleman, and had served originally in the Danish army before applying for a commission in the Prussian army. In 1823 he entered the General War School, and then held a variety of staff appointments, including acting as adviser to the Turkish army. Moltke spoke English and French, was a keen military historian, and was an early supporter of railroads. In the 1850s Moltke had attracted the attention of Prince William, and served as aide-de-camp to his only son, Prince Frederick William. It was through these connections and the reputation he gained as an efficient staff officer which led to Moltke's appointment as acting chief of the general staff, which was confirmed as permanent in 1858.

As deputy to his brother, and then as Regent, Prince William began a reorganization of the army aimed at increasing its size, improving its efficiency and controlling the *Landwehr*. This reorganization brought the king into direct conflict with the lower chamber of the Prussian parliament which objected to increased military expenditure and the reduction of the militia nature of the *Landwehr*. Prince William was impressed by a paper written by General Albrecht von Roon, submitted in July 1858, which proposed to increase the size of the standing army by returning to a system of three year conscript service. Roon recommended an annual call up of 63,000 men, and this and a three year period of service would permit the establishment of an active army of 200,000 men with substantial reserves. The other major aim of Roon's proposal was to raise the standard of effectiveness of the *Landwehr* and at the same time bring it firmly under the control of the regular army. The *Landwehr* was to be amalgamated with the regular army's reserves and thus lose its autonomous position.

To circumvent the more cautious officers in the War Ministry, in 1859 Prince William appointed Roon to head a special Military Commission to draft reform proposals to be presented to parliament. In December 1859 Roon was appointed War Minister, and a fierce parliamentary struggle began over the necessary grants for military expenditure, and it was only with the appointment of Otto von Bismarck as Minister President of Prussia in September 1862 that the deadlock was resolved in favor of William, who had become king in 1860 following his brother's death. Bismarck took the view that as there was a gap in the constitution between, on the one side the king, and the conservative upper house in favor of expenditure, and on the other hand the lower house which was against expenditure, the crown was entitled to take such action as it deemed necessary for the welfare of the state. Although it was not until a retrospective bill was passed in 1867 that the reorganization of the army and the altered terms of service were made legal, the king and Roon had already gone ahead with their own recommendations.

Under Roon's reforms, the army was expanded, and divided between the standing army and the *Landwehr*. But the *Landwehr* no longer provided regiments for service alongside those of the regular army. Instead, it constituted both a second line reserve of reinforcements and a pool of reserve divisions. Furthermore, there was the *Landsturm* which consisted of men liable for military service but who had not undertaken full time service in

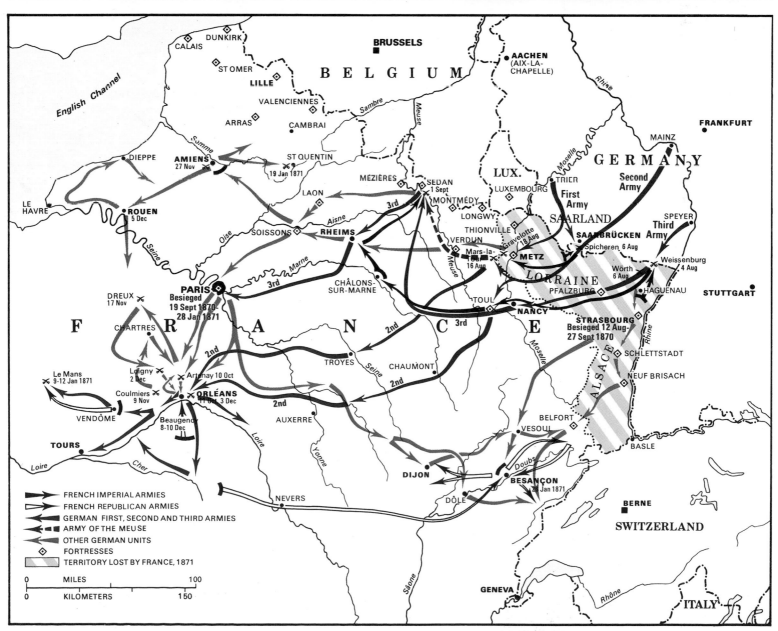

History of The German Army

The I Bavarian Corps storming a railway embankment on the outskirts of Orleans, 1870.

History of The German Army

the monarchy and Prussian institutions to protect its privileges, believing that its interests were indivisible from those of Prussia. The parliamentary opposition to such military independence and the clash over the budget was to be a continual problem for successive Prussian and German governments. Reactionary officers had achieved a firmer grip over both the personnel and administrative organization of the army. In 1859 Prince William had formally revived the old Military Cabinet with Manteuffel as its head, and made it responsible for all officer appointments. Selection of officer candidates was to be based on social background and political reliability, with a special emphasis placed on the reactionary officer cadet schools which consisted largely of the sons of the poor nobility.

As chief of the general staff, Moltke had not been directly involved with the military reorganization controversy. Instead, he concentrated on the organization of the general staff and strategic problems. In 1859 Moltke reorganized the general staff into four departments combining the geographical and functional systems. The Eastern Department dealt with Russia, Austria-Hungary, Sweden and Turkey. The German Department was concerned with the German states, including Austria, and other European countries. A new Railroads Department was established to consider the use of railways for mobilization and operational deployment. The fourth department, that of Military History, provided information and support to the other departments.

The Prussian army faced a test of its organization, mobilization plans and ability to deploy in the spring of 1859 when war broke out between Austria and the kingdom of Sardinia. France supported Sardinia, and the French Emperor, Napoleon III, led a French army against the Austrians in northern Italy. The Austrian Emperor, Franz Joseph, appealed to the Prussians for help against

the army. A conscript was now liable to seven years military service, three with the colors and then four with the regular army reserve. After seven years his name remained on the *Landwehr* lists for a further five years.

The crisis over the reorganization of the army between 1859 and 1862 appeared to have been resolved in favor of King William and his military advisers. Although the power of the monarchy to control the army seemed to have been reaffirmed, in practice, the army controlled itself, and the officer corps was prepared to use

Above left: Civilian resistance – a German lancer dragging in a Frenchman who has disrupted communications by cutting telegraph wires.
Right: The decisive battle of Sedan.
Below: Prussian siege guns firing on Paris, 1871.

the French. Although an active war between Prussia and France was prevented by the Austrians and French reaching a settlement in July, nevertheless, the Prussian army was mobilized and concentrated in the Rhineland. The large scale confusion resulting from this mobilization enabled Moltke to learn a number of lessons concerning the use of railroads and the need for meticulous planning. Moltke undertook a detailed study of the 1859 Italian campaign, and the results of both areas of experience were demonstrated in the summer maneuvers of 1862. These maneuvers were based on a railroad mobilization and transportation exercise directed toward the possibility of a war in northern Germany or against Denmark. In contrast to 1859, the mobilization and deployment in 1862 showed a marked improvement. The lessons Moltke had drawn from the Italian campaign confirmed his belief that a field commander should be given general aims related to clear objectives, and then instructed to take aggressive action against the enemy.

The Italian War of 1859 had been fought between armies mainly armed with muzzle-loading rifles and using the tactics of the Napoleonic war. Only gradually were armies adapting to the technical developments in weapon technology which nineteenth century advances in metallurgy, ballistics and precision engineering were simultaneously making possible. In particular, the development of breech-loading rifles and artillery would radically effect tactics and produce a volume of firepower and a degree of

accuracy hitherto unobtainable. The Prussian army had led the way in adopting the breech loading rifle, the Dreyse needle gun. In 1848 the uniform and equipment of the Prussian soldier was also substantially adapted. Based on Russian influences, the *Pickelhaube*, or spiked helmet replaced the shako, the blue coatee was replaced by a blue tunic, and the new Virchow belted equipment was introduced. From 1864 the uniform also included low boots, into which the trousers were tucked when in the field. The distinctive image of the Prussian, and later the German soldier had been established.

Between 1862 and 1864 there was considerable rivalry and antagonism involving Austria and Prussia over the German Confederation. Bismarck was determined to promote Prussia as the dominant power in Germany and to exclude Austria. However, both states were forced to act in concert over Danish claims to Schleswig-Holstein in 1863. In December 1863 both powers approved the dispatch of a federal army of Saxon and Hanoverian contingents into Holstein, while Danish troops occupied Schleswig. When the Danes refused to withdraw from Schleswig, the Austrians and Prussians sent a joint invasion force into Schleswig under the command of the obstinate, reactionary old *beau sabreur*, Field Marshal von Wrangel.

In the pre-war conferences, Wrangel had contemptuously refused the advice of Moltke and the general staff, and rejected the suggestion that any member of that organization should serve

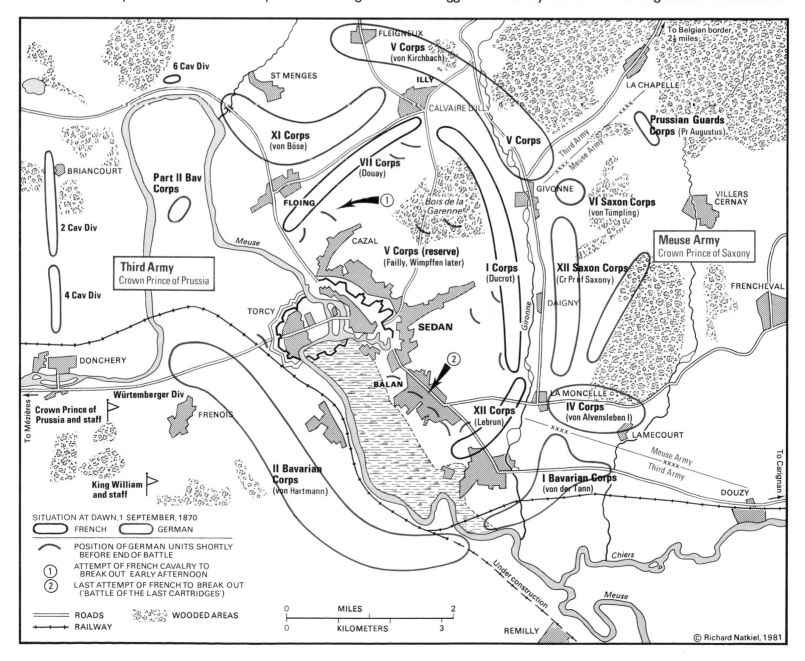

SITUATION AT DAWN, 1 SEPTEMBER, 1870
FRENCH   GERMAN

POSITION OF GERMAN UNITS SHORTLY BEFORE END OF BATTLE

(1) ATTEMPT OF FRENCH CAVALRY TO BREAK OUT EARLY AFTERNOON

(2) LAST ATTEMPT OF FRENCH TO BREAK OUT ('BATTLE OF THE LAST CARTRIDGES')

ROADS   WOODED AREAS
RAILWAY

MILES 0 — 2
KILOMETERS 0 — 3

© Richard Natkiel, 1981

History of The German Army

Above: German soldiers examine a captured French mitrailleuse, 1870. Faulty tactics meant that, when these early machine guns, a French secret weapon, were brought into action, they were usually quickly knocked out by the efficient Prussian artillery.
Right: Fierce street fighting in Bazeilles during the battle of Sedan.

limited war to force Austria to accept Prussia's aims. Although Austria could count on the support of the majority of the German states, Moltke calculated that the Prussian army could be mobilized and deployed faster and more decisively than Austria and her allies could concentrate their overwhelming numerical superiority. The smaller German states could be discounted because many of their officers were impressed by the Prussian army and were reluctant to fight against it. Moltke planned to

as his chief of staff. As Moltke had foreseen the Danes fell back from the frontier avoiding a major battle, and withdrew to the fortifications of Düppel in eastern Schleswig. Wrangel proposed to avoid a direct assault on the Danish fortifications by invading Jutland. William was persuaded, as a result of Wrangel's inefficiency and lack of judgement, to send Moltke to act as his chief of staff. Bismarck refused to accept Moltke's advice to starve Düppel into surrender, demanding a resounding victory to help the complicated international negotiations which had begun. So on 18 April 1864 the Prussians stormed the fortifications and won for Bismarck a resounding diplomatic victory.

In late April negotiations began following an agreement to a month's armistice which at the end of May was renewed for a second month. William was persuaded to relieve Wrangel diplomatically from the command of the allied army and replace him with Prince Frederick Charles. Anticipating the failure of negotiations, Moltke prepared plans for a speedy occupation of Jutland. When the war was renewed on 28 June the Prussians moved, and within a fortnight Jutland had been occupied and Denmark sued for peace.

The Danish War had begun badly for Prussia, and there had been considerable confusion and a lack of a clear military aim. Foreign observers had made uncomplimentary remarks about the Prussian army in comparison to the Austrian. However, Moltke's appointment as Wrangel's chief of staff had established the system of coordination which linked the chief of the general staff to the chiefs of staff of subordinate commands. The victory at Düppel was also important in establishing Prussia as the leading military exponent of German nationalism, and in making the Prussian army an object of admiration in the eyes of the Prussian people. Following the battle of Düppel, a parade of Prussian soldiers who had taken part in the assault was held in Berlin and a Victory Column erected commemorating the battle.

Both Bismarck and Moltke were determined that Prussia should annex Schleswig-Holstein and believed that war with Austria was inevitable. In 1865 Moltke worked on a plan for a

concentrate the main body of the Prussian army, some 250,000 men, against the Austrians in Bohemia, leaving 50,000 troops to deal with Bavaria, Baden and Württemberg. Meanwhile, Bismarck used all his diplomatic skills to neutralize France and Russia and to inveigle Italy into threatening Austria's southern flank.

In the spring of 1866 there was a rush for mobilization amongst the German states who feared a sudden Prussian attack, and on 7 June Prussian troops occupied Holstein, having been mobilized on 8 May. Prussia never declared war but began hostilities against Austria and her allies from 15 June. Moltke's influence had increased during the weeks of crisis, and on the 2 June the king had issued an historic order authorizing the chief of the general staff to issue orders directly to subordinate units of the Prussian army without having first obtained permission from either the king or the War Minister. At least for the duration of the war, the chief of the general staff was temporarily in command, ending the rivalry

between the general staff, the War Ministry and the Military Cabinet.

The war with Austria and her allies was over in seven weeks, following what many Prussian officers believed had been a risky strategy. The Prussian army was deployed according to Moltke's dictum of 'march separately, fight together.' Moltke correctly judged that new techniques and technology enabled such an innovation to be put into operation. The railways and improved roads meant that units of the Prussian army could be moved rapidly from one theater of operations to another. The telegraph had greatly improved communications, and indeed during the preliminary moves, it had allowed Moltke to remain in Berlin and yet keep in touch with the field army. Finally, the needle gun had increased the firepower of the Prussian infantrymen and made them less vulnerable to attack.

By the beginning of June, the Prussians had begun to consolidate their three main armies in Bohemia, with the intention of encircling and destroying the Austrian army under the command of General August Benedek. Although Moltke was able to bring the Austrians and their Saxon allies to battle at Königgrätz on 3 July 1866, he was unable to achieve the encirclement planned. This was because both the Austrians and Saxons fought well, and the Austrian artillery and cavalry were able to slow down the advance of the Prussian infantry. Moltke was unsuccessful in his attempts to coordinate the movements of the three Prussian armies, and this enabled the Austrians to withdraw on the fortress of Königgrätz.

Below: Winter fighting – Prussians in action against the French at Montbeliard, December 1870.

The Prussians, exhausted by intensive marching and fighting, were in no position to pursue the Austrians, whose casualties had amounted to 40,000 against 10,000 Prussian. As well as defeating the Austrians, the Prussians had also defeated their German allies in a dramatic way.

Bismarck accepted the mediation of Napoleon III, and in August 1866 a peace treaty was signed between Prussia and Austria. The War of 1866 resulted in Prussia becoming the dominant power in Germany with Austria excluded. Prussia annexed Hanover, Hesse-Cassel, Nassau and other minor states, adding to Prussia a population of 4,200,000. All the states north of the Main now formed the North German Confederation under Prussian leadership.

The armies of the newly incorporated states were partly disbanded, reorganized and reformed, being placed on the same establishments as that of Prussia. The king of Prussia was commander-in-chief of the armies of the North German Confederation. In 1867, approval was given to the 'law on the obligation to military service,' which extended the Prussian military system to all contingents in the Confederation. Large numbers of Prussian officers and NCOs were drafted into non-Prussian regiments, and in turn many former officers from Hanover, Hesse-Cassel and Nassau were posted into Prussian regiments. Allies of Prussia outside the Confederation, Bavaria, Württemberg, Baden and Hesse-Darmstadt, all of whom maintained their own armies, adopted Prussian military institutions, tactics, drill and weapons. By 1869 the peacetime strength of the Prussian army was 300,000 and the wartime strength 552,000.

Despite the victory over Austria, Moltke was far from satisfied

with the performance of the Prussian army, the general staff or himself. He began a critical analysis of the weaknesses revealed in the war, especially with regard to the failure of the cavalry at reconnaissance and pursuit, and the deficiencies of the artillery with regard to the requirement for steel, rifled, breech-loading cannon, and to deploy artillery well forward in support of the infantry. Moltke stressed the importance at all levels for commanders to coordinate their actions and to maintain operational control. Moltke had no power on his own authority to implement many changes, but he worked through Roon, the War Minister, and the arms inspectors. Moltke also made some changes in the organization of the general staff, and after 1867 it was divided between the *Haupetat*, or Main Establishment, and the *Nebenetat*, or Supporting Establishment.

Following the defeat of Austria considerable tension developed between France and Prussia. Napoleon III was very sensitive to Prussian territorial ambitions along the Rhine, and Bismarck looked for an opportunity to provoke the French into war. Moltke paid increasing attention to building new railroads to hasten the movement of the army toward the French frontier. He calculated that the Prussians and their allies could mobilize more quickly and with greater numbers of troops than could the French. He was aware also that the French army had no field headquarters and staff comparable to that of the Prussian army.

Bismarck successfully provoked the French into war in July 1870 over the question of a successor to the Spanish throne. Within eighteen days of mobilization, the Prussians and their allies had 1,200,000 men in uniform, with nearly 500,000 concentrating on the Rhine. King William entered the field as commander-in-chief, with Moltke, Roon, and a large entourage. Moltke took with him only a small fraction of the general staff from Berlin, and these formed a field general staff to control the unwieldy Prussian armies.

The main Prussian invasion force consisted of three armies, at first widely dispersed. In the center was the Second Army, under Prince Frederick Charles, which advanced through Saarbrücken; on the right was the First Army under General Steinmetz advancing towards Saarlouis; and on the left, the Third Army under the Crown Prince, moving on Strasbourg. Moltke planned to encircle and annihilate the French army north of the Saar where it was assembling in some confusion. But the Prussian army commanders could not move their forces with sufficient speed, and Steinmetz was unwilling to submit to Moltke's authority.

In fact Marshal Bazaine's Army of the Rhine fought exceptionally well in a series of major battles throughout August. French *élan* and the Chassepot rifle came as a nasty surprise to the Prussians, and there were a number of incidents where Prussian units, particularly those drawn from their German allies, broke in battle. But Prussian determination to attack the French could also lead to some heroic but costly actions. At the battle of Rezonville on 16 August the 16th Lancers and the 7th Magdeburg Cuirassiers made their famous *Todesritt*, or Death Ride. The two regiments of 600 men charged two lines of French artillery before being charged in turn by two French cavalry brigades. They lost over 400 men but the charge became a spectacular military tradition. At Saint-Privat, a Prussian infantry charge was decimated with losses of 8230 men out of an original total of 32,000. Such actions were splendid and heroic, but demonstrated the effect of modern firepower against traditional tactics. By the 19 August the Prussians had surrounded Bazaine's army in Metz and begun a siege.

Near Châlons, Marshal MacMahon had started to form what became known as the Army of Châlons. Amongst the confusion of new units and three corps from the Army of the Rhine was Napoleon III. Moltke was able to discover MacMahon's intentions through reading Parisian newspapers, and realized that he intended marching to join Bazaine at Metz. Leaving a force to cover Metz, Moltke concentrated the Prussian Third Army and a new Army of the Meuse against MacMahon at Sedan. On 1 September

1870, the Prussians attacked and the French were unable to withstand the devastating artillery fire. The French began to surrender in large numbers, and in the evening, Napoleon III requested an armistice. Sedan was a major Prussian victory with the capitulation of a French army and the capture of the Emperor Napoleon III.

With the surrender of Napoleon III, Bismarck and Moltke assumed the war was over, but to their horror and frustration, the news of Sedan led to a revolution in Paris, the overthrow of the Second Empire, and a new government of National Defense. Although the new French government were defiant they could offer little serious resistance to the Prussians, beyond hastily raised scratch forces. By 20 September the Prussians had surrounded Paris and begun a conventional siege. On 28 October Bazaine capitulated to an inferior Prussian army at Metz.

But Bismarck and Moltke began to worry that a decisive victory was eluding them, and with continued French resistance there was the increasing possibility of foreign intervention which would cheat Prussia of its rightful reward. Furthermore, the Prussian army was tied down besieging Paris and conducting major operations in northern France. Although the armies of the new French government were militarily insignificant, the *levée en masse* had produced the *franc-tireurs*, or irregular guerrillas, who attacked the Prussian lines of communication across the Rhine. Bismarck and Moltke feared the revolutionary nature of French resistance and were concerned to reach a peace settlement with a stable, conservative government, which could honor its obligations and maintain order.

Paris, threatened by internal civil insurrection, surrendered, and an armistice was signed on 28 January 1871. A peace settlement was finally concluded in May, and France was forced to cede Alsace-Lorraine, Metz and Strasbourg and pay a large war indemnity. On 18 January, in the Hall of Mirrors in the Palace of Versailles, King William I of Prussia was proclaimed Emperor of Germany. William was far from enthusiastic about becoming *Kaiser* and viewed his position with considerable distaste. Nonetheless, Prussia formed the core of the new *Kaiserreich*, and the Prussian army that of the new *Kaiserheer*.

Below: German victory parade along the Champs Elysees, Paris, 1 March 1871.

The Kaiser's Army

History of The German Army

The Prussian army finished the war in 1871 with an enhanced reputation both at home and abroad, and was seen as having been responsible for the success of the Wars of Unification – 1864, 1866 and 1870-71. The Prussian army was widely respected and admired both by German nationalists as a symbol of the new nation state, and by foreign military observers as combining the brains of the general staff with the discipline and fighting ability of its soldiers. This awesome reputation meant that within Germany the army became an object of national veneration, and its status was such that no civilian could significantly question its power and influence. Increasingly, the officers of the general staff came to believe in their own judgement and ability to such an extent that their overbearing confidence and arrogance set them at odds with Clausewitz's concept of the relationship between the civil and military authorities within the state.

In the *Kaiserreich*, the *Kaiserheer* was organized into eighteen army corps, thirteen from Prussia, two from Bavaria, one from Württemberg and one from Saxony. One army corps was a mixed contingent and was based in Alsace-Lorraine. In theory there were four separate state armies making up the *Kaiserheer*, each with its own War Ministry and general staff. In practice, the Prussian army dominated the *Kaiserheer*, and the Prussian general staff became the German general staff. The *Kaiserheer* owed its loyalty and obedience to William I who was 'Supreme War Leader.'

After 1871, the *Kaiserheer* became the model for many foreign armies in terms of organization, uniforms, weapons and doctrine. The success of the general staff encouraged foreign imitators, so that in 1872 France established its own general staff closely modelled on the Prussian example. The Austrians had a general

Previous page: German *Schutztruppen* in action against the Hereros in Southwest Africa in 1906.
Below: Great Military Tattoo in Berlin, 7 September 1872. Such parades helped inspire the growth of German nationalist feeling.

staff before 1866, but it had been mainly an association for military preferment. In 1875 the old Austrian general staff was abolished and a new one created on the lines of the Prussian example. The Russians continued to adapt and improve their general staff, and eventually the British and Americans were to form general staffs very much on Prussian lines. Foreign armies copied Prussian uniforms and equipment, and with the expansion of the German armaments business, German weapons were much in demand.

German military advisers began to train foreign armies such as the Japanese, Turkish and Bulgarian armies who in turn armed themselves with weapons and equipment from Krupp factories. The German government hoped that such contacts would assist diplomacy and trade and enhance German influence. In the case of Turkey and Bulgaria, this was correct, and in the First World War both these countries were to fight on the side of the Central Powers, their armies trained and staffed by German officers.

The Wars of Unification and the establishment of the *Kaiserreich* had not lessened external threats, rather they had transformed them from traditional Prussian fears of encirclement into German ones. After the Franco-Prussian War, Moltke and the general staff were concerned at the possibility of an alliance between France and Russia, which would realize the danger of a two-front war. Since the reign of Frederick the Great, Prussia had faced the danger of a two-front war, and at first Moltke concluded that the answer to the problem was to concentrate an overwhelming force against France to gain a quick decisive victory, before turning against Russia. Moltke was aware of the dangers of such a strategy which relied for success upon the ability of the Germans to mobilize faster than either the French or Russians, and that the Russians would be so slow and disorganized that the Germans would be able to concentrate the greater part of their army against France.

Bismarck hoped to lessen the dangers to Germany through diplomatic rather than military policy. He tried to isolate France

war plans. Schlieffen was an intensely professional, hard working staff officer who soon came to the conclusion that the decision to give Russia priority in offensive action in a two-front war was strategically unsound. Schlieffen concluded that it was necessary for Germany to achieve a quick and decisive victory. This would not be possible if Germany concentrated against Russia, because France was the greater danger, and campaigning in Russia would involve operations similar to those which had led Napoleon to disaster. The new war plan reverted to the early Moltke one of concentrating the greater part of the army against France while leaving a small covering force against Russia.

The basis of Schlieffen's strategic thought was the concept of maneuver and the double envelopment. He was convinced that it was only through such action that a decisive strategic victory could be achieved. Schlieffen's model of the perfect tactical battle of maneuver and envelopment, in which an army with inferior numbers was able to bring superior strength to bear against both flanks of a stronger opponent, was Hannibal's classic double envelopment victory at Cannae in 216 B.C. Schlieffen was to write a study of Cannae, in which he showed how Frederick the Great, Napoleon and Moltke had all successfully applied this method in strategic as well as tactical operations.

Schlieffen's war plan, which was adopted in 1894, concentrated nine-tenths of the army against France to seek a decisive victory before the French were mobilized and deployed. By achieving surprise, using mobility and maneuver, Schlieffen planned to envelop and destroy the French army before Russia could mobilize or some foreign power like Britain could intervene. Before the First World War there were to be four versions of the Schlieffen Plan reflecting the changing circumstances. Schlieffen pressed continually for increases in the strength of the army, and there was a need to consider the balance of forces between the two flanks in the west, the balance of forces between west and east, and to take into account French and Russian war plans.

Above: General Alfred von Waldersee, Chief of the General Staff, 1888-91.
Right: Colonel-General Alfred von Schlieffen, Chief of the General Staff, 1891-1906.

through the *Dreikaiserbund*, or League of the Three Emperors – Prussia, Austria-Hungary and Russia. But this informal alliance collapsed, and when Germany became more closely allied with Austria, Russia was pushed into an alliance with France. Bismarck's careful diplomacy was continually undermined by the bellicose attitude of the general staff who pressed for a preventive war. After William II became *Kaiser* in 1888, he abandoned Bismarck and enthusiastically adopted the bombastic attitude of the officer corps.

Moltke and the general staff were concerned with other problems relating to a two-front war. They had to take into account the possibility that the Russians might mobilize and concentrate their armies quickly and this necessitated a substantial increase in the size of the *Kaiserheer*. An expansion of the *Kaiserheer* was also necessary to take into account the new fortification system the French had begun to build along their border with Germany which enhanced both their offensive and defensive capabilities. Even the military alliance after 1879 with Austria did not alleviate the problems of fighting a two-front war, as the general staff, far from thinking that the Austro-Hungarian army would be an asset against Russia, were convinced that it would be a liability and would need German assistance. The result was a new plan to concentrate the greater part of the *Kaiserheer* against Russia, while a smaller force delayed the French in the west.

When Moltke retired as an elderly, senile legend in 1888, he was succeeded by his deputy, General Alfred von Waldersee, who in his three years as chief of the general staff did little to alter Moltke's strategic plans, preferring instead to concentrate on political and military intrigue. But Waldersee's successor, General von Schlieffen, did begin a fundamental reassessment of Moltke's

In 1906, Schlieffen left a final revised version of his plan to his successor, General von Moltke the Younger. It was based upon a mobilized army of 84 regular and reserve divisions, to be strengthened after mobilization by twelve *ersatz*, or newly created divisions. Schlieffen envisaged placing some 96 percent of the entire mobilized field strength of the army in the west. He calculated in 1905 that the Russians would take several weeks to mobilize and would be distracted by an Austrian offensive into Poland. East Prussia would be covered by a small force of garrison and *Landwehr* troops who would be reinforced eventually by units returning from the west after the successful six week campaign against France.

In the west, only ten divisions were allocated south of Metz to cover Alsace-Lorraine, whilst to the north some 71 divisions would be deployed. Those divisions south of Metz would blunt the expected French offensive while those in the north would form the massive envelopment movement which would sweep through Holland and Belgium toward Lille and Amiens, envelop Paris and encircle the French armies against the German forces and the fortresses of Alsace-Lorraine.

Moltke the Younger amended the Schlieffen Plan in several important ways. He decided not to violate Dutch territory, but instead to capture the Belgian fortified town of Liège, and then to push two German armies through the narrow gap between the Ardennes and the Dutch frontier. Moltke altered the balance of forces, not only between west and east, but between the left wing and the right wing in the west. The German forces in the east were strengthened by removing six divisions from the right wing

Left: Kaiser William II as Colonel of the Death's Head Hussars.
Below: The First Regiment of Foot Guards of the *Kaiserheer* on a route march shortly before World War I.

in the west. Additional divisions made available after increased manpower allocations were placed south rather than north of Metz.

The result of Moltke's decision was to weaken the right wing of the proposed envelopment movement in the west. Instead of the 71 divisions originally allocated, there were to be only 55. After his retirement, Schlieffen continued to refine his plan and became obsessed with the need to place all available strength on the right wing in the west. After the failure in 1914, many officers blamed Moltke for altering the balance of forces within the Schlieffen Plan and thus condemning it to failure. But even without Moltke's alterations, the Schlieffen Plan remained flawed as a strategic concept.

Schlieffen appeared indifferent to the political consequences of attacking neutral Holland and Belgium, and dismissed the threat of British military intervention. Although Schlieffen was very aware of the problems posed by Belgian and French fortifications and took a great interest in the development of mobile siege artillery, neither he nor his successor was seriously concerned that the envelopment movement of the right wing would be delayed by such fortifications. Schlieffen was aware of the problems of command and control of such a massive envelopment, but he appeared to think that the efficiency of the general staff would enable the chief of the general staff to exercise his authority. Both Schlieffen and Moltke assumed that the German divisions on the right wing would be able to march and fight and be supplied with food and ammunition in a wheeling movement which would cover some three hundred miles.

The fact that the Schlieffen Plan depended upon the speed with which the army was mobilized and deployed, meant that there was always pressure by the general staff to mobilize at the slightest sign of tension, and some were in favor of a preventive

war. An additional pressure in this respect was the progress made by the Russian army and developments in the Russian rail system in the years immediately before 1914. These undoubtedly increased the speed of the Russian mobilization and threatened the German advantage in this field. In many respects the Schlieffen Plan was a symptom of the 'encirclement paranoia' which affected both the *Kaiserreich* and the *Kaiserheer*.

The Schlieffen Plan depended for its success upon having a large enough army. After 1871 the general staff pressed successive Chancellors for increases in the military budget and the size of the army. Bismarck's constitution for the new *Kaiserreich* had given budgetary rights and thus control of military expenditure to the *Reichstag*, or Imperial Parliament.

He had considered this as a necessary gesture to obtain the support of the German liberals for a Prussian dominated, autocratic *Reich*. But almost immediately, Bismarck had attempted to circumvent parliamentary control of the army. He suggested an *Aeternat*, or Eternal Law, by which the size of the army would be permanently decided and the *Reichstag* would have no control over expenditure for arms and equipment. When the *Reichstag* rejected this proposal, Bismarck compromised with the *Septennat*, or Seven Year Bill, which became law on the 20 April 1874. This law increased military expenditure and also the size of the army to just over 400,000 men.

Further attempts to pass a second and third *Septennat* produced uproar in the *Reichstag*, where there was considerable opposition to increasing military expenditure and the size of the army. Bismarck was forced to call an election in 1887 based upon

Below: Kaiserheer railway battalion at work. Railway troops played a vital role in mobilization plans. In the event of a successful advance into enemy territory they would be expected to assist by repairing any demolitions made by the retreating forces as well as by managing all traffic within the war zone.

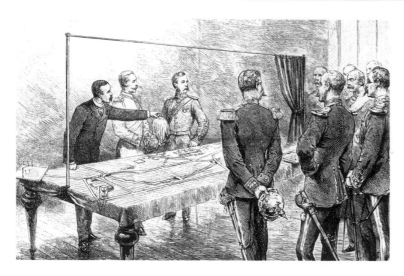

an expanding navy during the Wilhelmine era. Under William I the *Kaisermarine* had been a small coastal defense force, but William II was encouraged by a powerful navy lobby to think in terms of a large oceanic navy which would effectively challenge Britain's Royal Navy. The army followed the navy's lead in mobilizing popular political support for its needs, and in 1912, the *Wehrverein*, or Army League was founded. It was symptomatic of Wilhelmine Germany that there was little coordination between the army and navy and both pursued separate and at times contradictory approaches toward the problems of national security.

The *Kaiserheer* officer corps bitterly resented parliamentary interference and control. There had always been a suspicion and hatred of bourgeois liberal parliaments and their desire to interfere with the army. But in the *Kaiserreich* there was now a socialist party represented in the *Reichstag*, and by the turn of the century the Social Democrat Party appeared to have a natural majority. The officer corps resented the fact that the Prussian War Minister, who was always a serving officer, had to explain the army's case in the *Reichstag*.

Moltke's deputy and successor as chief of the general staff, Waldersee, was a born political intriguer, and was determined that the general staff should not be subordinate to the War Ministry and thus parliamentary control. Waldersee worked with General von Albedyll, the head of the Military Cabinet, to seek the independence of the general staff and the Military Cabinet from the War Ministry. This they achieved in 1883 when General

patriotic hysteria before a new *Reichstag* voted for the increases. Successive Chancellors were able to push through further increases, attempting to overcome parliamentary opposition by exaggerating the fear of encirclement. In 1899 the army was increased to 612,000 men and by 1913 the strength stood at 700,000 men.

The question of the military budget was complicated further for the army by the fact that it had to compete for resources with

von Kameke, the War Minister who opposed their plans, was forced to resign and was replaced by General Bronsart, who agreed to take over the appointment, but with reduced powers. In March 1883, an Imperial Decree was issued abolishing the Department of Personnel in the War Ministry, and formally transferring all military personnel matters to the Military Cabinet. On 24 May another Imperial Decree granted the chief of the general staff and his deputy *Immediatvortrag*, or the right of immediate access to the emperor.

Although in practice the power of the Military Cabinet had been established already, and Moltke had had *Immediatvortrag* before and during the Franco-Prussian War, these Imperial Decrees re-established the authority and power of the monarchy over the army, and removed it from parliament. William II believed that he was a soldier-king in the style of Frederick the Great, and his irrational and emotional interference in military questions was to exasperate the general staff. During the Franco-Prussian War there had been several important disagreements over policy between Bismarck and Moltke. Moltke refused to let Bismarck interfere in military matters even when there were political considerations which were of paramount importance.

Above left: The *Kaiser* and General Staff officers watch a demonstration of a new War Game.
Right: The field uniform and the parade uniform worn by Grenadiers of the Prussian Guard in the 1890s.
Below: The final parade of the *Kaisermanöver*, October 1883.

After 1871 the officer corps criticized Bismarck for refusing to listen to their demands for a preventive war and for being far too conciliatory towards the *Reichstag*. This hostile attitude was to become even more intense under Bismarck's successors as Chancellor.

Under Schlieffen, the general staff had become isolated from political realities and it became an introverted group of professional technicians. It was unfortunate that Moltke the Younger had little experience of service with the general staff, and was regarded with suspicion by its members. Indeed. Moltke was aware of his own deficiencies and this affected his self-confidence. By 1914 the number of officers on the general staff had increased to 625, reflecting not only the size of the army, but also the technical complexities of modern warfare. Membership of the general staff had become an essential prerequisite for a successful military career in the *Kaiserheer*. The competition for applicants to the *Kriegsakademie* was severe, and the course itself intense. However, the rewards of success were considerable, and it was estimated that membership of the general staff put an average of eight years on to an officer's seniority. Although the general staff was still the preserve of the old nobility, it was not merely sufficient to have the right social background to gain admittance. Increasingly, the officers who dominated the general staff were militarily proficient, but came from obscure social backgrounds, such as Erich Ludendorff and Wilhelm Groener.

The officer corps' fear of liberal parliamentary nationalism became transferred after 1871 to a fear of a socialist industrialized working class. In 1871 the population of Germany was 41 million, which by 1910 had risen to 65 million, with the greatest increase in the industrial working class. In less than thirty years Germany was to move dramatically from an agriculturally based economy to an industrially based economy. The 'enemy within' was the socialist industrialized working class. The officer corps was frightened that the army was being undermined by socialists which might one day impede its ability to crush a workers' revolt.

After 1871, large sections of the German bourgeoisie were absorbed into the military aristocratic value system of Prussia.

This was because many German liberals who had been suspicious of Prussia, and the Prussian army, were converted overnight into strident nationalists by the Wars of Unification. The German bourgeoisie, like the old landed nobility, feared the rise of a socialist industrialized working class, and was prepared to embrace an aristocratic value system. In their turn, the old nobility was forced reluctantly to admit certain elements of the bourgeoisie to strengthen its own position against a greater threat.

The vehicle by which sufficient candidates fulfilling the necessary social, educational and political background could enter the German military establishment was the *Reserveoffizierskorps*, or Reserve Officers Corps. The officer corps had hated and despised the *Landwehr* officers because they were bourgeois liberals who had dangerous notions of political and military independence. By 1886 the *Landwehr* had been reorganized so that the reserves were better coordinated with the regular army and under its effective control. The old liberal *Landwehr* officer was replaced by the reactionary reserve officer, who although bourgeois, was to ape the manners, attitude and life-style of the traditional Prussian army officer. In Wilhelmine Germany the greatest ambition of any member of the bourgeoisie was to become 'an officer of the reserve.' Indeed, to gain employment within the government's service and advancement in many professions, it became a *conditio sine qua non* to be a *Reserveoffizier*. The power and prestige of wearing an officer's uniform turned a young officer into a god, and a reserve officer into a demi-god. Chancellor Bethmann Hollweg took every opportunity to appear in his reserve officer's uniform and gain the respect which he might not have achieved from wearing civilian dress.

In the *Kaiserreich*, civilians had an obsequious respect for an officer's uniform which could be taken to ridiculous lengths. A lady walking along a path would step into the street to allow an officer to walk past. The socialist opposition parties mocked this attitude and rejoiced on the occasion before 1914 when a baker dressed up as an officer, and for a brief period of time acted as a tyrant in a small town. The incident of the 'Captain from Köpenick' symbolized the extent to which the *Kaiserreich* had become a militarized society.

Above: Staff officers at the War Ministry, Berlin, 1900. The carmine uniform decorations were the mark of the General Staff.
Main picture: 'Discipline, drill, obedience and pride' – the *Kaiserheer* at a march past.
Above right: Field artillery on maneuvers, 1907.

Above: Moving a Bavarian field gun up a hill on maneuvers, 1909.
Left: Horses of an artillery battery are watered whilst infantry march past during maneuvers.
Above right: Colonel-General Helmuth von Moltke, the Younger, Chief of the General Staff, 1906-14.

As far as possible, the regular officer corps was selected from the traditional landed class, but increasingly there were bourgeois officers to be found in the regular army, particularly in the non-Prussian regiments and in the technical arms. But the officer corps preferred to have a shortage of officers, as it did in 1913, rather than accept candidates from undesirable backgrounds.

To counter the increase in conscripts drawn from the industrialized working class and thus prevent the army becoming 'infected' with socialism, the War Ministry took a higher percentage of its recruits from the rural areas. Professional army officers have always argued that rural recruits are healthier and make better disciplined soldiers than those from urban areas. So in 1911, when 42 percent of the German population lived on the land, some 64 percent of recruits were from rural areas. In fact the German army's annual intake of recruits was never equal to the legally permitted maximum. Large numbers of men were rejected annually because the army's establishment did not permit it to recruit all who were capable of bearing arms.

Between 1871 and 1893 the peacetime organization of the *Kaiserheer* was established by the constitution and a series of military conventions. After 1893 every German male was liable to serve his country over a 27-year period from the end of his 17th to his 45th year of age. At the age of seventeen a man was enrolled in the *Landsturm*, and at the age of twenty he undertook two years with the regular army and five years with its reserves. For those men serving in the cavalry or the horse artillery it was three

years with the regular army and only four with the reserves. Between the ages of 27 and 39, a man joined the *Landwehr*, after that he served in the *Landsturm* until he was 45. It was the expansion and increase in the reserves of the *Kaiserheer* which gave the Germans the ability to mobilize and deploy a massive field army.

Germany was divided into *Wehrkreise*, or military districts, within which were stationed regiments, brigades, divisions and corps, which came together as formed units in the event of mobilization. Before 1914 the general staff and the War Ministry perfected a system of mobilization which was practiced frequently. In August 1914 the regular army expanded in six days from 700,000 men to 3,840,000, with 2,100,000 in the field army. Postal and telegraphic communications were of paramount importance for notifying reservists with their mobilization orders, and the general staff continued to take a close interest in the planning and efficiency of the railroads.

Both strategically and tactically, the *Kaiserheer* was committed to the offensive. The Germans believed that strategy was the art of preparing, mobilizing, concentrating, moving and deploying resources and forces between theaters of war, or within a theater, with a view to success in battle. Unlike the French or Anglo-Saxon tradition, the Germans then considered operations, an intermediate stage between strategy and tactics. Operations concerned separate tactical engagements which developed by degrees into prolonged battles covering wide areas and involving substantial numbers of troops. Tactics was the art of fighting battles in contact with the enemy.

Moltke had concluded that for a chief of the general staff to command and control a large field army in modern war it was necessary to have a uniform doctrine and a reliability of action by subordinate commanders and staff which could only be attained

Above: Anti-military cartoon, 1914 – Officers sensitive as to their honor hear a civilian calling them a 'Silly ass!' – a reference to an incident at Zabern in formerly-French Alsace.

through training and experience. The members of the general staff were products of a very intense course at the *Kriegsakademie* which taught them to evaluate a situation quickly, to draw from it the essence of the problem, and then to make a clear decision. By alternating regimental and staff appointments it was hoped to balance the academic and the practical in the experience of a general staff officer. It was much more difficult to influence the majority of officers who did not serve on the general staff and yet many of them would hold important command appointments. A balance had to be found between adopting a uniform doctrine and allowing initiative to subordinate commanders.

The Germans found the answer through *Auftragstaktik,* or mission-orientated command. Under the system of *Auftragstaktik* commanders were trained to tell their subordinates what to do, but not how to do it. Provided only that subordinates kept within the general plan, wide latitude was granted to them to carry out their own measures. It was the responsibility of every German soldier to take whatever action was required in any military situation, without waiting for orders, and even to disobey orders if they were not consistent with the immediate situation. *Auftragstaktik* was the culmination of the military thinking and experience of Scharnhorst, Gneisenau and Moltke, and was to provide the legendary 'flexibility' of the German army.

Considerable emphasis was placed on continuous training in the *Kaiserheer.* The military year began on 1 October with the intake of new recruits. Basic training was completed in the first six months so that by the following spring, complete battalions could undertake field training. This was followed by regimental and divisional field exercises, culminating in late summer with the *Kaisermanöver.* Here William II participated and it was always necessary to allow the forces he commanded to win. The *Kaisermanöver* were unrealistic but a useful public display of German military power. This ended the military year, and time expired soldiers were discharged and a new intake of recruits arrived. Reserve troops were recalled for two weeks training in each year, and this occurred in September.

Tactics were based on the aggressive offensive. By 1914, the infantry attack consisted of three stages. Firstly, the *Aufmarsch,* forming up, which was the change from marching column into the line or column for the attack. Secondly, the *Entfaltung,* or deployment which broadened the front. Thirdly, the *Entwickelung,* or extension, in which the whole unit moved into skirmishing lines, again extending the front. The final attack formation consisted of a firing line, its supports and reserves. The doctrine of the attack meant that the emphasis was on the offensive and speed was

essential. The principal task of the artillery was to support the infantry attack with direct fire. German cavalry were used as the main reconnaissance force of the army, and although still trained for mounted shock action, they were moving toward being used as mounted infantry by 1914.

The *Kaiserheer* was generously armed and equipped with the products of the German armaments industry, which was organized in large cartels. The industrial expansion of the Ruhr and Silesia formed the basis of the German armaments industry. There were close political, economic and social connections between German industry, the armed forces and the nationalist political parties. The most famous company, Krupp, gained immense profits from Prussia's wars and established major contracts with the *Kaiserheer* and *Kaisermarine.*

After 1871, the *Kaiserheer* began to receive a new generation of quick-firing rifles and guns. In 1871, the first Mauser rifle with a bolt breech action began to replace the Dreyse needle gun, and in 1884, a tubular magazine in which the cartridges were carried in a tube in the stock under the barrel was applied to the rifle. Then the pattern was changed again to the box magazine in 1893, and the 1898 model Mauser rifle became the standard infantry weapon of the *Kaiserheer.* In theory, the rifle had a range of 2000 meters, and a trained soldier was capable of discharging 10-15 aimed shots per minute, and a rapid rate of fire of 30 rounds per minute was achieved by marksmen.

The *Kaiserheer* was one of the first armies to realize the effect the machine gun would have on the battlefield. After a series of experiments in the 1890s, the machine gun was adopted by the *Kaiserheer* in 1908. By 1914 there were some 2400 of them in service and they were regarded as weapons of maneuver.

German artillery was divided between light pieces in the Field artillery and medium and heavy weapons in the Foot artillery. The *Kaiserheer* possessed a wide range of artillery pieces which reflected technical innovation and the expansion of the army. The principal weapons of the Field artillery were the 7.7cm field guns and the 10.5cm howitzers. The main armament of the Foot artillery were the 15cm and 21cm howitzers. Heavy siege howitzers were also introduced in the period 1909-12, when the general staff were requiring siege guns to demolish Belgian and French fortifications.

The *Kaiserheer* experimented with aircraft and Zeppelins before 1914, and they were used for reconnaissance, but were regarded as frivolous toys by the majority of officers.

Although in 1914 the *Kaiserheer* possessed some 4000 motor vehicles, the basic transport of the field army was provided by the horse-drawn wagon. The ability to supply the field army on the march away from its advanced depots supplied by rail depended upon the ability to organize and deploy vast supply columns of horse-drawn wagons. At this time, the *Kaiserheer* was not unique in relying upon horse-drawn wagons, but it would be a critical factor in the maintenance of any large-scale envelopment movement as was envisaged in the Schlieffen Plan.

Like other armies, the *Kaiserheer* found it difficult to assess the impact automatic firepower from modern rifles, machine guns and quickfiring artillery would have on traditional tactics. The ability of soldiers to move around the battlefield in linear formations or dense columns had already been inhibited by such developments as illustrated in the American Civil War, the Franco-Prussian War and the South African (Boer) War. German military observers in the Russo-Japanese War 1904-05 did analyze the impact of firepower, but concluded that it would aid a determined attacker rather than the defender. Apart from very peripheral experiences

Top right: German hussars indulge in a charge on maneuvers. Such dramatic set pieces were often a concluding feature of the annual *Kaisermanöver* being staged for the Kaiser's benefit rather than for their military utility.
Right: 'The Captain of Köpenick,' a cartoon from the anti-military magazine *Simplicissimus.*
Far right: A *Simplicissimus* caricature of the Kaiser as the 'military expert' on maneuvers.

against the Boxers in China in 1900-01 and against the Hereros in South West Africa in 1904-07, the *Kaiserheer* had no direct experience of modern warfare. The *Kaiserheer* was convinced that its strategy, tactics, training and discipline had proved successful in the Franco-Prussian War, and with slight modifications would prove successful in any future war.

The public image of the *Kaiserheer* was one of parades, military splendor, glittering uniforms and accoutrements. Prussian militarism and arrogance were symbolized by what was commonly called 'the goosestep.' In fact, this was the *Exerzierschritt*, or drill step of the Prussian army. It consisted of raising the leg, and whilst keeping it straight and unbent, bringing it down slowly on to the ground with the foot pointed at an angle. The origins of the *Exerzierschritt* cannot be accurately determined, but it may have been introduced into the Prussian army from Russia after the War of Liberation. Throughout the nineteenth century there were official attempts to prevent the *Exerzierschritt* developing into a drill movement whereby the outstretched foot was brought crashing down onto the ground. However, this was never achieved, and in 1922 it was officially accepted as a drill step. The jackboot and the goosestep were soon to represent the public image of the German soldier.

William II was eager to link the past glories of the Prussian army with the *Kaiserheer*. Military traditions from the time of Frederick the Great and the War of Liberation all legitimized the *Kaiserheer*. William II went to considerable lengths to establish a continuity of traditions between the *Kaiserheer* and the armies of the pre-unification German states. In 1899 he allowed the regiments of the X Corps, which was recruited in Hanover, to become the *Traditionsträger*, or tradition holders of the battle honors formerly borne by the Hanoverian regiments of the

Above: German *askari* (native soldier) in East Africa. Native troops formed the majority of von Lettow-Vorbeck's force which fought the epic campaign in East Africa during World War I.
Right: A German Zeppelin forced down by bad weather in 1912.
Below right: German infantry of a Bavarian unit pursuing Boxers in China in 1900.
Below: A company of German *askaris* attacked during a local rebellion in East Africa in 1905.

Above: New recruits are mustered for initial training, c 1900
Above left: Bavarian machine gun troops on maneuvers in the last years before World War I.
Below left: Patriotic painting showing German soldiers attacking a Boxer stronghold in China, 1900.

independent kingdom. As Hanover had supported Austria in 1866, the whole of the Hanoverian army had been disbanded in 1867 and new regiments created from the Hanoverian *Wehrkreis*, based on drafts from Prussian regiments. Thus, the Hanoverian 73rd Fusilier and 79th Infantry Regiments and the 10th Jäger Battalion were authorized to wear a 'Gibraltar' cuffband on their sleeve, in honor of those Hanoverian regiments who formed part of the British garrison during the great siege of 1780-83. This artificial tradition was despite three clear breaks in the line: between the X Corps and the Hanoverian army in 1867, between the reformed Hanoverian army and the King's German Legion in 1816, and between the King's German Legion and the old Hanoverian army in 1803.

Despite the range of flamboyant dress uniforms and accoutrements adopted by the *Kaiserheer*, it became obvious by the late 1880s that the time-honored dark blue uniform of the Prussian soldier was likely to prove a liability on the modern battlefield. In 1892 the first steps were taken toward adapting the uniform of the German soldier to the requirements of the modern battlefield with the introduction of rush green linen covers for the headdress. During the Boxer Rebellion in China 1900-01, soldiers of the German contingent wore a khaki drill uniform with a system of colored piping known as *Waffenfarbe* to indicate arm of service. Between 1907 and 1910, the *Kaiserheer* finally adopted the new *feldgrau*, or field gray pattern uniform, which was to be worn in the field and on maneuvers. By 1914, the regular army, and most of the reserve and *Landwehr* formations were dressed in *feldgrau*, and this uniform included a cloth cover for the spiked helmet and shako, the cover being designed both to protect the helmet and prevent any tell-tale reflections from badges.

The *Kaiserheer* in 1914 was an extension of the old Prussian army but it had been influenced by political, social and techno-logical developments in Wilhelmine Germany which the reactionary officer corps had tried to control. The *Kaiserheer* combined the conservative, almost feudal traditions of pre-unification Germany with modern managerial and industrial techniques. Despite the fact that there was little contact between reactionary officers and socialist conscripts, patriotism and discipline produced a cohesive military machine. The professional efficiency of the *Kaiserheer* largely depended upon the 100,000 NCOs. But a combination of German arrogance and insecurity during the Wilhelmine era had produced an army that was eager to fight a preventive war against both potentially hostile foreign powers, and at home against a potentially hostile working class infected by socialism. In either case, the politicians and diplomats only had a limited ability to control the desire of the officer corps for decisive action. This desire was all too clearly reflected in the Schlieffen Plan. Above all the plan was based on the belief that overwhelming victory in a decisive battle was the only possible strategic aim.

Below: The new field gray uniforms of the *Kaiserheer* as worn in 1914.

War and Revolution

History of The German Army

The summer crisis of 1914, provoked by the assassination of the Austrian Archduke Franz Ferdinand by Serbian nationalists on 28 June, was welcomed by the German officer corps. The general staff calculated that this provided Germany with the opportunity to initiate a preventive war. The *Kaiserheer* was well trained and armed, the reservists available as they were preparing for the summer maneuvers, and there was total confidence in the Schlieffen Plan. Moltke urged the Austrians to take decisive action against Serbia, and when the Russians made threatening moves, urged the Austrians to stand firm against them. The German officer corps was anxious to initiate a preventive war in 1914, and the only plan they had available was the Schlieffen Plan, which meant that a local war became a European war, with Germany attacking France whatever the circumstances.

The mobilization of the Austrian and Russian armies provided the German general staff with the excuse required, and on 1 August Germany mobilized and the Schlieffen Plan was put into operation. Moltke as chief of the general staff, became on mobilization chief of staff of the army in the field and head of the *Oberst Heeresleitung* (OHL), or Army High Command. Although William II, as Supreme War Leader, was the titular head of the *Kaiserheer*, he was to exercise little direct influence over operations. Almost immediately it became apparent that Moltke would have serious problems maintaining command and control over the armies in the field. Directly responsible for the conduct

Previous page: German storm troops advancing in March 1918.
Below: German women support the war effort, 1914.

of the war in the west, he had responsibility also for the war in the east which was soon to become an area of crisis. Above all Moltke faced the problem of maintaining communications between the steadily advancing field armies and coordinating the envelopment movement of the right wing in the west.

Although through *Auftragstaktik* Moltke allowed his field commanders considerable independence, there was a great danger that the Schlieffen Plan would disintegrate into a series of uncoordinated marches. Moltke neither had the strength of character, decisive intellect, nor even the physical means to communicate with his army commanders, who were ambitious men in any case, thirsting for personal glory. In practical terms, control and coordination depended upon the general staff at OHL and the chiefs of staff of formations in the field.

At first, the Schlieffen Plan appeared to be working satisfactorily, with the army mobilizing and deploying quickly and efficiently. In the west, the right wing of the enveloping movement occupied Luxembourg on 2 August and then moved into Belgium. The French army deployed as the Germans had assumed it would, and the French C-in-C, General Joffre, concentrated the greater part of his army for an offensive in Alsace-Lorraine against the German left flank. The French deployed relatively few forces farther north.

But within three weeks, the Schlieffen Plan had been badly affected by what Clausewitz had referred to as the 'friction' of war; something which the general staff had failed to take sufficiently into account. The Belgian army put up a surprisingly determined resistance and the fortress of Liège took longer to subdue than had been expected. The arrival in France of a British Expeditionary Force and its deployment along the Belgian frontier came as a surprise to the Germans.

Then events in the east dramatically impinged upon those in the west. The Russians, responding to a French appeal, had mobilized faster than the Germans had expected, and had inflicted not only defeats on the Austrians in Galicia, but had also invaded East Prussia with two armies. The small German army in East Prussia fought a drawn battle with the Russian First Army at Gumbinnen on 20 August. Faced with this disturbing news and under considerable pressure to defend East Prussia, Moltke made two decisions. He replaced Prittwitz, the commander in East Prussia, with the retired General Paul von Hindenburg, and appointed the able and ambitious Erich Ludendorff as his chief of staff. He then withdrew two corps from the west and sent them to reinforce the east. These two corps were lost to the right wing in the west at a crucial moment, and arrived too late to be used in the decisive battles in the east.

By the time Hindenburg and Ludendorff arrived in East Prussia, Hoffmann, the senior staff planner there, had made already the necessary dispositions to destroy, firstly, the Russian Second Army, and then secondly, the Russian First Army, using the excellent German rail system to transfer troops from one position to another. Hindenburg and Ludendorff reached a similar conclusion with regard to the deployment of their forces, and between 23 and 28 August the Germans trapped the Russian Second Army in a massive envelopment which became known as the Battle of Tannenberg. The Russians lost over 120,000 men and were forced to retreat, and the victory made national heroes out of Hindenburg and Ludendorff, the more so because German national territory had been threatened.

In the west, the right wing of the *Kaiserheer* triumphantly pushed south forcing the British and French to retreat and seemingly exposing Paris to capture. On 2 September, Moltke ordered General von Kluck, the commander of the First Army, to avoid Paris and pursue the allies further southeast. At this point the German envelopment plan began to come apart. Joffre had gradually realized the danger to his left flank and had begun to move reinforcements to his left wing. The Germans were exhausted by their long route marches, and in shortening the sweep of the right wing, exposed their open flank to an allied counter-offensive along the Marne on 6 September. The German armies on the right wing were forced to retreat to the Aisne with the consequence that the Schlieffen Plan could no longer achieve the decisive envelopment of the French army.

Bitter recriminations occurred between the army commanders and their staffs and in turn between them and OHL. It became obvious that Moltke no longer enjoyed the confidence of the *Kaiser* or the army, and on 14 September he was replaced by the War Minister, General von Falkenhayn. Falkenhayn was a tough, forthright officer who decided to combine the offices of War Minister and chief of the general staff. Despite the reverses in France, Falkenhayn still believed that the war could be won in the west. He attempted to transfer his forces toward the far right wing and attempt an envelopment of the allies through Flanders. But the allies had reinforced their position along the Channel coast and in turn were considering an offensive. Unable to achieve an envelopment of the allies, Falkenhayn reverted to a classic encounter battle attacking the allies to the north and south of Ypres in October and November. Despite a series of heroic attacks, the Germans were unable to break through the allied defensive positions, and suffered heavy casualties, particularly among the untrained volunteers put into the attack at Langemarck.

Both sides were exhausted, and by 20 November 1914 the Germans and the allies confronted each other from behind a series of field entrenchments that stretched from the Channel to the Swiss border. The Germans had failed to achieve the decisive battle of annihilation which they had eagerly sought for the previous thirty years, had suffered nearly 900,000 casualties, and

Right: 'May God protect you, goodbye until we meet again.' A patriotic postcard issued to German troops in World War I
Below: German troops street fighting against Russians in East Prussia, 1914.

faced the prospect of a war of encirclement against powerful enemies.

There developed then a fierce strategic argument between Falkenhayn as chief of the general staff and War Minister and Hindenburg and Ludendorff in Army Command East. Falkenhayn advocated *Ermattungsstrategie*, or a strategy of attrition, whilst Hindenburg and Ludendorff still affirmed Schlieffen's *Vernichtungsstrategie*, or strategy of annihilation. Falkenhayn wanted to wear down Germany's opponents, particularly France, through limited operations, while Hindenburg and Ludendorff pressed for a war of annihilation, particularly against Russia. Falkenhayn was forced to accede to Hindenburg and Ludendorff's strategy in 1915 because they persuaded the *Kaiser* to support the idea and because it was imperative for Germany to prop up Austria on the Eastern front. So in 1915 the Germans and the Austrians launched a series of major offensives on the Eastern front aimed at encircling and destroying the Russian army. But although they had occupied most of Poland by the end of the year and inflicted massive losses on the Russians, they failed to destroy the Russian army which retreated beyond their embrace. Falkenhayn was distracted continually by allied offensives on the Western front, in the Artois, Champagne and at Loos. Furthermore, the Germans were forced to help the Austrians who were faced with difficulties in Serbia and on the new Italian front.

In January 1916, Falkenhayn faced a dilemma in that a decisive victory in the east was impossible nor were limited operations in the west likely to break the will of the allies. So he decided to combine the strategies of attrition and annihilation by forcing the French to defend the fortress of Verdun, a place of symbolic importance, which would draw in most of their army which would

Below: An officer reads the Mobilization Order to a Berlin crowd, 1 August 1914. As in each European capital the decision to go to war was greeted with widespread public rejoicing.

Right: A German artillery battery moving through a French village in 1914 on the eve of the battle of the Marne.
Below right: The failure of the Schlieffen Plan.

be destroyed by artillery fire and limited attacks. But in the battle of Verdun, which began on 21 February and did not finish until 18 December 1916, not only was the French army wasted away, but so was the German army, in a long, horrible attritional battle. What Falkenhayn had failed to see was that Verdun would become in turn a symbol for Germany, and once the attritional battle had begun it was very difficult to limit the commitment. The French lost over 500,000 men and the Germans 434,000 during the course of the battle. By the end of the terrible struggle the position of the front line was little altered.

The German failure at Verdun was compounded by the fact that on 1 July an Anglo-French offensive began along the Somme with the aim of breaking through the German lines. The battle of the Somme developed into another attritional battle, and although the Germans lost very little territory and inflicted over 600,000 casualties on the allies, they suffered another 500,000 casualties in the process. Concurrently with the allied offensive on the Somme, the Russians launched a major offensive against the Austrians in Galicia taking 200,000 prisoners, the situation only being stabilized by the arrival of German reinforcements.

Criticism of Falkenhayn had been mounting even before the failure of his strategy became apparent in the summer of 1916, and it culminated in his dismissal on 29 August and the appointment of Hindenburg as chief of the general staff and Ludendorff as First Quartermaster General. The appointment of Hindenburg and Ludendorff was regarded by the political, economic and military establishment as being fundamentally important if Germany was to win a decisive victory and thus contain the internal social divisions which were widening under the strain of war.

Germany had gone to war in 1914 in the spirit of *Burgfrieden*, or national unity, with all the major parties, apart from the Independent Socialists, supporting the government. Patriotism and war enthusiasm had swept Germany as it had other belligerent powers, and the reservists and the volunteers had flocked to the colors. But with mounting casualties, food shortages and inflation there was a breakdown of the *Burgfrieden* by 1916, and the beginning of widespread industrial disputes. With the appointment of Hindenburg and Ludendorff Germany moved towards total war, with a substantial increase in the production of war materials, the control and allocation of raw materials and labor, and punitive action taken against strikers.

From August 1916 OHL under Hindenburg and Ludendorff began to mobilize all areas of German society, giving advice and aid, which was reciprocated, to right wing political parties, working in close cooperation with industrialists and bankers, and having a decisive say in the formulation of government policy, including foreign affairs. The *Kaiser*'s power and influence declined even with regard to the traditional royal prerogative and authority over the army. Hindenburg and Ludendorff were able to force the resignation of Chancellor Bethmann Hollweg, who was regarded as a proponent of a negotiated peace, and approved the appointment of Michaelis as his successor. By threatening to resign, Hindenburg and Ludendorff were able to establish their own veto over wide areas of government policy to the extent that politics, foreign policy, economic affairs and industrial relations were all subordinated to the war aims of the general staff. Hindenburg and Ludendorff had set their faces firmly against any form of negotiated peace, instead they advocated a 'Hindenburg Victory,' based upon total war and an increasingly far fetched policy of annexation of occupied territory.

Despite their public optimism, Hindenburg and Ludendorff were prepared to admit in private in the autumn of 1916 that the war had become in fact one of attrition and exhaustion, and that victory would go to the side which could hold on the longest. Hindenburg and Ludendorff were determined to break the

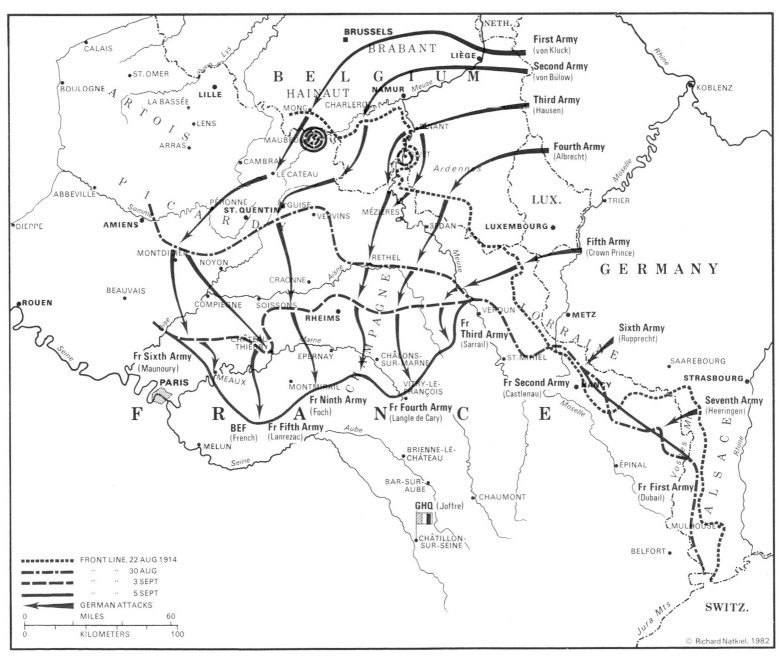

First Army
(von Kluck)

Second Army
(von Bülow)

Third Army
(Hausen)

Fourth Army
(Albrecht)

Fifth Army
(Crown Prince)

Sixth Army
(Rupprecht)

Seventh Army
(Heeringen)

Fr Sixth Army
(Maunoury)

Fr Ninth Army
(Foch)

Fr Fourth Army
(Langle de Cary)

Fr Third Army
(Sarrail)

Fr Second Army
(Castlenau)

Fr Fifth Army
(Lanrezac)

BEF
(French)

Fr First Army
(Dubail)

GHQ (Joffre)

NETH.

BRUSSELS

BRABANT

LIÈGE

BELGIUM

HAINAUT

NAMUR

CHARLEROI

MONS

MAUBEUGE

DINANT

Ardennes

LUX.

LUXEMBOURG

GERMANY

KOBLENZ

TRIER

METZ

LORRAINE

SAAREBOURG

STRASBOURG

ALSACE

CALAIS

ST. OMER

BOULOGNE

LILLE

LA BASSÉE

LENS

ARRAS

ARTOIS

CAMBRAI

LE CATEAU

PÉRONNE

GUISE

ST. QUENTIN

VERVINS

MÉZIÈRES

SEDAN

ABBEVILLE

PICARDY

DIEPPE

AMIENS

MONTDIDIER

NOYON

RETHEL

VERDUN

ST. MIHIEL

NANCY

CRAONNE

SOISSONS

RHEIMS

CHAMPAGNE

CHÂLONS-SUR-MARNE

BEAUVAIS

COMPIÈGNE

ROUEN

CHÂTEAU-THIERRY

ÉPERNAY

MONTMIRAIL

VITRY-LE-FRANÇOIS

EPINAL

MULHOUSE

BELFORT

PARIS

MEAUX

MELUN

FRANCE

AUBE

BRIENNE-LE-CHÂTEAU

BAR-SUR-AUBE

CHAUMONT

CHÂTILLON-SUR-SEINE

Seine

Somme

Oise

Aisne

Marne

Seine

Meuse

Meuse

Moselle

Moselle

Rhine

Rhine

Lys

Vosges Mts

Jura Mts

SWITZ.

- - - - - - - FRONT LINE, 22 AUG 1914
— ·· — ·· —   ''   ''   30 AUG
— — — —   ''   ''   3 SEPT
— — —   ''   ''   5 SEPT
⟵⟵⟵   GERMAN ATTACKS

0 ———————— 60
     MILES

0 ———————— 100
   KILOMETERS

© Richard Natkiel, 1982

morale of the allies, and were a receptive audience to the navy's suggestion of unrestricted submarine warfare. This offered the prospect of breaking the tight allied naval blockade of Germany and at the same time starving Britain into submission. Those German foreign office officials and army officers who had visited the United States pointed out that such a policy would bring that country inevitably into the war on the side of the allies. These objections were brushed aside, and this strategically important decision was left to OHL who gave the order for unrestricted submarine warfare, and this prompted the United States to declare war on Germany on 6 April 1917.

In 1914 the *Kaiserheer* had gone to war with its tactical training emphasizing aggressive offensive action, and machine guns and artillery were regarded as weapons to support that action. Like other European armies, the *Kaiserheer* had not spent much time on defensive training. The failure of the Schlieffen Plan, the impact of modern firepower against extended infantry attacks, and the subsequent development of positional warfare forced the Germans to reassess their tactical doctrine.

Contrary to popular belief, the *Kaiserheer* did not start the war in 1914 with a vast stock of weapons and equipment suitable for protracted positional warfare. Only 20 percent of artillery was of a heavy variety, and there was an almost complete lack of weapons suitable for close fighting. The Germans did have a stock of weapons and equipment suitable for besieging Belgian and French fortresses, but these were insufficient for the requirements of trench warfare after September 1914. New types of weapons and equipment had to be introduced to meet the requirements of trench warfare. A new, lighter machine gun was introduced in 1915 which allowed it to be fired from the shoulder, and in place of the heavy sledge there was a bipod. The Germans were quick to realize how important the machine gun was as a defensive weapon in trench warfare, and increased the production of the Maxim gun. In 1914 the Germans already possessed a stock of hand and rifle grenades in anticipation of siege warfare.

Above: 'The fight for a French regimental color' – the reality of war was somewhat different by 1915.
Left: Christmas presents for German soldiers – from a field post card.
Below: 'Shoulder to shoulder' – German propaganda showing Austrian and German military cooperation.

Schulter an Schulter

This gave them an advantage over other combatants during the first six months of trench warfare. By 1918 they had produced over 300 million grenades, and the familiar stick grenade replaced most other patterns.

Trench mortars had been developed by the *Kaiserheer* before 1914, and a small number of *minenwerfer* were available for employment. Artillery came to dominate trench warfare, and the Germans produced a wide range of medium and heavy artillery pieces, particularly howitzers for use in positional warfare. Flame throwers, which could be used either in the defensive or offensive role had also been accepted into service with the *Kaiserheer* before 1914. They were used for the first time in February 1915, and by 1917 a lighter model had been produced which gave the operator mobility. In their search for weapons to break the trench deadlock, the Germans experimented with gas. There were three methods of discharging gas; released directly from cylinders, projected from *Gaswurfminen*, or delivered by shell. The consequence of using gas was the need to provide gas masks, which became standard issue after August 1915.

Although the *Kaiserheer* had examined a number of armored vehicles before 1916, interest in the tank as a weapon only became widespread after the British use of tanks on the Somme in September 1916. At first the Germans used a number of converted, captured British models, and it was not until May 1917 that a German designed tank was demonstrated. Surprisingly, Ludendorff, who had always taken a keen interest in new weapons, had no particular enthusiasm for tanks.

The uniform and personal equipment of the German soldier was gradually adapted between 1914 and 1916, reflecting the nature of the war and the need for severe economy in clothing. In September 1915, a new field uniform was introduced which was both simple and functional, and slowly the *Stahlhelm*, or steel helmet replaced the *Pickelhaube*. By 1916, the German front line soldier in his field blouse, knee length boots or puttees and wearing his distinctive steel helmet, had taken on the image which was to symbolize the German army in two World wars.

Although after November 1914 the Germans spent a considerable period of time on the defensive on the Western front, frequently they had the advantage of occupying ground according tactical advantages. Unlike the allies, the Germans were occupying enemy territory, and could adjust the line to suit the tactical circumstances. Throughout the war, the *Kaiserheer* gained a formidable reputation for the strength, depth and comfort of its trenches and dugouts.

General Alexander von Kluck, commander of the First Army in the West, 1914.

line, and during the battle of the Somme the Germans suffered heavy casualties from the British artillery bombardment. Many German officers referred to the Somme as *die Materialschlacht*, or battle of materiel, and they realized that the allies would win any battle of attrition, and the *Kaiserheer* would have to develop tactics to conserve its strength.

With the arrival of Hindenburg and Ludendorff at OHL in August 1916, there began a major reassessment of the organization, training and tactics of the field army. This became a corporate effort, and although Ludendorff provided the impetus and determination, the development of a new German tactical doctrine was the result of an exchange of ideas and opinions between officers of the general staff at OHL, and staff and regimental officers in the field. As a result, OHL published *The Principles of Command in the Defensive Battle in Position Warfare December 1916*. This document provided general guidance, and with subsequent editions, it became the German doctrine of defense for the rest of the war.

The new German elastic defense in depth was aimed at nullifying the effects of allied artillery bombardment and destroying the impetus of the infantry attack. The defense now consisted of three successive zones – the outpost zone, the battle zone and the rearward zone. The main area of defense would be in the battle zone which would usually be beyond the range of allied artillery observation. The whole defense in depth was considered fluid, with the emphasis placed on the defenders' ability to use tactical features and strongpoints, and to withdraw or advance depending upon the circumstances. Defense in depth also included a very aggressive and offensive response with an emphasis placed on the counter-attack, usually at that moment when the attackers had not yet consolidated their gains. This new tactical doctrine reinforced the principle of *Auftragstaktik*, as a great deal of initiative was left to local commanders. While continually adapting the new defensive tactics in the light of experience, OHL also began to reorganize the army.

In the period 1916-17, the German infantry division was reduced to three infantry regiments and battalion strengths were correspondingly reduced, creating surplus manpower to form new divisions. Within the battalion, greater emphasis was placed on specialized units such as machine-gunners, sharpshooters and trench mortar-men. The nurturing of an aggressive spirit in the defense was also considered important in maintaining the morale and fighting spirit of the German soldier who would otherwise become passive through positional warfare. It was recognized that a particular type of soldier and unit was required for the aggressive counter-attack in the elastic defense in depth. Luden-

Initially, the Germans were fully committed to defending ground according to the principle, *'Halten, was zu halten ist'*, meaning, 'Hold on to whatever can be held.' But the experience of being attacked by the British and French in 1915 and 1916 forced them to modify their tactics and develop new concepts. They began to copy the French example of establishing a defense in depth which could absorb enemy artillery fire and infantry assaults. But Falkenhayn insisted on holding the forward defense

Left: Early trench warfare – German Maxim machine guns in position on the Eastern Front, 1915.
Below: German infantry and supply wagons advance along a dust road in western Russia, 1916.

War and Revolution

Patriotic German print showing Bavarian infantry storming a Russian trench.

dorff directed that the field army should apply the concept and organization of special assault troops, who had been employed on a small scale by a number of German units since 1914. He was greatly impressed by the *Sturmbataillon*, or Storm battalion, developed by a Captain Willy Rohr.

Unlike the pre-war tactical doctrine of advancing in a broad firing line with the infantry mainly armed with rifles, Rohr organized attack forces in small groups deployed in depth, armed with grenades, trench mortars, light machine guns, rifles, pistols, flamethrowers and light artillery pieces. Training was conducted under live-firing conditions and his battalion extensively practised with supporting artillery in order to coordinate movement with supporting fire. The basic unit of the *Sturmbataillon* was the *Stosstrupp*, or assault squad, and the *Stosstruppen* were recruited from among the toughest and most aggressive soldiers.

Whilst the Germans were developing their elastic defense tactics on the Western front, Ludendorff was considering ways to take the strategic initiative on the Eastern front to win a decisive

Left: An early German trench on the Western Front in 1914. The German defenses soon became much more elaborate.
Below: Cheerful German walking wounded captured by the British on the Somme, July 1916.

victory against Russia which would release German troops for a major offensive in the west. The entry of Rumania into the war on the side of the allies in the autumn of 1916 gave the Germans an opportunity to win a quick victory and at the same time bolster up the sagging morale of the Austrians. In December 1916, a joint Austrian, Bulgarian and German army under Falkenhayn's command defeated and occupied Rumania. In February 1917, the Tsar's government was overthrown and replaced by a liberal bourgeois government which was committed to continuing the war on the side of the allies. Recognizing that Russia was close to collapse, and that the Bolsheviks wanted peace, Hindenburg and Ludendorff facilitated the return of Lenin and his supporters from exile across German controlled territory in April 1917. OHL seemed unaware of the dangers to Germany of encouraging a proletarian revolution in Russia.

In November 1917 the Bolsheviks and their supporters overthrew the Kerensky government and at the same time the Russian army began to disintegrate. At the end of the month the Bolsheviks asked for a general armistice, and on 22 December, a conference was opened at Brest-Litovsk to discuss the matter. German demands as put forward by representatives from OHL included the annexation of Lithuania and Courland, and the Russian evacuation of much of western Russia, and the payment of

a huge indemnity. When the Bolsheviks prevaricated, the Germans began to advance eastwards on 17 February 1918 encountering little resistance. In March 1918 the Bolsheviks reluctantly accepted the German peace terms at Brest-Litovsk, by which Germany and Austria annexed large areas of Russia and indirectly ruled areas like the Ukraine through puppet regimes. The armistice in the east in November 1917 had enabled the Germans to transfer some of their best divisions to the west. But Brest-Litovsk did not end the war in the east, and the Germans continued to maintain some twenty divisions in Russia for occupation duties and for furthering grandiose political and economic schemes to establish a colonial empire as far as the Caucasus, laying the guidelines for future Nazi policy.

By the early months of 1918, OHL felt reasonably confident that a decisive victory could be obtained in the west. The defeat of Russia and Rumania had released many divisions, and the Italians had been badly beaten at Caporetto in October 1917, forcing the British and French to divert troops to Italy. On the Western front throughout 1917 the Germans had successfully implemented their elastic defense in depth tactics. As a result, the allies had failed to break the German line in two major offensives, Nivelle's French offensive along the Aisne in April, and Haig's British offensive at Ypres between July and November. The failure of

History of The German Army

Left: German cartoon showing Hindenburg's offensive in the East ending a debate in the Russian Duma, 1916.
Above: General Erich von Falkenhayn, Chief of the General Staff, 1914-16.
Below right: German artillery in action on the Western Front, 1916. The developing importance of counter-battery artillery fire and the great efforts made to spot enemy gun positions from the air and by other means soon made it essential for artillery positions to be well camouflaged like the one shown here.

carefully coordinated attack relying on surprise. OHL realized that it was impossible to achieve the destruction of all enemy forces in a deep penetration attack, instead they planned to disrupt enemy units and communications and by maintaining the initiative keep up the momentum of the advance. Coordination between all arms was emphasized in what can best be described as 'infiltration tactics.'

The attack in depth required a new organizational basis for the *Kaiserheer* and careful planning and training. To maintain the momentum of the attack, it was decided that OHL would reinforce only success, and that leading units were to continue without relief, but were to avoid strongpoints and bypass them and leave them for the attention of follow on units. The leading units were to be based on the *Stosstruppen* developed for the counter-attack of the defense in depth. Such *Stosstruppen* began to teach other German units the technique of small unit organization and tactics which required a considerable degree of aggressive initiative among all ranks. The *Kaiserheer*, however, could not train or equip every division for the offensive, and by March 1918 only 56 out of 192 divisions in the west were described as *Stossdivisionen*, or attack divisions. Significantly, the rest were referred to as *Stellungsdivisionen*, or trench divisions, which denoted a static capability and a passive attitude amongst the troops.

Artillery support was carefully integrated into the assault plan. The Germans wanted to avoid any prolonged artillery bombardment which would destroy the element of surprise, require a vast stockpile of munitions, and cause massive destruction to the terrain which would impede a quick German advance. Instead, the Germans developed a fire plan which would produce fast and accurate neutralizing fire with an emphasis placed on the use of gas shells against a wide variety of specific targets. Such methods had been developed by Georg Brüchmuller, a German artillery officer, who had successfully used them at Riga in July 1917, and again at Caporetto in October. So successful were these methods that the Germans referred to *'Durchbrüchmuller'*, or 'Breakthrough Muller,' a pun on the inventor's name.

The German offensive began on 21 March 1918 against the British position along the Somme. Following a short, but very intense artillery bombardment which confused and dislocated the British, small German assault squads infiltrated through the British positions, bypassing and isolating strongpoints. The German attack in depth tactics secured them 140 square miles in the first twenty-four hours for the cost of 39,000 casualties. The majority of British casualties were prisoners reflecting the disruption and confusion caused by the German tactics. But despite such tactical

Nivelle's offensive after much foolish optimism caused widespread mutinies in the French army and the inconclusive nature of the attritional fighting at Ypres temporarily broke the offensive capability of the British.

Ludendorff believed that Germany would have one great opportunity to defeat the allies in the spring of 1918 before the Americans arrived in any significant numbers. Between October 1917 and March 1918 the German divisional strength in the west increased from 150 to 192. Their defensive tactics in the west in 1917 had taught them how *not* to attack and their experiences of mounting offensives in Russia and Italy had taught them how *to* attack. A combination of an intensive study by the general staff and lessons learned from the experiences of 1917 culminated in OHL publishing in January 1918 *The Attack in Position Warfare*, which became the basic document for the German offensives in 1918.

The objective of the spring offensive was to achieve a breakthrough after penetrating the allied line and divide the British and French armies forcing them to retreat and sue for peace. The Germans did not seek a solution to the problem of achieving a breakthrough either in the form of the failed heavy artillery bombardment or through the use of tanks. Rather, they chose to accomplish the attack in depth with existing combat means in a

mile front. Six German divisions collapsed, many prisoners were taken and discipline in the *Kaiserheer* broke down. Reinforcements marching to the front were jeered and accused of being 'strike breakers' by troops relieved. From this point Ludendorff was in a state of nervous collapse and although by the end of September he had come to realize that an armistice would have to be sought, he still had wild notions that this could give Germany a breathing space and that a policy of massive territorial annexation was still possible.

But Germany's ability to continue the war was being undermined on all sides. Her allies were exhausted and sought peace, with Bulgaria signing an armistice on 30 September, Turkey capitulating on 30 October and the Austrians requesting an armistice the same day. Although the German field army on the Western front fought a tough, defensive retreat and most front line formations maintained their discipline after the collapse on 8 August, there was widespread dissatisfaction in the army rear area and amongst the troops in the east. On the home front, there was a desperate war weariness and considerable industrial unrest promoted by the Independent Socialists and the communists who had been inspired by the Bolshevik victory in Russia.

In the face of such grim realities, Hindenburg and Ludendorff decided to transfer the blame and the consequences for what had happened to a civilian government. Above all else they wanted to protect the officer corps and maintain discipline within the army. On 3 October the *Kaiser* invited the liberal Prince Max of Baden to become Chancellor and to negotiate peace terms. Prince Max began to negotiate with the American President Woodrow Wilson, who soon intimated that there could be no negotiations with the military and monarchical masters of Germany. On 28 October Ludendorff resigned and was replaced by General Wilhelm Groener who saw his main task as the preservation of

Above: General Wilhelm Groener, Ludendorff's successor.
Right: Ludendorff, Hindenburg and Hoffmann (L to R) with staff officers on the Eastern Front, 1915.

successes, the Germans were unable to achieve a strategic breakthrough. The British conducted a skillful and dogged retreat, and by 4 April the impetus had gone out of the offensive. Apart from the defensive tactics of the allies, including French support for the British, the German failure was due to a number of factors. The Germans did not have sufficient mechanical transport to supply their advancing troops, and their artillery was unable to keep up with the advancing infantry. Many of the best German assault troops were killed and the remainder began to lose their aggressive spirit as a consequence of heavy casualties. Finally, in the face of the abundance of supplies found in captured allied dumps, discipline amongst German troops broke down, and widespread looting developed.

Ludendorff was to attempt four more major offensives against the allies each one more desperate and each one successively weaker in strength and impetus. In April the Germans attacked the British along the Lys, then in May the French along the Aisne, and again the French between Noyon and Montdidier, and finally, along the Marne in July 1918. As a result of these offensives, the Germans had made impressive territorial gains and inflicted heavy casualties on the allies and achieved some spectacular tactical successes, but they had failed to achieve the decisive breakthrough and split the allies. The *Kaiserheer* had suffered 500,000 casualties and was exhausted, and Ludendorff had run out of strategic options.

In fact the strategic initiative in the west had passed to the allies, and on 18 July Marshal Foch launched a Franco-American offensive towards Soissons. Although the Germans were able to stabilize the front, a far more serious blow occurred on 8 August, on what Ludendorff was to call, 'the black day of the German army.' A major British offensive on the Somme using large numbers of tanks penetrated seven miles into the German lines along a fifteen

Above: German 38cm railway gun on the Western Front, 1917.
Right: German soldiers relaxing over a game of cards behind the lines on the Western Front, 1917.

the officer corps and the army against the dangers of a Bolshevik revolution. On 4 November sailors from the German High Seas Fleet mutinied at Kiel on learning that they might be ordered to sail on a suicide mission against the allies. The mutiny spread to Hamburg and Bremen, and on 7 November revolution broke out in Munich and a Bavarian Soviet Republic was proclaimed. Revolution and disorder swept across Germany and everywhere the institutions of the *Kaiserreich* were swept aside.

Demands for the *Kaiser*'s abdication had caused William II to flee to OHL, where Groener informed him on 8 November that he no longer enjoyed the confidence of the army. Groener advised the *Kaiser* to abdicate as he believed that this might help to save the officer corps. In fact the decision was made for the *Kaiser* by Prince Max who announced his abdication and at the same time his own resignation. On 9 November the *Kaiser* appointed Hindenburg his successor as Supreme Commander of the German armed forces, and Groener became *de facto* acting chief of the general staff. For Groener, the collapse of Germany was the responsibility of the home front, 'The army stands splendidly; the poison comes from home.' The first words of the 'stab in the back' legend that was to play such a part in the revival of German nationalism had been spoken.

The First World War changed and then destroyed the *Kaiser-heer*. In 1914 the army was extremely conservative in outlook and imbued with a strong sense of patriotism and loyalty to the *Kaiser*. The regular officer corps was recruited traditionally from the landed class, and although the reserve officer corps was mainly bourgeois, it aped the social behavior and attitude of the regulars. The backbone of the *Kaiserheer* in 1914 had been its NCOs, whose superb discipline and professionalism was the envy of other armies. The War Ministry had made sure that a disproportionate number of conscripts was recruited from rural areas and imbued with obedience, discipline and patriotism.

Casualties and an increase in the *Kaiserheer*'s establishment affected its composition and homogeneity. From a divisional

Below: German machine gun detachments training for the March offensive, 1918.

strength in 1914 of fifty, the *Kaiserheer* had expanded to 212 in 1918. After 1914, more and more men were conscripted, taking in that very element which previously it had tried to exclude, the urban industrial workers. Undoubtedly, many of these workers made reluctant soldiers and increasingly they were receptive to the anti-war and revolutionary propaganda of the Independent Socialists and the communists. The military authorities also made a fundamental error when they conscripted striking workers into the army as a punishment, thus bringing into the army more disaffected elements. Conscription had also brought in men from Alsace-Lorraine and Poland who were reluctant citizens of the *Kaiserreich* and even more reluctant soldiers in the *Kaiserheer*. After the Bolshevik revolution and the armistice on the Eastern front in November 1917, there was widespread fraternization between German and Russian soldiers, and German troops transferred to the Western front were, in the words of one officer, 'badly infected with the virus of Bolshevism.'

Casualties and an increase in the *Kaiserheer*'s establishment did not dramatically affect traditional officer recruitment. The regular officer corps was doubled to 45,923 during the war, of whom 11,357 were killed. During the same period the number of reserve officers increased to 226,130. The officer corps refused to alter its standards, even in wartime, and to overcome the severe shortages among junior officers, it resorted to the expedient of giving NCOs the responsibility and authority of junior officers, but not their status, hence the special rank of *Offizierstellvertreter*, or sergeant-lieutenant. By the end of the

Above: Colonel Paul von Lettow-Vorbeck, second from right, commander of the *Shutztruppen* in East Africa, 1914-18.
Left: German War Loan poster showing an idealized portrait of a storm troop fighter, 1918.

war the majority of battalions were officered by reserve officers and *Offizierstellvertreters*, all of whom regarded themselves as members of the officer corps.

As in other armies, there developed a division between the front line troops and the *Etappe*, or base. In the *Etappe* were to be found some of the least well disciplined units whose soldiers indulged in political disaffection and who called the front line troops, 'trench hogs.' Reinforcements passing through the *Etappe*, particularly at the end of the war, often absorbed their anti-war and revolutionary sentiments.

The development of the *Stosstruppen* also affected the establishment and ethos of the *Kaiserheer*. By recruiting the best officers, NCOs and men into *Sturmbataillonen*, OHL correspondingly weakened other battalions who lost their natural leaders. Within the *Sturmbataillonen* a new discipline emerged with a much less formal and a much closer relationship between all ranks. Independence, initiative and personal bravery were encouraged and the *Stosstruppen* took on the characteristics of the old mercenaries with a personal loyalty and devotion to the *Stosstruppführer* rather than to the *Kaiser* or OHL. Leadership devolved upon very young junior officers, men like Ernst Jünger, Erwin Rommel and Ferdinand Schörner, all of whom were decorated with the Pour le Mérite.

It was the German NCO who largely determined the discipline and combat performance of the *Kaiserheer* during the First World War. By 1917, many of the pre-war NCOs had become casualties after the attritional battles of Verdun and the Somme. By 1918 a young NCO might find himself in command of a company because of the shortage of officers. The attitude of these NCOs was crucial to the cohesion of the *Kaiserheer* as they either maintained discipline and combat determination or encouraged disaffection and urged surrender.

Some eleven million Germans were mobilized to serve in the *Kaiserheer* of whom six million became casualties. The old *Kaiserheer* was destroyed or dispersed after 1916, and increasingly the most aggressive elements were concentrated into *Sturmbataillonen*. But the fighting performance of the army was also determined by its arms and equipment. After the launch of the 'Hindenburg Program' in 1916, war industry began to supply the army with sufficient weapons and equipment, but by the summer of 1918 that program had collapsed and the army suffered severe shortages which affected its combat efficiency.

There is a widespread belief that in the First World War the *Kaiserheer* had fought against overwhelming odds, and that the individual combat effectiveness of the German soldier and the tactical skill of the general staff had been far superior to those of their opponents. The German soldier certainly displayed many characteristics which reflected his patriotism and cultural background and the fact that his training emphasized duty, and instilled in him discipline and determination. The various drills in the use of specific weapons and basic procedures were ingrained in the *Kaiserheer* through thorough training and repetition, but the application of these techniques in the conditions of battle was not done in a rigid fashion. The Germans introduced new tactical doctrines to meet the conditions of positional warfare and demonstrated that the *Kaiserheer* could instill techniques by inflexibility and repetition, whilst developing a sense of tactics through flexibility, good judgement and creativity.

It was the lack of strategic and political judgement which was to lead to the defeat of Germany, and this was mainly the responsibility of OHL and the general staff. Before 1914 the general staff had adopted a strategic plan which fitted their concept of a preventive war, but in practice was inflexible and unable to overcome the 'friction' in war. The sharp differences of opinion within the general staff between the advocates of the strategy of attrition and those of annihilation were basically over means rather than ends. After August 1916 Hindenburg and Ludendorff were able to dictate or veto government policy and to ignore the repercussions of their decisions, such as the introduction of unrestricted submarine warfare. The general staff, and in turn the German government, adopted an increasingly unrealistic policy of territorial annexation, and the occupation policy and behavior of the army in Belgium, northern France, Poland and Russia was to give it a reputation for brutality which foreshadowed that of the *Führerheer* in the Second World War.

Given the fact that the Schlieffen Plan relied upon achieving a quick decisive victory in western Europe, little consideration had been given to wider strategic questions. The *Kaisermarine* was to plan and fight a separate war, and ironically the numerically least significant part of its pre-war strength, commerce raiders and submarines, were the most effective weapons used against the allies. Although the High Seas Fleet was able successfully to challenge the Royal Navy, it spent most of the war in port, where harsh discipline, poor food and conditions and an abysmal relationship between officers and men was to lead to the mutinies on 4 November 1918.

Limited numbers of German naval vessels and military personnel were to play a disproportionately important part in tying down allied resources away from the Western front. Although the majority of Germany's colonial territories were quickly occupied by the allies, in East Africa Colonel Paul von Lettow-Vorbeck, commander of the *Schutztruppen*, was to fight a brilliant diversionary war for four years, and did not finally surrender until after the armistice. Lettow-Vorbeck had soon realized that his job was to force the allies to divert resources against him and away from other theaters. Instead of merely attempting to defend the territory of East Africa, he made the maintenance of the integrity and independence of his small army his main objective. So although the British had occupied German East Africa by the end of 1917, Lettow-Vorbeck had removed his army into Portuguese East Africa and continued the war from there. He managed to maintain the loyalty and fighting ability of a force of 11,000 men, the majority of whom consisted of native *askaris*. Although strategically largely irrelevant to the outcome of the war, Lettow-Vorbeck's exploits gave the Germans a considerable morale boost, and in December 1918 he returned to Germany as, 'the only undefeated German soldier.'

German military advisers to the Turkish army were also responsible for causing the allies considerable problems. A German military mission had been active before the war training and equipping the Turkish army, and after 1914, German military personnel were to play a key role acting as advisers and specialists. General Liman von Sanders helped to organize the Turkish defense of Gallipoli in 1915, and later in Palestine. The Germans were to demonstrate in the Balkans at Salonika that given the flexibility provided by interior rail communications and the deployment of a limited number of troops, they could bolster up their Bulgarian allies and prevent the British and French from conducting a successful eastern policy. But this was only a holding operation, and ultimately the Germans were unable to prevent the political and military collapse of the Turks and Bulgarians in the autumn of 1918 which was to have dramatic consequences for Germany itself.

The collapse of the old order of the *Kaiserreich* was so complete that on 9 November 1918 a German Socialist Republic was proclaimed. The Independent Socialists and the Spartacist-Communists wanted to establish a Soviet Republic and found themselves in conflict with the moderate Social Democrats who made up the majority of the new government. Throughout Germany workers' and soldiers' councils were being established to run local government and to challenge authority within the army. Ebert, the new Chancellor of the provisional government, agreed to the sovietizing of the army with the election of commanders under the control of the soldiers' committees, the abolition of all formality and distinction and the establishment of a people's militia. But on 9 November Groener contacted Ebert and offered him the support of the army and promised to return it to Germany in good order. In return, he told Ebert, OHL

Above: German tanks in action against the French, June 1918.
Above right: The German offensives in 1918.

expected the government to help it retain discipline and to stop the spread of Bolshevism. Ebert was only too grateful to accept this support and pledged his government to do all it could to prevent the spread of disorder.

Ebert and the majority of the Social Democrat Party were committed to gradual constitutional reform and were horrified by the collapse of the *Kaiserreich* and the outbreak of revolutionary violence. Groener was the perfect man to negotiate on behalf of the officer corps, as he himself was a man of humble origins who had become an outstanding technocrat on the general staff and who liked to think he was more politically aware than other officers. Hindenburg had been only too pleased to leave the distasteful tasks of persuading the *Kaiser* to abdicate and negotiating with the Social Democrats to Groener.

Groener and the general staff arranged the rapid and orderly withdrawal of three million German troops eastward across the Rhine following the armistice on 11 November 1918. The

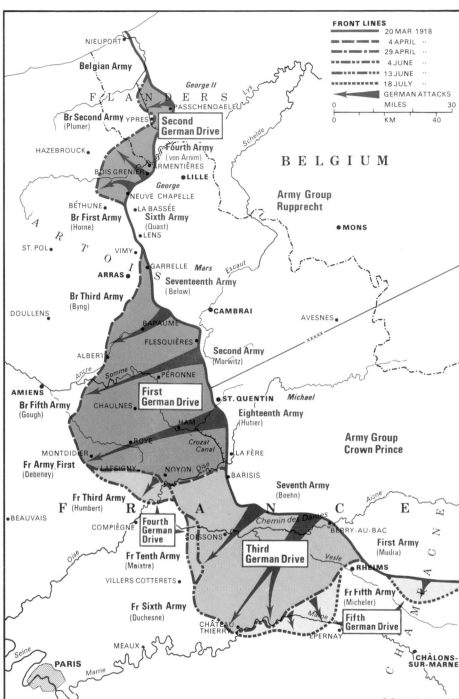

© Richard Natkiel, 1982

German army in the west returned home believing that it was undefeated and that victory had been denied to it by the traitorous disaffection of the home front. Ebert reinforced this conviction when he addressed a march past of troops in Berlin on 11 December, referring to them as 'an unvanquished army.' This combined with the fact that the provisional republican government had had to begin the armistice negotiations, provided the officer corps with a most useful alibi. On arriving home the German army fell apart as the mass of the rank and file deserted to their homes. The withdrawal of the one million German soldiers from the east was a complete rout, and so by the middle of December 1918, apart from a few scattered units there was no such thing as a German army. For the provisional government, there was the real danger that the Independent Socialists and the Spartacist Communists would try and seize power, something which was to happen in Berlin on 27 December.

The Independent Socialists and the Spartacist Communists were determined to maintain the momentum of the revolution, and the workers' and soldiers' councils provided the leadership of what they hoped would become a 'German Red Army.' In Berlin

their most effective military force was made up of sailors of the People's Naval Division, who seized public buildings, including the Imperial Palace. Groener ordered the commander of military forces in the Potsdam-Berlin area to suppress the uprising, but his demoralized soldiers were put to flight by the People's Naval Division and a massive public demonstration. This was undoubtedly the nadir of the German army when it was unable to disperse a badly organized and weakly armed force of revolutionary sailors.

But a new military force was at the disposal of the government and OHL. Over the previous month individual commanders had begun to form independent units recruited by voluntary enlistment from amongst unemployed veterans, students and right wing political activists. These independent military units soon became known as *Freikorps*, and were organized by officers, industrialists and landowners to protect property, and in the east to maintain control of the Baltic and to fight the Poles in Silesia. The recruiting nuclei of the *Freikorps* were sometimes based on the remnants of some old *Kaiserheer* formation, but more often than not they were raised by an individual officer to whom *Freikorps* members gave their personal allegiance. Recruits were

less concerned with politics than in retaining the camaraderie of wartime and being able to indulge in widespread violence. Discipline was very lax, and although the *Freikorps* were to fight under the overall direction of OHL and the government, individual *Freikorps* soldiers held little allegiance to either organization. *Freikorps* units were a throwback to the mercenary bands of the Middle Ages and the Renaissance, and their recruitment and employment indicated just how far authority had collapsed.

Ebert nominated Gustav Noske as his liaison man with Groener. Noske was a veteran Social Democrat who was considered the party's military expert and whom the officer corps had cultivated during the war. Noske regarded himself as the government's 'bloodhound,' and with Groener, organized the *Freikorps* to suppress the revolutionary uprisings which had spread throughout Germany. In January 1919, the *Freikorps* brutally crushed the Spartacist uprising in Berlin and murdered two leading members, Rosa Luxemburg and Karl Liebknecht. Throughout Germany the *Freikorps* destroyed the revolutionary movement and conducted a savage civil war against the Independent Socialists and the Communists. The power of the workers' and soldiers' committees was destroyed, and the first constitutional assembly of the provisional Republic met at Weimar under *Freikorps* protection.

In the Baltic, *Freikorps* units were initially allowed to operate against the Soviets by the allies so that local governments could be established in independent states. The *Freikorps* helped to defeat the Soviets, but their subsequent attempts to establish German rule were defeated by local forces and allied pressure.

The National Assembly meeting at Weimar had produced a provisional *Reichswehr*, or armed forces, law, by which the old *Kaiserheer* would be dissolved formally and a new Defense Ministry established with Noske the first minister. Hindenburg and Groener planned to convert the *Freikorps* into the new *Reichsheer*. They planned to have a peacetime strength of 300,000 men by 1920. But this planning was overtaken by events, when on 7 May 1919 the allies presented their peace terms to the German representatives at Versailles.

Under the terms of the Versailles Treaty, the German army was to be limited to a strength of 100,000 manned by voluntary recruitment. There were to be no combat aircraft, heavy artillery, tanks or other offensive weapons. The navy was to be reduced to a coastal defense force. The general staff, the *Kriegsakademie* and all officer cadet schools were to be dissolved. The allied occupation of the Rhineland was to continue and in addition there was to be a demilitarized strip of territory fifty kilometers to the east of the occupied zone. All of these provisions were to be enforced by an Allied Control Commission. These terms, along with other allied demands, had a unifying effect upon the German people. Before the deadline of 20 June the general staff considered the possibility of rejecting the demands and even organizing a military

Above: An armored car of the Revolutionary Soldiers' Council beside the Berliner Schloss, November 1918.
Above left: Revolutionary soldiers and sailors at the Brandenburg Gate in Berlin, November 1918.
Right: General Hans von Seeckt, *Chef der Heeresleitung,* 1920-26.

putsch. But it was obvious that Germany had no alternative but to accept the terms and sign the peace treaty which included admitting to Germany's war guilt.

Hindenburg refused to be associated with this, and on 24 June resigned, once again leaving Groener to shoulder the responsibility and blame. For the German officer corps, the Treaty of Versailles was a document of shame because it legitimized the destruction of the *Kaiserheer* and reduced the army to 100,000 men and restricted their professional ambitions by only permitting an establishment of 4000 officers. For many civilians, the army remained above reproach, and the consequences of defeat and national degradation were blamed unfairly upon the Social Democrats and the new Weimar Republic.

Groener suggested to Noske that the government set up a Preparatory Commission for a Peace Army and proposed Major-General Hans von Seeckt as its President. Noske agreed, and the commission formally met on 5 July. Although Ebert wanted Groener to remain on the active list and head the new *Reichsheer*, he refused, and retired from the army in the autumn of 1919, taking up the cabinet post of minister of transport.

The Reichsheer and Politics

History of The German Army

Between the establishment of a provisional *Reichswehr* in March 1919 and its transformation into a permanent *Reichswehr* in March 1921, there was an uneasy period of reorganization and the failure of a military putsch. In accordance with the new constitution of the Weimar Republic adopted in August 1919, the President of the Reich was made Supreme Head of the armed forces with the right to nominate and dismiss all general officers.

Members of the *Reichswehr* had to take an oath of allegiance to the constitution, and were subject, except in time of war, to civil, rather than military courts. The exclusive right of legislation with respect to the army was transferred from the provinces to the *Reich*, and the separate state war ministries and contingents were abolished, and the administration of the army was to be handled by a central *Reichswehr* ministry whose minister would be a member of the cabinet and answerable to the *Reichstag*.

The majority of the delegates at the Weimar National Assembly were content to leave the internal administration and control of the new *Reichsheer* in the hands of the old officer corps once democratic control had been established. On 1 October 1919, the four war ministries of the old *Kaiserreich* were abolished and replaced by the *Reichswehr* ministry in the Bendlerstrasse in Berlin with Noske as minister, and comprising the *Heeresleitung* and *Marineleitung*, or army and navy administrative offices. Colonel Reinhard became the first *Chef der Heeresleitung*, effectively Commander-in-Chief of the *Reichsheer*, and Seeckt was head of the *Truppenamt*, or Troop Office, which fulfilled the role of the now disbanded general staff.

Real power in the provisional *Reichsheer* lay with Seeckt, who not only carried out most of the reorganization but maintained links with the *Freikorps* leaders and right wing politicians. Seeckt came from a traditional Prussian aristocratic military background and had been commissioned as a Guards officer. He had been a member of the general staff, and had held a number of responsible staff appointments during the war, finally serving as acting chief of staff for the Turkish army. His objective with the *Reichsheer* was to create a *Kaiserheer* in miniature, and to protect the army from the dangerous revolutionary sentiments of the Weimar Republic. Although reluctant to involve the *Reichsheer* directly in politics he maintained an ambivalent loyalty toward the republican government.

The loyalty of the Provisional *Reichsheer* was tested over the winter of 1920. Seething discontent grew amongst certain serving officers and members of the *Freikorps* over a succession of incidents: allied demands for the government to hand over a number of Germans accused of being war criminals, the evacuation of *Freikorps* troops from the Baltic, and finally, the demands of the Allied Control Commission for the immediate demobilization of a number of notorious *Freikorps* units, including the Ehrhardt naval brigade. The commander of the *Reichsheer* forces in Berlin, General von Lüttwitz, was the unofficial spokesman for those officers and *Freikorps'* leaders who were opposed to the allied demands and 'government complicity.' On 12 March 1920, Lüttwitz initiated a putsch in Berlin against the government, supported by *Freikorps* units and right wing political groups, and established a provisional government under the leadership of a civil servant named Kapp. Ebert and the Social Democrat government ordered the *Reichsheer* to put down the putsch, but Seeckt refused saying, '*Reichsheer* do not fire on *Reichsheer*.' Although Seeckt wanted to prevent the *Reichsheer* from being divided between the supporters of Kapp and the supporters of the legal government, he was prepared to accept the possibility that the putsch might succeed. In the event, the putsch failed not

Previous page: The *Reichsheer* parading with regimental colors from the *Kaiserheer*.
Right: *Freikorps* soldiers of the Erhardt Brigade in Berlin during the Kapp Putsch, 1920.
Below: General von Epp inspects recruits of his Bavarian *Freikorps*, 1919.

The German Army

because of the opposition of the *Reichsheer*, but as a result of the government calling a general strike throughout the country on 14 March which forced the leaders of the putsch to capitulate.

But one unforeseen consequence of the Kapp putsch and the general strike was that the Independent Socialists and the Communists seized power in many areas of the Ruhr announcing that they would defend the Republic against the monarchists and the militarists. Faced with this new crisis, Ebert appointed Seeckt as *Chef der Heeresleitung*, and gave him the responsibility of crushing the revolutionary uprising. Seeckt used *Reichsheer* units and *Freikorps* troops, many of whom had participated in the Kapp putsch, and moved against the Ruhr, and by the middle of May had succeeded in brutally putting down the disorders.

The Kapp putsch indicated the high level of pro-monarchist and anti-republican feeling prevalent in the *Reichsheer*'s officer corps and their close links with the *Freikorps*. Seeckt had demonstrated that while he was not prepared to use the *Reichsheer* against disloyal units and right wing activists, he was quite prepared to use it against the revolutionary left. The ghost of the *Kaiserheer* haunted the *Reichsheer* and made it a reluctant servant of the Weimar Republic.

From 1920 until 1926 Seeckt as *Chef de Heeresleitung* was effectively both C-in-C and chief of staff of the *Reichsheer*. His ideas and methods were to mold the *Reichsheer* and his successors were officers brought up in his shadow. The size and organization of the *Reichsheer* had been determined by the allies, and the 100,000 strong army was divided into two army groups, of seven infantry and three cavalry divisions. It was intended only for border police duties and internal security. Although Seeckt

Above: President Ebert, with Gustav Noske behind him, inspecting *Reichsheer* officers in 1919.

Left: Freikorps soldiers display the *Kaiserreich* flag in Berlin, 1920.
Below: The Communist 'Red Army' in the Ruhr, 1920.

was concerned about the possibility of communist disorders and the Bavarian separatist movement, his main worry was the security of the German border, particularly those areas vulnerable to French and Polish incursions.

Effectively Seeckt established his own authority over the *Reichsheer* and remained independent of Gessler, the new *Reichswehr* minister. Seeckt had every intention of evading the restrictions imposed by the Versailles Treaty and the activities of the Allied Control Commission. Under the direction of Major-General Otto Hasse, the *Truppenamt* carried on the duties of the old general staff, with sections dealing with developments in armored warfare disguised as transportation, and even main-

History of The German Army

Above: Communist wall poster denouncing capitalism and the *Reichsheer*, 1920.
Above right: A crippled officer begs in Berlin in the twenties. Such everyday
sights emphasized Germany's changed military status.

taining a small air planning staff. Those staff officers serving outside the *Truppenamt* were called *Führergehilfen*, or command assistants. Although the *Kriegsakademie* had closed, a covert system of staff preparation and training was devised whereby students trained for many staff duties within the divisions and the *Truppenamt*.

The arms balance within the *Reichsheer* was unwieldy with 18 regiments of cavalry to only 21 regiments of infantry. So Seeckt used the cavalry to conceal motor and horse transport battalions as well as a number of technical units. Forbidden any regular reserves or militia, Seeckt was reduced to all kinds of subterfuges to strengthen the *Reichsheer*. Large numbers of officers and soldiers who could not be found places in the *Reichsheer* joined the Republican *Landespolizei*, which with its para-military role became a substitute force for maintaining internal order. Border clashes with the Poles in Silesia provided Seeckt with the opportunity to set up a covert para-military organization known as *Grenzschutz Ost*, which was sponsored by the *Reichsheer*. Membership was drawn from amongst the *Stahlhelm*, the largest ex-servicemen's association. These and other para-military units who were the successors to the *Freikorps* became known as the 'Black' *Reichsheer*.

Seeckt was to claim later that the success of the *Reichsheer* was due to the retention of the pre-war officer corps, particularly those former members of the general staff. With an officer corps limited to only 4000, Seeckt was able to pick his officers with care, laying emphasis on social as well as professional and military criteria. Inevitably, the majority of officers were pro-monarchist and strongly anti-Republican and disliked parliamentary control. Seeckt retained very few officers who had received wartime commissions, and was not interested in the majority of *Freikorps* officers. Many of these wartime officers became embittered, not only against the Republic but also against the professional and social exclusiveness of the *Reichsheer*, and continued to play at being officers in right wing para-military organizations. The post-war intake of officers inevitably came from bourgeois or landed backgrounds and they went through a vigorous four year system of professional and social selection before ultimately being commissioned.

As far as possible, Seeckt attempted to maintain the social exclusiveness of the *Reichsheer*'s officer corps, and if anything, it was more so than in the old *Kaiserheer*. But although the officers of the *Reichsheer* were by no means representative of their age group in Weimar Germany, they did maintain a closer relationship with their troops than had the pre-war officer corps.

Recruits for the *Reichsheer* were volunteers and had to serve

for a minimum of twelve years. The acceptance standards were high and recruits were generally taken from rural rather than urban areas as they were regarded as being physically fitter and more conservative in outlook, an attitude similar to the pre-war *Kaiserheer*. Although discipline was strict in the *Reichsheer*, it was not as rigid as that of the *Kaiserheer*, and emphasis was placed on developing initiative.

Seeckt was determined to maintain the traditions of the *Kaiserheer* within the *Reichsheer* as a basis for a future expansion and a return to the old monarchial army. Despite the fact that the *Kaiserheer* had disintegrated in 1918, and that the *Reichsheer* was the immediate successor to the *Freikorps*, he linked the 18 cavalry and 21 infantry regiments of the republic with the 110 cavalry and 217 foot regiments and 45 independent infantry battalions of the *Kaiserheer*. Seeckt ordered that squadrons and companies of the *Reichsheer* were to be the *Traditionsträger*, or tradition holders of the regiments of the *Kaiserheer*, and were to keep alive their history and traditions and be linked with their veterans' associations. Thus, for example, the 9th Regiment became *Traditionsträger* of the 1st Foot Guards, and acquired the nickname *Graf Neun* because of its attraction for aristocratic officers. The *Traditionsträger* of the *Reichsheer* made it a very suspect organization in the eyes of many republican politicians.

Under Groener's guidance, the general staff had begun its assessment of the operational experience of the First World War almost immediately following the armistice. Seeckt continued this study through the *Truppenamt*, with his staff concentrating on why the Schlieffen Plan had failed in the west; the success at Tannenberg; the use of tanks and aircraft; and the success and failure of breakthrough attempts. The conclusions from these studies were fairly orthodox and predictable, for Seeckt was a reactionary officer who looked back with pride and nostalgia to the era of Moltke and Schlieffen. Seeckt believed that any future war would be won by the small professional *Reichsheer*, consisting of cavalry and infantry striking deep into the enemy's rear using an envelopment plan, with the defense of the homeland in the hands of short service conscripts and a militia. He wanted to see developments in heavy artillery, gas, aircraft and armored cars, but these were seen as support weapons. Too much emphasis has been paid to the work and influence of the advocates of armored warfare like Captain Heinz Guderian. Seeckt was not really very interested in tanks beyond their use as infantry support weapons.

In the 1920's, Seeckt was interested in establishing cooperation with the Soviet Union, which like Germany was a 'pariah' state of the Versailles settlement. The Germans and the Soviets had a joint interest in controling the ambitions of Poland, and wanted to exchange military expertise for training facilities. By 1922 negotiations had reached the stage whereby the Germans were prepared to build a number of factories for the manufacture of aircraft, tanks and gas in the Soviet Union, in exchange for allowing military personnel to train with these weapons. These commercial and military negotiations were conducted with the private agreement of the German government and their public denial. There was a certain irony in the fact that Seeckt the monarchist and violently anti-Bolshevik officer should conduct negotiations with the Soviet government seeking the cooperation of the Red Army.

German public opinion was sharply divided in its attitude toward the experience of the First World War, the role of the officer corps and the general staff and the image of the *Reichsheer*. While many patriotic Germans and right wing political parties accepted the officer corps' interpretation of the war, other Germans, including the left wing parties, believed that Germany's defeat was due to the dictatorship of the general staff, and suspected that the *Reichsheer* was the *Kaiserheer* under a different name. The anti-war and anti-military sentiment in Germany in the 1920's is symbolized by Erich Maria Remarque's novel *All Quiet on the Western Front*, which viewed the war and the *Kaiserheer* through the eyes of a young student volunteer who becomes progressively disillusioned with life as a front line 'trench hog.' Remarque's novel attacked the image of the heroic German soldier which had been romantically described by many patriotic writers. Equally influential, however, was Ernst Jünger's

Right: Hitler and the Nazi party's 'Blood Flag' at an SA Parade.
Below: Armed troops of the SA during the Beer Hall Putsch in Munich, 1923. Note this early use of the swastika emblem.

memoir *The Storm of Steel*, which along with other books he wrote gave a very realistic view of life at the front but glorified the role of the trench fighter and the *Stosstruppen*. Jünger was to influence a whole generation of German youth who were to form the basis for Hitler's *Führerheer*.

The most serious political crisis faced by Seeckt's *Reichsheer* was in 1923. At the beginning of that year the French and the Belgians occupied the Ruhr because the Germans were in default in their reparation payments. The *Reichsheer* could not prevent the allied action, and Seeckt feared that the French intended to encourage separatist movements in Bavaria and the Rhineland, and the Poles to take action in Silesia. Within Germany, right wing nationalists as well as the communists were preparing to overthrow the government and seize power. Matters came to a head in October 1923 when Bavaria was on the edge of secession under the virtual dictatorship of Gustav von Kahr. The commander of the *Reichsheer* in Bavaria, General Otto von Lossow, supported Kahr and refused to obey Seeckt's orders. At the same time a number of extreme right wing parties, including the Nazis led by Adolf Hitler and with the support of Ludendorff, decided to seize power in Bavaria.

The result was the Beer Hall Putsch of 8 November 1923 when Hitler attempted to take over the leadership in Bavaria preparatory to a march on Berlin. The putsch was defeated, not by the *Reichsheer*, but by the Munich police, and Hitler was

Below: Men of the SA, armed with a machine gun, in Neustadt during the Beer Hall Putsch.

wounded and captured. But the national government faced with a crisis in Bavaria, communist uprisings in Saxony and Thuringia, and clashes with the Poles in Silesia, decided to declare a state of emergency, giving Seeckt dictatorial powers. After Lossow was dismissed, the *Reichsheer* in Bavaria responded to Seeckt's orders, and over the next few months was deployed with other *Reichsheer* units in stamping out the communist insurrection. Once again the *Reichsheer* had proved to be an instrument of dubious loyalty when faced with a challenge from the right, but a reliable force when crushing the left.

In 1925 President Ebert died and he was succeeded by the aged Field Marshal Hindenburg, who became for many Germans an *ersatz Kaiser*, or substitute monarch. Relations between Seeckt and Hindenburg were cool, and when Seeckt made the error of allowing Prince William of Prussia to attend military maneuvers in the autumn of 1926, Hindenburg did nothing to prevent the demand for his resignation by the government. Seeckt was forced to submit his resignation and went into retirement.

Seeckt's greatest achievement was that he took what others had salvaged from the remnants of the *Kaiserheer* and created the *Reichsheer*. But he was politically reactionary and professionally conservative. Although he claimed that the *Reichsheer* was '*Überparteilichkeit*,' or 'above politics,' he supported right wing groups, was ardently anti-republican, and in 1920 and 1923 had an ambivalent attitude toward right wing putschs. Seeckt promoted to senior positions in the *Reichsheer* a clique of officers from whom he demanded unquestioning obedience rather than original thought. Far from seeing the *Reichsheer* as the basis of a mass conscript army, he believed in the need for a small professional force. Despite all his subterfuges to stockpile weapons, maintain illicit reserves of manpower and experiment with tanks and aircraft in Russia, he left a *Reichsheer* that was little more than a gendarmerie, or what one of his military contemporaries referred to as 'a bandbox army,' unable to defend Germany's frontiers against even limited French and Polish incursions. Although Seeckt liked to give the impression that he was a completely apolitical soldier, he was a born intriguer who gave some of his subordinates an unfortunate example.

With the departure of Seeckt, the leadership of the *Reichsheer* passed into the hands of a younger generation of staff officers who had been promoted because they were obedient technicians. As *Chef der Heeresleitung*, Wilhelm Heye was a genial, moderate officer, affectionately known as 'Papa' or 'Uncle,' and who did little to change the direction of policy. In any case, Heye was overawed by the presence of Hindenburg, who as a former chief of staff and now President took a personal interest in all aspects of the *Reichsheer*. In political terms, the most important senior *Reichsheer* officer after Seeckt's resignation, was Kurt von Schleicher, who was known as the '*Kardinal in politicis.*'

Schleicher came from an old Prussian family, and had been commissioned into the 3rd Foot Guards in the *Kaiserheer*, a regiment which also included at one time or another Paul von Hindenburg and his son Oskar, Kurt von Hammerstein-Equord, Walther von Brauchitsch and Erich von Manstein. Schleicher served on the general staff during the First World War and gained the favorable attention of Groener. Although Seeckt had little personal regard for Schleicher, he appointed him to serve as a liaison officer between the *Reichswehr* Ministry and the armed forces. Schleicher, a born intriguer, fully exploited his personal contacts with Hindenburg. So when the *Reichswehr* Minister Gessler was forced to resign in 1927 because of his association with a financial scandal, Schleicher recommended Groener as his replacement. Hindenburg duly appointed Groener in January 1928, and in turn he appointed Schleicher to head his *Ministeramt*, or Ministry Office, concerned with all policy affecting the armed forces and with liaison between the government and political parties. Thus in the Weimar Republic after 1928, an 'old comrades association' from the *Kaiserheer* controled the President's office, the *Reichswehr* Ministry and the *Reichsheer*. In 1929, Schleicher's

Above: Hindenburg, Hitler and Blomberg in conversation at Potsdam in March 1933.

'old regimental friend,' Hammerstein-Equord, was appointed head of the *Truppenamt*, and then in 1930, through Schleicher's influence head of the *Heeresleitung*.

In fact, Schleicher became increasingly unpopular amongst the *Reichsheer*'s officer corps who resented his politicking and his promotion of a small circle of cronies. However, Schleicher was also closely involved in influencing Hindenburg on the appointment of successive Chancellors, already maneuvering for his own political advantage. By 1930, Germany was in serious political and economic turmoil with the collapse of business confidence, mass unemployment and widespread violence between the paramilitary forces of the Communist and Nazi Parties.

Although the majority of *Reichsheer* officers were violently anti-communist and had little affection for the Social Democrats or the Weimar Republic, few of them supported the Nazis who were regarded as vulgar street fighters who wanted to radicalize society. Hitler was seen as a loud-mouthed former corporal, and the sympathy of the officer corps lay with the more traditional

Below: Papen, sitting second from right, with the members of his Cabinet in 1932 – Schleicher in uniform stands on the right. Konstantin von Neurath, later Hitler's foreign minister sits at Papen's left.

Above: Hindenburg, Hitler and Blomberg in conversation at Potsdam in March 1933.

right wing parties. In 1930 three junior officers belonging to an artillery regiment at Fulda were put on trial for conspiring to commit high treason through their support for the Nazis. Groener was furious at this political activity, and was critical of their commanding officer, Colonel Ludwig Beck, for appearing in their defense alongside Hitler. Increasingly over the next three years more and more officers were converted to the aims of the Nazi Party and were impressed by Hitler.

In the 1930 *Reichstag* elections the Nazis and their allies gained 148 seats whilst the Social Democrats and the Communists gained 220 seats, which meant that Chancellor Brüning and his supporters from the center parties could not govern. Brüning was obliged to rule by presidential decree, which meant that ultimately his government depended upon the support of Hindenburg, who prevaricated and was influenced by his son Oskar and Schleicher. Groener was appointed Minister of the Interior in addition to *Reichswehr* Minister, and was quite prepared to take firm action against all the para-military groups who were undermining democracy and the rule of law. But the ambitious Schleicher was secretly having talks with Hitler and Goebbels, looking for a way by which he could use the Nazis to oust Brüning and replace him with a more reactionary government.

In 1932 Hindenburg was re-elected as President, beating Hitler and several other candidates. Groener persuaded Hindenburg to order the banning of the Nazi *Sturm Abteilung*, SA, or Storm Squads' brown-shirted uniforms. This caused an immediate uproar, and Schleicher told Groener that he no longer had the support of the *Reichsheer*. Groener then discovered that he did not have Hindenburg's support over this issue. On 13 May Groener resigned, and seventeen days later Hindenburg dismissed Brüning, and on Schleicher's recommendation, appointed the right wing political light-weight Franz von Papen as Chancellor. In turn, Papen appointed Schleicher as *Reichswehr* Minister. The Papen government had little support in the *Reichstag*, and despite Schleicher successfully persuading Hindenburg to lift the ban on the SA, the Nazis were not so easily bought. In July 1932, Papen was forced to call an election, and after

Above: Reichsheer cavalry on maneuvers.
Below: Reichsheer machine gun deployed in an anti-aircraft role during training in the early 1930s.

a violent campaign, the Nazis became the largest party in the *Reichstag*.

Hindenburg refused to appoint Hitler as Chancellor and the Nazis would not enter into a coalition government. New elections in November slightly reduced the Nazi strength but did not break the political deadlock. Schleicher was involved in some complicated political maneuvering, alternatively working for and against both Papen and Hitler. In desperation, Hindenburg appointed Schleicher Chancellor in December 1932, but without any support in the *Reichstag* and unable to gain Hindenburg's agreement to rule by emergency decree, Schleicher was forced to resign on 28 January 1933. He was replaced, finally, by a coalition government, with Hitler as Chancellor and Papen as his deputy. Papen and the conservatives believed that they would be able to control and use Hitler and the Nazis. In this belief they were to deceive themselves, as Hitler was not prepared to conduct politics by the old party methods.

Schleicher had been replaced as *Reichswehr* Minister by another serving officer, General Werner von Blomberg, who was sympathetic to the Nazis. When confirmed in his new post, Blomberg appointed as head of his *Ministeramt*, Colonel Walther von Reichenau, an intelligent, articulate and ardent pro-Nazi officer. The influence of Hammerstein-Equord as *Chef der Heeresleitung* had been already compromised because of his close connections with Schleicher. In October 1933, Blomberg suggested to Hindenburg that on the retirement of the self-effacing General Adam as head of the *Truppenamt*, he should be replaced by Lieutenant General Ludwig Beck. This was approved, and Beck took up his new appointment in the knowledge that he was regarded by his brother officers as a brilliant thinker but also a Nazi sympathizer. In February 1934, Hammerstein-Equord was succeeded as *Chef de Heeresleitung* by Lieutenant-General Werner von Fritsch, one of Seeckt's protégés, and an officer who accepted his appointment with some misgivings.

After becoming Chancellor, Hitler began to consolidate his power by a frantic campaign of intimidation and illegal actions. The *Reichstag* fire on 27 February 1933 had provided the excuse to suppress the communists, and Hitler acquired dictatorial powers, whilst throughout Germany the Nazi Party and the SA established a grip on the bureaucracy, judiciary, police and local government. Hitler also began an intensive campaign to win the support of the *Reichswehr*. Although many senior officers still regarded him with personal distaste, they warmed to his stated objectives of over-turning the Versailles settlement and supporting the expansion of the *Reichswehr*. They were also relieved to hear Hitler announce that the Nazi Party and the *Reichswehr* were the twin pillars of the new state. Increasingly, junior officers were captivated by his strident nationalism and his vision of a new Germany.

The leaders of the *Reichsheer* were quite prepared to support many of the new laws passed by the Nazis which were anti-semitic or aimed at restricting civil liberties. Blomberg and Fritsch worked hard for closer relations between officers and Nazi Party officials. A symbol of the link between the *Reichswehr* and the Party came in February 1934 when Blomberg ordered that the Nazi Party's emblem of the swastika carried by an eagle with outstretched wings was to be worn on the uniforms of all members of the armed forces.

But there were serious disagreements between the *Reichsheer* and the SA over the expansion, leadership and the very ethos of the army. For some time the SA had been demanding a major role, not only in what it saw as the maintenance of internal security, but also in border control and national defense. Captain Ernst Röhm, the SA chief of staff, was a former officer and *Freikorps* activist who wanted to replace the small professional, conservative *Reichsheer*, with a Nazi people's militia based on the SA, with himself in command. Many SA leaders were former officers who were frustrated at their lack of employment and demanded a further revolution in Germany.

Right: Stahlhelm members on parade, 1933. Veterans organizations like the *Stahlhelm* generally aided the Nazi rise to power.
Below: Reichsheer infantry battalion marches past at the end of maneuvers in the 1920s. The limitations on the size of the *Reichsheer* meant that its leaders were able to select a very high standard of officers and other ranks which helped facilitate the expansion following Hitler's accession to power.

History of The German Army

Although the *Reichsheer* had been pleased to give the SA some military training and to regard it as a useful reserve, it had no intention of being supplanted as the 'sole bearer of arms' in Germany. In February 1934, Hitler rejected Röhm's proposal to use the SA as the basis for a new army, believing that such a militia would be inadequate for his requirements of building up an army capable of undertaking offensive action. Hitler intended expanding the *Reichsheer* through conscription.

The split between the *Reichsheer* and the SA came at a time when other Nazi leaders, including Hermann Göring and Heinrich Himmler, the head of the *Schutz-Staffel*, SS, or Protection Squads, a rival but subordinate organization to the SA, were planning to eliminate Röhm and reduce the SA to impotence.

Throughout the spring of 1934 the outspoken criticism of Röhm and senior SA officers, combined with the provocative actions by the SA caused the leaders of the *Reichsheer* to fear an SA putsch. Reichenau had been undertaking secret negotiations with Himmler and gathering information from his officers attached to the SA. In June, the SA were sent on a month's leave, and over the next few weeks Hitler was persuaded by Göring and Himmler that Röhm planned a putsch. On 30 June Himmler's SS squads moved against the SA, and Röhm and other senior SA commanders were arrested. Many senior SA officers were murdered, and other 'enemies of the state,' including Schleicher and his wife and two of Papen's assistants were shot down. What became known as 'the Night of the Long Knives' was the murder or arrest of a wide range of Hitler's opponents both inside and outside the Nazi Party, and the scoring off of old grudges by individual Nazis. Röhm and several other SA commanders were executed a few days later. The *Reichsheer* provided weapons and facilities for some of the SS murder squads, and many officers approved of what had happened as it removed a threat to the independent power of the *Reichsheer*. In doing so they were unwittingly to help replace the SA with the SS, potentially a much greater threat.

On 2 August 1934, Hindenburg died and Hitler abolished the post of President and assumed the far more significant position of *Führer*. The *Reichswehr* were required to swear a new oath of allegiance. Under the Republic's constitution, the troops had sworn loyalty 'to the Reich constitution, the Reich and its lawful institutions,' with obedience to the holder of the Presidential office and to the soldiers' superiors. In December 1933 Hitler had had the oath revised so that a recruit no longer swore allegiance to the President, constitution, institutions or superior officers, but 'to the people and Fatherland.' In August 1934, all officers and men were ordered to swear 'unconditional obedience to Adolf Hitler as *Führer* of the German *Reich* and Commander-in-Chief of the armed forces.' With this oath, Hitler bound the armed forces to his person and hamstrung all those soldiers who were to have reservations about his policy.

Hitler had gained office in January 1933 partly as a result of Schleicher's political intrigues, and had capitalized on the anti-socialist sentiment of the officer corps and its lack of loyalty to the Republic. The officer corps of the *Reichsheer* claimed to be 'above politics,' but had sympathized with conservatives like Papen who were convinced they could use Hitler and the Nazis to destroy the socialists. But Hitler used the conservatives, and with the assistance of certain pro-Nazi officers and the sympathy of an increasingly large number of officers, was able to convert the *Reichsheer* into supporting many of his policies.

Main picture: Dummy tanks of the *Reichsheer*, 1928.
Above right: Hindenburg greeting Red Army officers attending *Reichsheer* maneuvers.

PzKwII

Preparing for Blitzkrieg

History of The German Army

Adolf Hitler was motivated by a few basic ideas. He regarded life as a struggle which could be determined only by conflict. In ideological terms, he saw the struggle as between on the one hand the Nazis and the best racial elements of the Germanic peoples and on the other Jews, communists, Christians and reactionaries. In foreign affairs it was a struggle between Germany, and rival powers such as France, Poland, Czechoslovakia, Britain and the Soviet Union. Hitler was determined to overthrow the Versailles settlement and rearm Germany. Few Germans disagreed with this policy, although some had doubts about the methods he advocated to achieve them, and some people were shocked by his ultimate aim of creating a 'Third *Reich*' based upon racial considerations which would go far beyond the boundaries of the *Kaiserreich*.

Hitler transferred the methods he used in domestic politics – bluff, daring, imagination, surprise and intimidation – and applied them to foreign affairs. He planned to isolate his enemies politically, undermine their morale by propaganda and sabotage, and finally, if necessary, knock them out with one sharp blow. Hitler wanted war, but after his own experiences as a front line soldier in the First World War, he was determined that it would not be a protracted attritional conflict. He intended to fight wars by *coups de main*, each one short and decisive and designed to annihilate one particular enemy. Hitler had no carefully prepared strategic plan apart from general objectives, and his ability and need to extemporize from one crisis to the next. Initially, he was rather reticent and indeed diffident in dealing with the leaders of the *Reichswehr* because he was unsure of his grasp of technical details,

but increasingly he was able to challenge the military experts until he believed his own judgment was superior. As his confidence grew and he established his authority as *Führer* Hitler became more impatient with what he believed was the reactionary attitude of senior members of the old officer corps, and individuals such as Fritsch and Beck were seen as obstacles in his path.

When Hitler had become Chancellor in January 1933 he had indicated immediately that the *Reichswehr* would be returned to its former position of influence and power, but he had no intention of letting the officer corps dictate policy. Hitler dazzled the officer corps with the prospects of rearmament, expansion, promotions and political brinkmanship, whilst proceeding gradually to convert the small professional armed forces into a National Socialist force.

Above: German recruits swear an oath of loyalty to Hitler on their regimental colors.
Left: Tracked carriers of the Motor Transport Corps training future tank crews for the *Führerheer*.
Page 126-127: Pz Kw II tanks of the *Führerheer* on exercise in 1937.

Preparations to expand the *Reichsheer* had already begun under the Weimar Republic. A paper scheme had been drawn up to create a reserve army, and in 1932 money had been allocated for rearmament. But little was achieved beyond these initial measures, and even after Hitler came to power Fritsch and Beck were only given some general guidelines to expand the army from 7 to 21 infantry divisions preparatory to the reintroduction of conscription.

The expansion of the *Reichsheer* after 1934 was achieved by doubling the number of infantry regiments in the first phase using as a basis for new regiments the third battalion and the training battalion of each old regiment, and tripling them in the second when each of the regiments created new battalions to replace those they had given up, while the new two-battalion regiments raised their own third and fourth battalions. Recruits for this expansion before conscription became law in 1935 were drawn from volunteers and through the incorporation of complete battalions of the para-military *Landespolizei*.

This expansion had to be carried out against the background of the formation of a separate *Luftwaffe*, or air force. Although Germany had been forbidden an air force by the Versailles settlement, a small nucleus of an air staff had been concealed in the *Truppenamt*, and between 1925 and 1933, 130 army fighter pilots and 80 observers had been trained at Lipetsk in Russia. An interest in military flying had also been preserved within the civil air transport ministry which included many former air force pilots. With the formation of the airline *Lufthansa*, an air transport and a permanent ground support organization had been set up which could be converted quickly into a military organization. In 1933 a *Reich* Air Ministry was set up under Göring, a former wartime pilot and leading Nazi, who, with his deputy Milch began to plan a separate *Luftwaffe*. Eventually, the *Luftwaffe* would lay claim not only to the army and navy air services, but also would acquire by 1935 the army's anti-aircraft artillery. Furthermore, the army had to transfer a number of officers to the air arm and was responsible for administering and training air personnel until the formal announcement of the creation of a *Luftwaffe* in 1935.

History of The German Army

From 1933 there was increased support for motorization and mechanization within the *Reichsheer*. The *Reichsheer* had been forbidden tanks, but this had not prevented it from experimenting in their use and conducting a wide debate about the future of motorized and mechanized troops. The first inspector of *Kraftfahrabteilungen*, or transport battalions in the *Reichsheer*, General Erich von Tschischwitz, together with his staff officer, Captain Guderian, began to alter the use of the seven transport battalions away from service tasks in favor of tactical experiments. In 1925 the German armored school opened at Kazan in Russia, and the first postwar tanks were manufactured in Germany and sent there in 1928. The influence of foreign theorists of armored warfare such as Liddell Hart and Fuller was probably limited, and Guderian was to write during the Second World War that the greatest influence was the British *Provisional Regulations Part II* of 1927. Between 1929 and 1931 the first motor-cycle and mechanized reconnaissance companies were formed in the *Reichsheer*.

After 1933, the new German panzer arm was formed from the *Kraftfahrabteilungen* of the *Reichsheer*, although these were reinforced in 1935 by units from the cavalry and infantry. In October 1935 the first three panzer divisions were formed, each consisting of a panzer brigade of two tank regiments, and a rifle brigade. By 1938 there were two further panzer divisions and two independent panzer brigades. In the same year Hitler ordered that all panzer troops, cavalry, infantry anti-tank and reconnaissance units were to be grouped together into *Schnelle Truppen*, or mobile troops, and Guderian was appointed the first Inspector. On mobilization in 1939 the *Führerheer* had five panzer divisions and four (cavalry) light divisions.

In the early days of raising the panzer troops there were few

Left: Pz Kw I tanks practicing a river crossing in 1936. Although designed as a training tank, this type saw considerable action in the early war years.
Below: Panzers parade past Hitler at the Brandenburg Gate. Dramatic parades played a large part in intimidating Hitler's enemies by their portrayal of German strength.

Above: Machine gun section of the SS *Leibstandarte Adolf Hitler*, 1935.

tanks or armored cars, and units had to train on tractors or tracked carriers. A light tank, the Pz Mk I had been ordered from Krupp in 1931, and by 1936, 3000 of these were in service. This two man tank with two machine guns, weighing about six tons, was entirely outmatched by the tanks then in service with the French or Red armies. But heavier models were soon produced, the Pz Mk II in 1935 with a crew of three, a 20mm gun and one machine gun, weighing eleven tons; the Pz Mk III in 1937 which had a 37mm gun and weighed over 20 tons and in 1938 the Pz Mk IV with a short-barrelled 75mm gun and weighing nearly 25 tons. The mechanical design of all these models was good, and from 1937 the optical and ancillary equipment excellent. However, the weaknesses of these early tanks were that they were underweight, under-gunned, under-armored, and the angle of their armor incorrect for proper protection. The design of the Pz III and IV did, however, permit updating with more powerful guns.

The development of the German panzer arm was a collective act by a number of officers from the early days of the *Reichsheer*. Officers such as Lutz, Guderian, Hoeppner, Hoth, Schmidt, Kleist, Vietinghoff, Schweppenburg, Harpe, Thoma, Weichs and Paulus all played their part, and many of them were to hold senior command appointments during the Second World War. Guderian provided many of the ideas which his superior, General Otto Lutz, the first *General der Panzertruppen*, transformed into practical projects. Lutz and Guderian determined the operative use of tanks in large formations. But the growth of panzer troops in the *Führerheer* during this period was not a simple matter, for many senior officers opposed the use of panzer formations in the offensive role seeing them merely as infantry support, whilst the traditional arms resented the competition for manpower and equipment.

Rearmament and the expansion of the army increased at a frantic pace after 1935. In that year Hitler publicly announced the existence of the *Luftwaffe* and the re-introduction of conscription. What also took the generals by surprise was his announcement that the army was to be increased to 36 divisions. The *Reichswehr* was renamed the *Wehrmacht*, and the *Reichsheer* became simply *das Heer*, along with a *Kriegsmarine* and *Luftwaffe*. A few months later Hitler announced that Blomberg the C-in-C of the Wehrmacht and the defense minister would henceforth be called the war minister. Fritsch now became C-in-C of the *Führerheer* and the *Heeresleitung* was designated *Oberkommando des Heeres*, OKH, or army high command, while Beck became chief of the general staff. Both the *Kriegsmarine* and the *Luftwaffe* also had their own high commands, and this meant that the *Führerheer* had to compete with them for resources and over strategic objectives.

Above: Hitler and Blomberg in 1936. Blomberg proved to be very subservient to Hitler's wishes.

From 1935 plans were prepared for raising a *Kriegsheer*, or war army, which was to consist of the peacetime *Feldheer*, or field army, and eventually, after mobilization, of the *Ersatzheer*, or replacement army. By 1937 the mobilization strength of the *Kriegsheer* stood at 36 infantry and 3 panzer divisions, one mountain and one cavalry brigade, all of the active army, and four reserve and 21 *Landwehr* divisions, a total of 66 formations. By midsummer 1939 the *Feldheer* order of battle stood at a total of 103 divisions, which meant that the army had expanded fifteen-fold in divisional strength in only six years. Manpower for these divisions had been acquired through conscription, the incorporation of the *Landespolizei* battalions in the Rhineland after the reoccupation in 1936, and the transfer of five divisions from the Austrian *Bundesheer* following the *Anschluss* in 1938. In fact, the strength of the *Feldheer* in 1939 was largely illusory because the trained manpower available would not have staffed more than half the divisions. Furthermore, the *Ersatzheer* remained seriously below strength and had insufficient replacements for the *Feldheer*.

Although the trained manpower of the *Reichsheer* had been a useful basis for the expansion of the *Führerheer*, within a few years this nucleus had been swamped by the induction of a mass of partially trained or untrained men. Of the original 4000 officers of the *Reichsheer*, some 450 were medical or veterinary personnel, whilst 500 of the remainder were released eventually for service with the *Luftwaffe*. To meet the *Führerheer*'s requirements, officers were provided by transferring members of the *Landespolizei* who had been officers in the *Kaiserheer*; re-employing officers who had been discharged after 1918; shortening the period required to take a commission; and commissioning a higher proportion of NCOs. While the expansion of the officer corps initially did not affect professional standards, it changed the social exclusiveness, and there was a much closer spirit of camaraderie between officers and soldiers, a feeling which was fostered and emphasized by the Nazi Party.

The rapid expansion of the *Führerheer* and the continual need

to split up old units to provide cadres for new ones caused considerable confusion and at times a lack of cohesion. Hitler was not in favor of re-establishing the *Traditionsträger* of the *Kaiserheer* as he wished to emphasize the National Socialist origins of the *Führerheer*. A degree of lip service was paid to these traditions, and they were used to reinforce Hitler's position and contemporary developments. Hitler was keen to establish a new military *esprit de corps*, and old ceremonial traditions were re-introduced and given a Nazi flavor. After 1935 new full dress, field service and fatigue uniforms were introduced, and a wide range of lanyards, chevrons, badges and medals awarded for proficiency, long-service, loyalty and to commemorate political and military victories. On 14 September 1936 the *Wehrmacht* received new colors on Hitler's orders, and in future the *Führerheer* held special parades on a wide range of anniversaries connected with German military history and Nazi mythology.

Another consequence of the rapid expansion of the *Führerheer* had been an acute shortage of weapons and equipment, especially motor transport. In 1939, even the panzer divisions were short of guns and vehicles, while only four of the infantry divisions were fully motorized. The remaining 86 divisions relied on horses for transportation, including the movement of artillery. There was a wide variety of weapons of early designs and numerous variants. The standard infantry rifle was the Type 98 which was based on the Mauser of 1898. There were at least five types of machine pistol, and many machine-guns were obsolete. It was not until 1940 that the infantry was fully equipped with a standard weapon, the MG 34. There were shortages of anti-tank and anti-aircraft weapons and even the divisional artillery employed modified developments of those weapons used in the First World War.

These weaknesses in manpower, weapons and equipment were a direct consequence of Hitler's decision to expand the size of the *Führerheer* as rapidly as possible. What Hitler required from rearmament was a mobilization of resources in breadth rather than in depth with a great deal of emphasis placed on building up a large number of units to win quick, overwhelming victories. As long as he was able to prevent his enemies from combining together and forcing him to fight an attritional war, Hitler could use a decisive superiority at the crucial point to achieve victory. Before 1939 Hitler's military strength was largely a question of bluff, with a brilliant use of highly publicized military maneuvers and propaganda which concealed the weaknesses in hasty rearmament. These methods combined with partial mobilization and bellicose behavior overwhelmed such weak opponents as Austria and Czechoslovakia. Hitler was prepared always to take risks, and in concentrating his main forces he relied upon *Landwehr*, Labor Corps and border troops to defend his otherwise vulnerable frontiers.

There are many misconceptions concerning *Blitzkrieg*, or lightning war, which is usually associated with the German development of a new operational doctrine based upon armor and close air support in the 1930s. The Germans never used the term *Blitzkrieg* until after it had been used by a journalist in 1939 to explain the short war of envelopment and annihilation against Poland. In fact German operational doctrine before 1939 was an extension of historical developments which included Moltke and Schlieffen's concepts of a strategy of annihilation based upon the double envelopment, and the lessons drawn from the experiences of the First World War. But the proponents of armored warfare in the *Führerheer* before 1939 did have a new concept in that they argued that the primary aim of modern warfare was to paralyze an enemy by deep thrusts into his rear areas which only armored formations could achieve. Guderian was to propound these theories in 1937 in his book *Achtung! Panzer!* Instead of having vast slow moving armies of marching infantry there would be fast moving columns of armored troops supported by mobile artillery which would be provided in the form of close air support from the *Luftwaffe*.

In fact the proponents of armored warfare were never entirely able to convince the majority of senior officers of the merits of their case. Although Hitler was to back the need for panzer forces, the panzer divisions of the *Führerheer* before 1939 were subordinated to the old strategy of decisive maneuver by a mass army. In any case, the hastily expanded *Führerheer* did not have the necessary armored vehicles or motor transport to translate Guderian's ideas into practice. It would take the impact of war before the operational doctrine and the organization of the *Führerheer* responded, and even then, there were to be bitter disputes between the advocates of armored supremacy and those who favored a more balanced mix between armor and the other service arms.

By 1939 the Germans had also established a small force of airborne troops. In April 1937 the *Führerheer* had raised a parachute infantry company while Göring formed a parachute battalion from a police unit. Göring was able to persuade Hitler that airborne troops were the responsibility of the *Luftwaffe*, and in January 1938, the military parachute battalion passed into the control of the *Luftwaffe*. The OKH was also suspicious of the formation of certain para-military SS units, collectively referred to as SS *Verfügungstruppen*, or Special Disposal Troops. These small formations were tasked to provide Hitler's personal bodyguard, and, along with SS *Totenkopfverbände* and *Ord-nungspolizei*, would maintain internal security on the home front when the *Führerheer* was at war. In 1939 Hitler permitted Himmler to allow some of these units to accompany the *Feldheer* in war and enable them to gain military experience and respect

Below: Potential staff officers in training at the *Kriegsakademie* in 1936.

Above: Hitler and Mussolini enjoying the crowd's salutes in Berlin, 1938.

which would help them in their primary duty of internal security. These SS formations would form the basis of what would eventually be known as the *Waffen SS*, or armed SS.

The *Führerheer* in 1939 was far from the powerful panzer force which contemporaries believed, and it had many operational and organizational weaknesses. Nevertheless, it was still a formidable military force which had been created in a remarkably short

period of time. The professional expertise and sheer hard work of the officers, NCOs and soldiers of the *Reichsheer*, and the enthusiasm of the new volunteers and conscripts helped to overcome many problems. The *Führerheer* evolved an organization which aimed at providing maximum support for the front-line soldier with a minimum of administration. There can be no doubt that Hitler, his ideology and the success of his policies were important factors in boosting morale, creating an *esprit de corps* and a pride in German military traditions within the *Führerheer*. But a number of senior officers had begun seriously to question how successful the rapid expansion of the army had been and had also considerable doubts as to the wisdom and morality of Hitler's aggressive foreign policy.

Both Fritsch, the C-in-C of the army, and Beck, the chief of the general staff, were alarmed at the manner in which Hitler had announced rearmament in 1935. They were worried that the military expansion was taking place too quickly and that quality was being sacrificed for quantity. With the consequence of disorganization, Fritsch and Beck believed that Germany was in no condition to fight a war if there was a crisis with either Poland or France. Neither Fritsch nor Beck opposed in principle Hitler's plans to prepare for military action against Czechoslovakia, they just questioned the timing. In 1936 Hitler decided to abrogate the Locarno Pact which had provided for the demilitarization of Germany's western frontier. Blomberg, Fritsch and Beck all opposed Hitler's decision to send German troops into the Rhineland. But on 7 March, after some last minute vacillation,

Left: Colonel-General Ludwig Beck, Chief of the General Staff, 1933-38.
Below: German troops receive a rapturous welcome as they march into the Rhineland, 1936.

Hitler ordered three infantry battalions to march into the Rhineland. They were greeted with wild enthusiasm by the local population, and there was no military reaction from either the French or British.

On 5 November 1937, Hitler addressed a conference at the Chancellory, consisting of Blomberg, Fritsch, Göring, Raeder the C-in-C of the *Kriegsmarine*, and Neurath the foreign minister. Hitler told his audience that the initiative for Germany in Europe would last for only a few years, and he left them in no doubt that he would risk world war to further his policy of expansion. Blomberg and Fritsch both warned of the dangers to Germany of fighting Britain and France, and Blomberg drew their attention to the strength of Czechoslovakia's defenses. As a result of this opposition Hitler was determined to remove those senior military officers who criticized his policy or delayed the *Wehrmacht*'s expansion.

The opportunity for Hitler to remove Blomberg came about by fortuitous circumstances. On 12 January 1938 Blomberg, a widower, married a woman who, it was later claimed, had a police record of immorality. At the same time, Himmler produced a file claiming homosexual practices against Fritsch. The whole matter was most convenient for Hitler, who wanted to remove both these officers; for Göring, who had ambitions to succeed Blomberg; and for Himmler who wanted to prove how useful he was to the *Führer*. Blomberg was persuaded to resign, and whilst Fritsch protested his innocence, talks were very soon begun to find his replacement.

Right: Colonel-General Werner von Fritsch, Army C-in-C, 1934-38.
Below: German troops march past General von Bock in Vienna, March 1938. The soldiers are from the 1st Division, VIII Corps.

Above: Brauchitsch (right) and Halder at work soon after Halder's appointment. Halder's pencil is poised ominously over Czechoslovakia.

On 4 February 1938 a public announcement listed a number of military and diplomatic retirements, including those of Blomberg and Fritsch. At the same time Hitler was able to extend his personal control over the *Wehrmacht*. He announced that he would succeed Blomberg as Supreme Commander of the *Wehrmacht* and as War Minister. Hitler set up the *Oberkommando der Wehrmacht*, OKW, or armed forces high command, and appointed as his deputy, Major General Wilhelm Keitel to act as *Chef der OKW*, and Colonel Alfred Jodl as head of the *Wehrmachtführungsamt*, or Operations Office. Schwedler, the head of the army personnel department, was succeeded by Keitel's younger brother, Bodewin, which gave Hitler greater control over officer appointments. Finally, Fritsch was succeeded as C-in-C of the army by General Walther von Brauchitsch. A total of 16 high ranking generals were relieved of their commands and 44 others, including a number of senior field commanders were transferred. Göring was placated in his failure to succeed Blomberg by being given the rank of *Generalfeldmarschall*, which in fact made this former air force captain, the senior officer of the *Wehrmacht*. Beck only survived because Hitler did not want to cause too much confusion by a total purge at the top of the *Führerheer*.

Although a number of senior officers were shocked at Fritsch's treatment, particularly when it was proved that the allegations were false and had been fabricated by the Gestapo, no positive steps were taken to protest to Hitler or to oppose the massive assumption of power now concentrated in his person. A number of military and civilian figures did talk about carrying out a putsch, but nothing came of this, which was to be the pattern of all such resistance to Hitler before 1939. The overwhelming majority of senior officers, even if they did have reservations about Hitler's policies, owed him a personal debt for expanding the army and accelerating their own promotion. The Fritsch affair was overshadowed by the occupation of Austria in March 1938, and then

became something of a forgotten cause since after that triumphant success Hitler's personal authority was even more secure.

After 4 February 1938, Hitler had concentrated political and military power in Germany in his person as *Führer*, Chancellor and Supreme Commander of the *Wehrmacht*. The creation of a unified OKW under Hitler might have supposed a greater coordination between the three services, but in fact it meant overlapping and competing areas of authority, confusion and mistrust. As Hitler's deputy, Keitel was merely a loyal functionary, who had proved himself a competent but none too imaginative officer in the *Kaiserheer* and the *Reichsheer* and then on Blomberg's staff. Keitel lived in Hitler's shadow, and soon gained the nickname, '*Lakaitel*,' or 'Lackey,' and showed little loyalty toward his brother officers. Jodl was an intelligent staff officer who soon became one of Hitler's foremost military advisers, but lacked the experience of field command. For the *Führerheer*, the appointment of Brauchitsch as C-in-C was something of a disaster, as he was under a great personal obligation to Hitler, who had allowed him to divorce his wife and marry a woman of dubious reputation and had given him a financial settlement. Brauchitsch was overawed by Hitler who despised him and publicly berated him for what he saw as objections to his policies by reactionary elements within the officer corps.

After 1938, senior officers in the *Führerheer* were promoted because they were either *treu ergeben*, personally loyal, or *Nursoldaten*, technicians. Either way, they were usually officers without strong political or personal opinions who could be relied upon to execute the *Führer*'s orders.

Beck lingered on as chief of the general staff until his resignation on 18 August 1938. Increasingly, he became more outspoken about Hitler's policies and the preparations for war. He opposed the military pressure brought to bear on Czechoslovakia and wrote several memoranda to Brauchitsch on the subject. Beck feared that Hitler's aggressive policies toward Czechoslovakia would inevitably lead to war with France, and he believed that Germany was unprepared for such a war and would be defeated by the impressive French army. Beck represented a minority view amongst senior officers, because Hitler was able to persuade them that his policy of bluff and intimidation worked, and after the *Anschluss* with Austria it appeared he was correct. Beck also urged his brother officers to defend the rule of law and resist the power of the Nazi Party.

Beck was succeeded by an equally outspoken critic of the *Führer*. Franz Halder was a Bavarian who had enjoyed an outstanding career as a staff officer, serving as Beck's deputy and chief of operations from 10 February 1938. A highly intelligent,

Below: Austrians enthusiastically welcome the *Führerheer* during the early stages of the *Anschluss* in March 1938.

hard working officer with a wide range of interests, Halder had advocated strong action against Hitler at the time of the Blomberg-Fritsch affair. Halder appears to have accepted his promotion to chief of the general staff as providing him with an opportunity to continue his opposition to Hitler's policies. This opposition crystallized around Hitler's plans to use military force against Czechoslovakia. A loose conspiracy of officers including Halder, Witzleben, Hoeppner, Karl-Heinrich von Stülpnagel and Colonel Oster of the *Abwehr*, planned to arrest Hitler as soon as the final order had been given for the invasion. But Hitler was able to achieve his objectives against Czechoslovakia through the Munich settlement on 29 September 1938. This caused the conspiracy to collapse, but it is doubtful in the event whether many officers would have supported such a putsch. After Munich, the doubters like Halder suppressed their political and moral qualms and proceeded to carry out what they understood as their professional duty as officers in assisting Hitler to prepare his expansionist war plans.

By 1938, OKH had already evolved into a war organization. Its main task was to provide a command organization for war, both in the field and at home, with the wartime *Ersatzheer* providing the men and materials to maintain the *Feldheer*. On mobilization, the OKH would divide into main, rear and replacement army headquarters. The main headquarters would consist of the C-in-C of the army and the chief of the general staff. The general staff in the main headquarters would include operations, intelligence and supply, and the chiefs of signals and intelligence. The rear

Right: Austrian soldiers are given their new German uniforms.
Below: After the *Anschluss*, the Austrian regiment *Hoch-und-Deutschmeister*, now incorporated into the *Führerheer*, parades past Hitler in Vienna.

headquarters at Zossen would consist of the second-echelon of the general staff departments. Finally, the other departments of the OKH including the arms inspectors, would come under the authority of General Friedrich Fromm, the C-in-C of the *Ersatzheer*, whose responsibilities would include the home army in the static *Wehrkreise* (military districts).

The Munich settlement which had given Germany the Sudetenland had 'cheated' Hitler of war, and even the German occupation of the rump of Czechoslovakia on 15 March 1939 was without opposition. But on 3 April, Hitler notified his service chiefs that they were to prepare for a war against Poland because of the intractable attitude of the Poles over Danzig and the Corridor. Planning for *Fall Weiss*, or Case White, began almost immediately. Halder and other members of the general staff were horrified by this decision, because they feared that while Germany became involved in a war with Poland, France and Britain would be able to attack in the west. Apart from the incomplete fortifications known as the *Westwall*, there would be few troops left to guard the frontier. They were worried also about the reaction of the Soviet Union. Hitler, however, was confident that by clever diplomacy he would be able to divide Britain and France from the Soviet Union.

The final OKH plan agreed to by Hitler was a double envelopment of the main grouping of the Polish army lying to the west of Warsaw in the bend of the Vistula between Krakow and Bromberg. One flank of the envelopment would consist of a thrust from Silesia and Slovakia northwards to meet a second thrust moving south from East Prussia. The main emphasis was to be on speed and mobility with the *Luftwaffe* destroying the Polish air force and then causing chaos and confusion in the Polish rear areas. Hitler also ordered Himmler's SS and Police to be responsible for special tasks behind the army front line, and SS *Einsatzkommandos* would deal with saboteurs, communists and Jews. In other words, carrying out mass arrests and executions of those deemed to be politically and racially undesirable. The SS had already gained experience of such operations during the *Anschluss* and the occupation of Czechoslovakia. The majority of officers regarded these operations with distaste, but ultimately as having nothing to do with the army as they concerned political questions.

On 23 August 1939 Hitler achieved a diplomatic coup and astounded his enemies at home and abroad by concluding a Non-Aggression Pact with the Soviet Union. This pact allocated German and Soviet spheres of interest in eastern Europe and guaranteed the division of Poland. But Hitler's major political error was his underestimation of the determination of Britain and France to guarantee Poland's territorial integrity. In the final week of August the decision to invade Poland was twice postponed as Hitler negotiated with the British. But on 1 September, after faking Polish attacks across the German border on the previous day, Hitler gave the order for the attack to commence. He calculated that by the time the *Wehrmacht* had defeated the Poles the British and the French would be barely mobilized and would probably agree to negotiate faced with a *fait accompli*. Influenced by his egotistical comparisons with Frederick the Great, Hitler launched his *Führerheer* on what he called his 'First Silesian War.'

Above right: Hitler signing the Munich Agreement, 30 September 1938. Mussolini and Göring converse in the background.
Above far right: German soldier decorated with flowers by an Austrian woman.
Right: German troops parade through Prague in March 1939 following the final occupation of Czechoslovakia.
Below: Hitler's victory drive through the Sudetenland, October 1938.

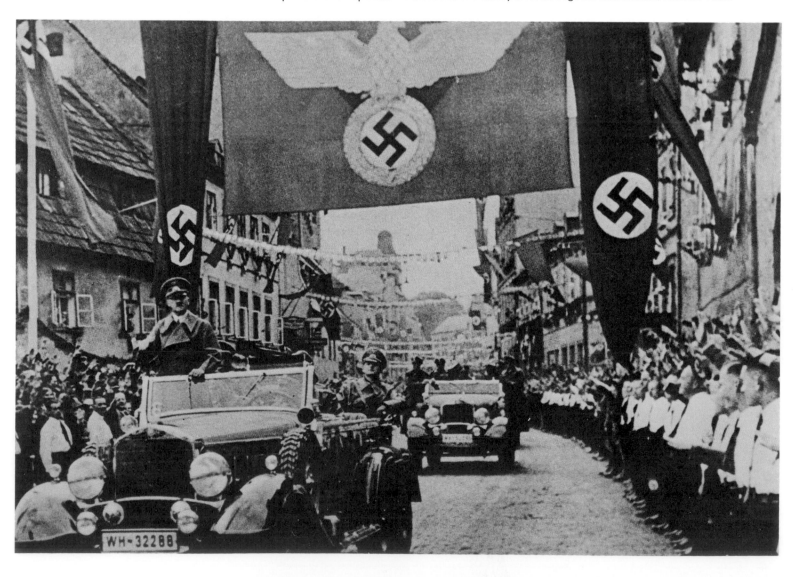

Hitler's Army
at War

History of The German Army

The overwhelming success of the *Führerheer* and the *Luftwaffe* against the Poles in September 1939 was helped by the Polish deployment. The Poles had been forced to divide their forces between both western and eastern Poland, and those in the west were deployed well forward in the vast bend of the Vistula, surrounded on three sides by German territory. The Polish deployment, their lack of mobility and the destruction of their communications and command headquarters by the *Luftwaffe*, combined with the rapid advance of the German ground forces from the north and the south meant that a large proportion of the Polish army was quickly encircled. By 17 September this encircled force was cut off behind the Vistula, and on the same day the Red army invaded Poland from the east and the Polish army began to distintegrate. The *Führerheer* rapidly reduced the remaining Polish fortified positions, and on 27 September, Warsaw surrendered, and the following day the Poles capitulated.

Although panzer and motorized formations had played an important part in the German victory, they had not been allowed really to operate independently as Guderian and other advocates had proposed. Instead, they had been tied to the advance of the infantry and were used as a means to facilitate the movement of the traditional arms. Some field commanders were fearful of allowing the panzers and the motorized troops to advance beyond the marching infantry and horse-drawn artillery because this would have divided their forces. Despite this limitation the Poles and the western allies believed the Germans had succeeded because they had fought with a new doctrine and new weapons,

Previous page: Infantry and a Panzer III of the Afrika Korps, 1941.
Below: German soldiers cross the Meuse in May 1940.

which combined with Nazi ruthlessness became *Blitzkrieg*. Certainly Hitler believed that close air support, the panzer breakthrough and the deep motorized envelopment was the way to conduct *Blitzfeldzug* (lightning campaigns) and win decisive victories.

Hitler had made little attempt to interfere with the conduct of operations in Poland and had left Brauchitsch and the OKH to fight the campaign. But Hitler had gone to the front with his first *Führerhauptquartier*, which consisted of Keitel and Jodl, various *Wehrmacht* liaison officers and a traveling circus of courtiers and party hacks. Although Hitler did not interfere with the operational side of the campaign, he was concerned with political questions, and had been far from pleased by Stalin's occupation of eastern Poland, and although an agreement was reached over the final division of the spoils, Hitler did not trust Stalin. Hitler was determined to see that the administration of the occupied territories would be in the hands of the Nazi Party and the SS and not the military. Individual field commanders, like General von Blaskowitz had protested already about the SS murdering Jews and Poles. But neither Brauchitsch nor Keitel was prepared to take any action, and the field commanders seemed relieved when their forces in Poland were transferred to the west. Some parts of Poland were incorporated into the Reich itself while in the remainder power was handed over to a Nazi administration.

While the Germans had been campaigning in Poland the British and the French had done little beyond mobilizing and deploying their forces. The French were established behind the Maginot Line watching the Germans behind the *Westwall* in what was soon to be called the '*Sitzkrieg.*' The British deployed a small expeditionary force in northern France, which along with a strong

mobile French force was concentrated to meet any German thrust through Belgium. The allies planned a gradual build up of their military strength and did not contemplate any serious offensive action in the west before 1941. Hitler, however, had determined on 23 September to attack in the west as soon as possible. The OKH were not enthusiastic, because they feared the strength and reputation of the French army, were depressed by the shortages in manpower, weapons and equipment in the *Führerheer*, and had noted that while a decisive victory had been obtained in Poland, many German troops had displayed unsteady symptoms in battle. Given the recent success against the Poles, his own increasing self-confidence and contempt for Brauchitsch and Halder, Hitler was determined that he would decide how the war in the west would be fought. In contrast to 1914, when strategy and operations had been determined by the general staff, in 1939 these were determined by Hitler as *Führer*, Chancellor and Supreme Commander of the *Wehrmacht*. The general staff had to compete with OKW, the other services and even individual field commanders for the *Führer*'s attention.

Hitler told the *Wehrmacht* leaders on 27 September 1939 that he intended to attack Belgium and seize the Channel coast which would guarantee the security of the Ruhr and enable the *Luftwaffe* to attack Britain, and that this offensive would take place as soon as possible. Brauchitsch and Halder were still very pessimistic and made their views known to Hitler. In fact Hitler was forced to postpone the campaign in the west until the following spring because of bad weather. But one result of the clash between

Right: German heavy artillery in France, May 1940.
Below: Exhausted German motor-cyclists in France in May 1940. The speed of the German advance made great demands on the troops.

Hitler and Brauchitsch, was that it reduced even further the influence of the OKH and increased that of Keitel and Jodl at the OKW.

Between October 1939 and May 1940 there were several fundamental revisions made to *Fall Gelb*, or Case Yellow, which covered the main attack in the west. These revisions were the result of Hitler's whims, a debate within the *Führerheer* concerning the *Schwerpunkt*, or center of gravity of the offensive, and the fact that a copy of the initial plan fell into allied hands. The original plan in October 1939 had given the main role to Bock's Army Group B in the north, consisting of four armies, including nine panzer and four motorized divisions, which would attack through Belgium. In the center Rundstedt's Army Group A, consisting of two armies, would cover Bock's left flank by advancing through the Ardennes. Finally, Leeb's Army Group C would have a passive role behind the *Westwall*. The OKH had decided that the main panzer thrust should be in the north, despite obstacles such as the Meuse, and the Albert Canal. They had considered a panzer thrust through the Ardennes based on Rundstedt's Army Group A, but decided that this wooded area would be too difficult in winter.

By the time the final revised plan had been adopted, the emphasis for the panzer thrust had switched from Bock's Army Group B to Rundstedt's Army Group A, with the *Schwerpunkt* based on the Ardennes and Sedan. Manstein, the chief of staff at Army Group A, has been credited with the concept of switching the panzer thrust to the Ardennes. But the change came about after Hitler had consulted a wide range of opinion, including Guderian and Manstein. Hitler quickly grasped the opportunity the change in emphasis offered to divide the French army and encircle the British and French forces in Flanders against the Channel coast.

Throughout the winter of 1939-40, Hitler busied himself with a wide range of military details. He was an enthusiastic supporter of using the *Luftwaffe*'s parachute troops and the *Führerheer*'s air landing units to carry out a *coup de main* against the Dutch bridges on the Maas and Rhine and the Belgian fortress of Eben Emael on the Albert Canal.

In May 1940 the strength of the *Führerheer* was 153 divisions, with in addition three *Waffen SS* divisions. The ten panzer and six motorized infantry divisions were all allocated to the west forming part of the 136 divisions available for the attack. Of the remainder, nine were in the east, three in the Reich and eight were in Scandinavia. In fact in total manpower and divisional strength the Germans only matched the combined armies of the western allies, and in armor had slightly less than the Anglo-French total. But the advantages the Germans had over the allies included the fact that the allies were divided and had little common coordination in doctrine, weapons and equipment, and allied armor was dispersed rather than concentrated. The allies were outnumbered in the air and had based their war plan on the assumption that the Germans would launch their main attack through Belgium. Finally, after 9 April, the Anglo-French command was diverted by its attempts to combat the German attack on Denmark and Norway.

As early as December 1939, Hitler had instructed Jodl to consider a plan to occupy Denmark and Norway. Hitler was perturbed about the possibility of Anglo-French intervention to help the Finns who had been attacked by the Soviets on 30 November. Such an allied move would threaten Germany's supplies of iron ore from Sweden via Norway. Without really informing the OKH, Hitler planned an attack on Denmark and Norway using a small military force, including naval and *Luftwaffe* units. The plan *Weserübung*, or Exercise Weser, was coordinated by the OKW, and the land forces were placed under the command of General von Falkenhorst. Halder advised against this operation as he regarded it very risky.

Left: On the road to Warsaw – German troops in Poland.
Below: Panzers in France, May 1940. The tanks shown are Czech-manufactured types, which made up a large part of the German strength.

The German landings in Norway and the occupation of Denmark on 9 April 1940 nearly ended in disaster. Although Denmark was speedily occupied with little resistance, the attack on Norway met fierce opposition and an Anglo-French expeditionary force which landed in the north surrounded German mountain troops at Narvik. Hitler had a crisis of nerves and wanted to evacuate these troops into Sweden where they would be interned rather than have the ignomiy of them surrendering to the British. In fact, Hitler's orders were never sent, and General Dietl, the commander at Narvik, conducted a determined and skilful defense until relieved by other German forces. Eventually, the allies were forced to withdraw from Norway. *Führerheer* and *Luftwaffe* casualties had been small, although the *Kriegsmarine* had lost a number of ships. This early success convinced Hitler that he had been correct in using the OKW and not the OKH for operational planning involving the three services.

The first phase of *Fall Gelb* was decided within five days of its implementation on 10 May. Although some of the *coup de main* operations in the north failed, the Germans were able to knock out the fortress of Eben Emael and capture some of the Dutch bridges. Bock's offensive into Holland and Belgium quickly destroyed the fighting ability of the Dutch and Belgian armies and attracted the mobile Anglo-French forces into Flanders. But the decisive breakthrough was through the Ardennes at Sedan where Kleist's panzer group smashed through the weak French defenses and began to advance toward the Channel coast. As a result of their faulty deployment of forces and without air support, the allied armies were divided into two groups by the German breakthrough at Sedan.

Hitler and the OKH were troubled by nagging doubts about the safety of the flanks of Kleist's panzer group which were well ahead of List's marching infantry. Although these fears were never

Above: German and Soviet officers consult a map to establish the demarcation line in Poland, October 1939.
Below: German anti-tank gun outside La Gare de l'Est in Paris, June 1940.

directly translated into a halt order for the panzers, they were an inhibition on thrusting commanders such as Guderian who yearned for independent action. The allies were in no position to attack the German flanks seriously, although a hastily organized British counter-attack at Arras did cause confusion to Rommel's 7th Panzer Division and Eicke's SS *Totenkopf* Division. On 20 May

Kleist reached Abbeville at the mouth of the Somme, and the Anglo-French forces in Flanders were trapped between Rundstedt's Army Group A to the south and Bock's Army Group B to the northeast.

Instead of moving north along the coast to destroy the allied forces, and to prevent a British evacuation through the local ports,

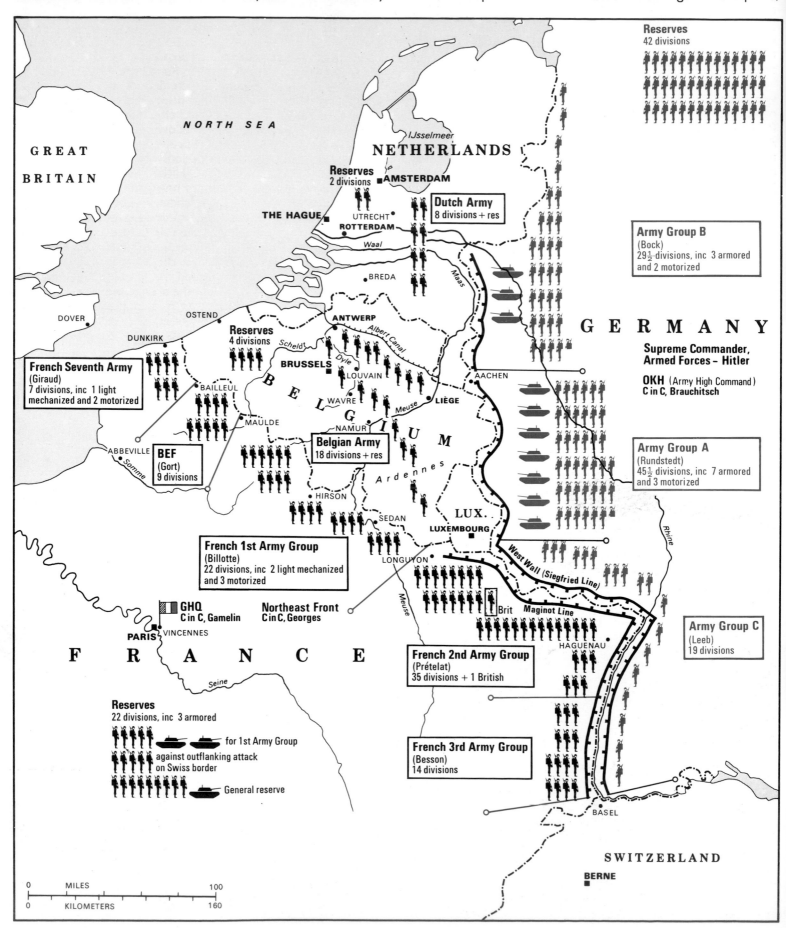

Reserves
42 divisions

NORTH SEA

GREAT BRITAIN

NETHERLANDS
IJsselmeer

Reserves
2 divisions
AMSTERDAM

Dutch Army
8 divisions + res

THE HAGUE
UTRECHT
ROTTERDAM

Waal

BREDA

Maas

Army Group B
(Bock)
29½ divisions, inc 3 armored and 2 motorized

GERMANY

Supreme Commander, Armed Forces – Hitler

OKH (Army High Command)
C in C, Brauchitsch

DOVER
OSTEND
ANTWERP
Albert Canal
AACHEN

DUNKIRK
Reserves
4 divisions
Scheldt
Dyle
BRUSSELS
LOUVAIN

French Seventh Army
(Giraud)
7 divisions, inc 1 light mechanized and 2 motorized

BAILLEUL
WAVRE
LIÈGE
Meuse

MAULDE
NAMUR

ABBEVILLE
BEF
(Gort)
9 divisions
Belgian Army
18 divisions + res
Ardennes

Somme
HIRSON
SEDAN
LUX.
LUXEMBOURG

Army Group A
(Rundstedt)
45½ divisions, inc 7 armored and 3 motorized

Rhine

French 1st Army Group
(Billotte)
22 divisions, inc 2 light mechanized and 3 motorized

LONGUYON

West Wall (Siegfried Line)

GHQ
C in C, Gamelin

Northeast Front
C in C, Georges

Meuse

PARIS VINCENNES

Brit
Maginot Line

FRANCE

French 2nd Army Group
(Prételat)
35 divisions + 1 British

HAGUENAU

Army Group C
(Leeb)
19 divisions

Seine

Reserves
22 divisions, inc 3 armored

for 1st Army Group

against outflanking attack on Swiss border

General reserve

French 3rd Army Group
(Besson)
14 divisions

BASEL

SWITZERLAND

BERNE

0   MILES   100
0   KILOMETERS   160

Kleist's panzers were finally halted on 24 May. After the war, surviving German generals blamed Hitler for this decision which allowed the British to evacuate some 336,000 troops from the area of Dunkirk. Whilst Hitler was responsible for the final decision, he was influenced by the advice of commanders including Brauchitsch, Halder and Rundstedt. A combination of factors influenced Hitler in this decision, including the belief that the panzers needed resting and that the terrain was difficult for tank operations, and the fact that Göring, Keitel and Jodl all advised him that the *Luftwaffe* and Bock's Army Group B could destroy the trapped allies.

Even before the final phase of *Fall Gelb* in the north, the OKH was preparing *Fall Rot*, which was the plan to destroy the remaining French forces south of the Somme. On 5 June Rundstedt's and Bock's Army Groups moved south and Leeb's Army Group C moved west against the Maginot Line. French resistance soon collapsed and the panzer formations raced south outdistancing the marching infantry. Paris was captured, and by 11 June the Germans were south of the Loire and had reached the Swiss frontier. With the armistice agreed on 22 June, all fighting came to an end in France.

The six week campaign in the west had resulted in an overwhelming German victory. Although the *Führerheer* had played a dominant role in this victory, it had to share the honors with the *Luftwaffe*. Brauchitsch and Halder at the OKH were totally eclipsed by Hitler, 'the greatest *Feldherr* of all time.' Given the size of the victory, German casualties of 166,000 appeared relatively insignificant. The German people, soldiers, foreign observers, and above all Hitler himself, believed that the *Führer* was the strategic genius responsible, The *Führerheer* appeared to have used brilliantly the new *Blitzkrieg* tactics of panzer and motorized thrusts combined with close air support. In reality, for most of the campaign, the panzers had been restrained by the

horse-drawn and marching infantry divisions and the timidity of conservative field commanders. Although the allies had often fought well in independent actions, overall they had lacked the leadership and determination necessary to fight the Germans effectively. Leadership, high morale and determination in all ranks of the armed forces had all played a part in helping to secure the German victory in 1940.

As Hitler celebrated his victory, something more than Moltke or Hindenburg and Ludendorff had achieved, he publicly thanked his generals. On 19 July Hitler promoted Göring to *Reichsmarschall*, and Keitel, Brauchitsch, Rundstedt, Leeb, Bock, List, Kluge, Witzleben, Reichenau, Milch, Sperrle and Kesselring to *Generalfeldmarschall*. Halder was promoted to colonel general and Jodl became a general of artillery. Many of these officers received secret *Donationen*, or endowments from Hitler in the form of gifts of money, land and property.

Invasion of Britain had never seriously been considered by the general staff, or for that matter Hitler. But on 13 July Hitler ordered Brauchitsch and Halder to begin planning *Unternehmen Seelöwe*, Operation Sealion, the landing in England. A prerequisite from the *Kriegsmarine*'s point of view was that the *Luftwaffe* had to gain air superiority over the RAF before an invasion fleet could attempt a Channel crossing. In fact, until 18 October when *Seelöwe* was definitely postponed, the planning for the landing appears to have been very muddled with considerable disagreement between the services over the area of operations and the support required. The *Führerheer* had no experience of such combined operations except for limited landings along the Baltic coast during the First World War. As early as June 1940, Hitler was looking eastward, and in July Brauchitsch and Halder were

Opposite: The opposing forces in 1940.
Below: Panzers refueling in France, June 1940.

Above: German infantry wait for the signal to attack in North Africa, 1941.
Below: German 2cm anti-aircraft gun mounted on a truck in North Africa. Both sides made considerable use of such improvised equipment in the North African campaigns.

ordered to study the problems of a campaign against the Soviet Union.

Hitler and the majority of senior officers regarded the Soviet Union as a threat to Nazi Germany and believed that Stalin would take the opportunity to seize more territory in the east while Germany was distracted by the war with Britain. Hitler had always had a pathological hatred of the Soviet Union because it was the center of world communism. But he also coveted its territories and resources and planned to establish a Nazi empire in the east. Initial estimates by the general staff were optimistic and reflected the overweening German confidence following the victories in the west and a corresponding contempt both for the Soviets and the Red army.

At the same time both the OKW and the OKH were distracted by having to prepare contingency plans for possible operations in the Mediterranean. For a time, Hitler considered an attack on Gibraltar, but Franco's lack of enthusiasm effectively stopped it at the planning stage. More serious were the difficulties faced by the Italians in North Africa following the commencement of a British counter-offensive from Egypt in December 1940. In January 1941, Hitler agreed to send German forces to Libya to assist the Italians and to form a *Sperrverband*, or blocking force. Eventually, this force, named the *Afrika Korps*, and under the command of Rommel, was to consist of three divisions whose limited role was to prevent a complete collapse of the Italian position. The hasty organization of the *Africa Korps* and its speedy deployment to a theater outside the German experience of operations was a typical example of the flexibility of the general staff.

Hitler was also fearful of a British landing in Greece, as the Italian invasion of that country in October 1940 had ground to a halt. This fear combined with suspicions of Soviet moves in the Balkans prompted Hitler to prepare a new plan, *Marita*, whereby the OKH prepared contingency plans for a possible occupation of Greece. So the preparations for what was to be a quick, decisive

German campaign against both Yugoslavia and Greece in April 1941, had been prepared already that winter, and German troops were deployed in Rumania and Bulgaria months before the invasion.

In December 1940 Hitler had signed Directive 21, *Fall Barbarossa*, which outlined how the Soviet Union was to be crushed in a short, decisive campaign planned for May 1941. Unfortunately, neither Hitler nor the OKH could decide on how this aim was to be achieved. Instead of concentrating either on one major thrust on Moscow after destroying the bulk of the Red army or alternatively seizing the Ukraine before redeploying north, the directive talked of general aims and the initial planning did not develop in detail beyond taking the *Führerheer* to Smolensk. Only after this had been achieved would future strategic options be considered. The OKH's preparation for *Barbarossa* was slapdash and in certain areas ignored inconvenient factors. There was a lack of detailed information concerning the political, military and economic strength of the Soviet Union and a failure to consider the problems of operating over a vast terrain quite different in extent and type from those which had been fought over in the previous two years. Halder suppressed a report by one of his own staff which detailed the transportation problems which would confront the *Führerheer* in such a campaign. Undoubtedly, some officers shared Hitler's political contempt for the Soviet regime and his racial contempt of the Russian *untermensch*.

By June 1941, although the German order of battle had seen the *Führerheer*'s divisional strength rise to 205, this was an illusory figure, for in terms of effective manpower and weapons it was no more powerful than the 153 divisions of May 1940. The number of panzer divisions had been doubled, but each division only had half the tank strength of the old divisions. There were shortages of motor transport and radio equipment and it was assumed that the campaign in Russia would be over before the onset of winter, and that therefore there was no requirement for warm clothing.

After the experience of campaigning in the west in 1940, it was decided to concentrate all motorized forces into four large panzer groups which would be capable of independent long-range action designed to tear open the Soviet front. To compensate the infantry for this withdrawal of panzer support the *Führerheer* began to introduce the *Sturmgeschütz*, or assault gun, which just to complicate the establishment was manned by the artillery.

Hitler was determined that the campaign against the Soviet Union would be an ideological and racial war, and he made plans to prevent the OKH from frustrating his policy. In May 1941, an agreement was reached between Himmler's deputy, Heydrich, and General Eduard Wagner from the OKH, whereby SS *Einsaztgruppen*, basically mobile murder groups, would operate behind the army front against Jews, communists, officials and suspected partisans. The *Führerheer* was also expected to hand over to the SS all Red army commissars. Although some senior

Below: A German motorized column passes through a Yugoslav village in April 1941.

officers, such as Leeb and Bock, were critics of this racial war, the majority either approved of the measures or preferred not to know about them, regarding the matter as a political rather than a military question. Once the front had moved forward, Hitler intended that the occupied territories would be administered by the Nazi Party and the SS.

In the spring of 1941 as a consequence of the British landing troops, Hitler decided to move against Greece. Hitler had spent some time trying to persuade Yugoslavia to join the Axis, and just when this appeared imminent, the government was overthrown by an anti-German coup. So an enraged Hitler ordered the immediate invasion and occupation of both Yugoslavia and Greece. The precautionary planning and movement of German units into the Balkans over the previous few months was a considerable help, but of the 33 divisions deployed, some 15 were brought from France. The three-week campaign against Yugoslavia and Greece in April 1941 was the final short *Blitzfeldzug* of the *Führerheer*. German panzer and air superiority combined with excellent staff work and offensive determination led to the speedy collapse of the Yugoslav and Greek armed forces and the hasty evacuation of the British force. Although casualties were light, the rough terrain and the distances covered meant that the panzer and motorized divisions already earmarked for *Barbarossa*, had to be refitted, thus causing a delay in the start date. In May the Germans successfully invaded Crete using *Luftwaffe* parachute troops and elements of two mountain divisions. But total German casualties of 8000 men persuaded Hitler that large airborne operations were too risky and costly. Along with the Italians, Hungarians and Bulgarians, the *Führerheer* had to provide troops for occupation duty in the Balkans.

From June 1941, Russia was to be the only theater of operations under the control of the OKH, all other theaters coming under the OKW. This division of command and responsibility was to cause endless confusion and a lack of control and was complicated further by the fact that the *Luftwaffe* and *Kriegsmarine* were able to operate independently under their own high commands. The strength of the *Führerheer* in May 1941 was 3,800,000 in the *Feldheer*, of whom 3,300,000 were deployed in the east, and the strength of the *Ersatzheer* was 1,200,000. The *Luftwaffe* numbered 1,700,000 men, the *Kriegsmarine* 400,000 and the *Waffen SS* 150,000. The divisional order of battle on 21 June was 145 in the east, with 38 in France, 12 in Norway, 2 in Libya, 1 in Denmark and 12 in the Balkans. But those in the east were up to full strength whilst many of those in the west were skeleton divisions. More importantly, nearly all the panzer and motorized troops were in the east.

To implement *Barbarossa*, the *Ostheer*, the *Führerheer* on the eastern front, was divided into three army groups each supported by an air fleet. Leeb's Army Group North consisted of two armies and one panzer group and was based in East Prussia. Its objective was to clear the Baltic states and advance on Leningrad. Bock's Army Group Center was the most powerful force consisting of two armies and two panzer groups. It was to attack north of the Pripet marshes toward Smolensk. Rundstedt's Army Group South was divided into two separate groups. One army and one panzer group in Poland was to attack toward Kiev with flank protection provided by one army. The second group consisted of one army and the Rumanian expeditionary force which would attack into Bessarabia. Concentrated along the western frontier of the Soviet Union were 150 Red army divisions who were

Left: Members of an SS cavalry unit on reconnaissance in Russia in the summer of 1941.
Right: MG 34 in action in the heavy machine gun role in North Africa. The first 'general purpose' machine gun to see widespread service in any army, the MG 34 could also be mounted on a bipod for use as a squad light machine gun.

Above: Hitler briefs the Rumanian head of state, Antonescu, while Keitel and Halder look on.
Right: German troops in Finland improvise anti-aircraft defense.
Opposite: The drive to Moscow, September-December 1941.

regarded by the *Führerheer* as having no real military significance following Stalin's purge of the officer corps and the debacle in the winter war against Finland in 1939-40.

On 22 June 1941 the *Ostheer* attacked the Soviet Union and within a few hours had achieved major successes against the Red army. By 29 June Hoth's and Guderian's panzer groups in the center had enveloped 300,000 Red army troops at Minsk. It appeared to Halder that the campaign was virtually over, and by 16 July Hoth and Guderian had reached Smolensk, only 200 miles from Moscow. At this point there was considerable confusion among the Germans about the next stage of the campaign. In retrospect, many senior officers blamed Hitler for failing to continue the advance on Moscow, but at the time there were bitter disputes between the OKH and among the field commanders. Hitler, far from having the 'iron willpower' he is credited with, was prone to listen to a variety of opinions and be influenced by the last person who spoke to him. Hitler was convinced that the campaign was almost over and was supported in this belief by some field commanders. He therefore ordered Hoth's Panzer Group North to assist Leeb in clearing the Baltic states, whilst Guderian was sent south to help encircle the Soviet position on the Dniepr. As a result, Army Group Center marked time at Smolensk, and did not renew its advance on Moscow until October.

Hoth's panzer group helped Leeb to isolate Leningrad while Guderian's met Kleist's at Kiev resulting in the encirclement of 700,000 Red army prisoners. In September, after listening to conflicting opinions among the field commanders and at the OKH, Hitler decided to redeploy Hoth's and Guderian's panzer groups to Army Group Center and to continue the advance on Moscow.

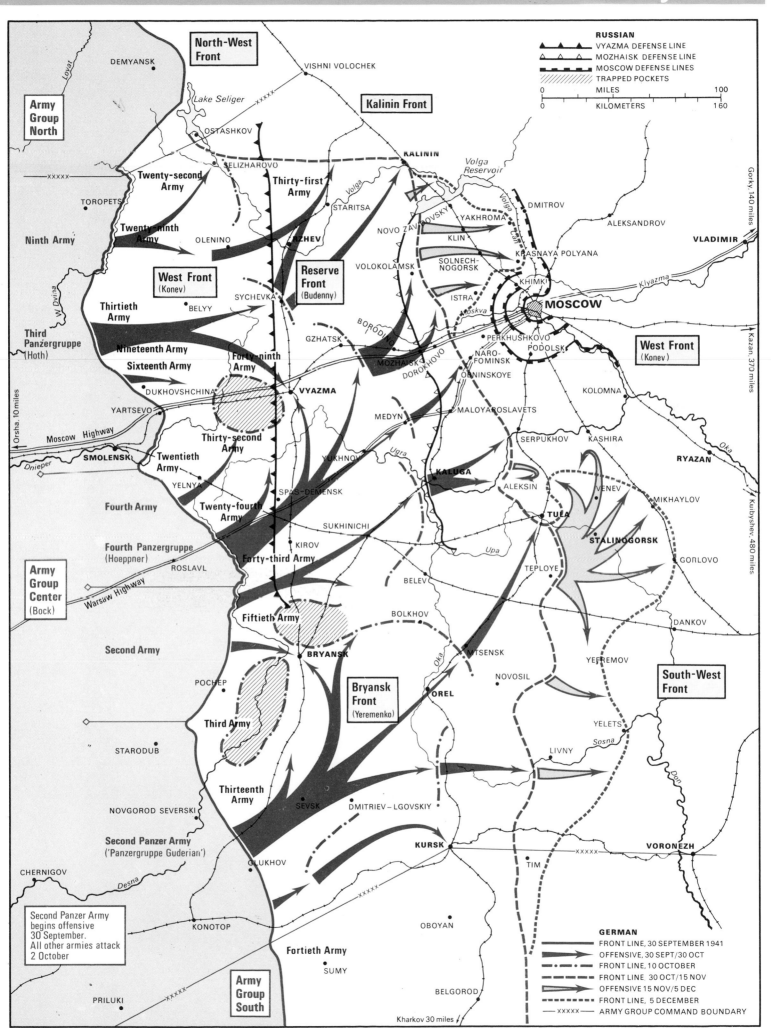

RUSSIAN

⎯⎯ VYAZMA DEFENSE LINE
⎯△⎯ MOZHAISK DEFENSE LINE
⎯⎯ MOSCOW DEFENSE LINES
///// TRAPPED POCKETS

0   MILES   100
0   KILOMETERS   160

North-West Front

Kalinin Front

Army Group North

Ninth Army

Third Panzergruppe (Hoth)

Twenty-second Army

Twenty-ninth Army

West Front (Konev)

Thirty-first Army

Reserve Front (Budenny)

Thirtieth Army

Nineteenth Army

Sixteenth Army

Forty-ninth Army

Thirty-second Army

Twentieth Army

Fourth Army

Fourth Panzergruppe (Hoeppner)

Twenty-fourth Army

Army Group Center (Bock)

Forty-third Army

West Front (Konev)

Fiftieth Army

Second Army

Bryansk Front (Yeremenko)

Third Army

South-West Front

Thirteenth Army

Second Panzer Army ('Panzergruppe Guderian')

Fortieth Army

Army Group South

Second Panzer Army begins offensive 30 September. All other armies attack 2 October

DEMYANSK, TOROPETS, OSTASHKOV, SELIZHAROVO, Lake Seliger, Lovat, VISHNI VOLOCHEK, KALININ, Volga Reservoir, DMITROV, ALEKSANDROV, VLADIMIR, Gorky, 140 miles, STARITSA, RZHEV, NOVO ZAVIDOVSKY, YAKHROMA, KLIN, KRASNAYA POLYANA, SOLNECH-NOGORSK, VOLOKOLAMSK, ISTRA, KHIMKI, MOSCOW, Klyazma, Kazan, 370 miles, OLENINO, BELYY, SYCHEVKA, BORODINO, GZHATSK, MOZHAISK, DOROKHOVO, PERKHUSHKOVO, PODOLSK, NARO-FOMINSK, OBNINSKOYE, KOLOMNA, KOLOMNA, Moskva, DUKHOVSHCHINA, VYAZMA, MALOYAROSLAVETS, Oka, RYAZAN, YARTSEVO, Moscow Highway, MEDYN, SERPUKHOV, KASHIRA, Orsha, 10 miles, SMOLENSK, Dnieper, YUKHNOV, Ugra, KALUGA, ALEKSIN, VENEV, MIKHAYLOV, Kuibyshev, 480 miles, YELNYA, SPAS-DEMENSK, TULA, Upa, STALINOGORSK, GORLOVO, KIROV, TEPLOYE, DANKOV, ROSLAVL, Warsaw Highway, SUKHINICHI, BELEV, YEFREMOV, BOLKHOV, Oka, MTSENSK, NOVOSIL, POCHEP, BRYANSK, OREL, YELETS, STARODUB, DMITRIEV-LGOVSKIY, LIVNY, Sosna, Don, SEVSK, NOVGOROD SEVERSKI, KURSK, VORONEZH, TIM, W Dvina, Desna, CHERNIGOV, GLUKHOV, KONOTOP, OBOYAN, BELGOROD, PRILUKI, SUMY, Kharkov 30 miles

GERMAN

⎯⎯ FRONT LINE, 30 SEPTEMBER 1941
⟶ OFFENSIVE, 30 SEPT/30 OCT
⎯·⎯ FRONT LINE, 10 OCTOBER
⎯··⎯ FRONT LINE, 30 OCT/15 NOV
⟹ OFFENSIVE 15 NOV/5 DEC
····· FRONT LINE, 5 DECEMBER
⎯XXXXX⎯ ARMY GROUP COMMAND BOUNDARY

But by this stage, the momentum of the German offensive was beginning to falter. Although the panzers had not suffered heavy battle casualties, they were greatly reduced in numbers because of mechanical problems. Difficult terrain, the lack of roads and the vast distances to be covered caused serious supply problems and the marching infantry had difficulty in keeping up. Despite predictions, the Red army had not collapsed even though it had suffered staggering casualties, and the endurance of the Russian soldiers amazed the *Ostheer*. In many cases, the leadership of the Red army was excellent, individual units fought with determination, and weapons like the T-34 tank came as a very nasty surprise to the Germans.

In the middle of October the weather broke and rain and sleet turned the whole countryside into a quagmire making movement extremely difficult. It was only when the bitter freezing winter began on 15 November that Army Group Center could move, and this offensive became known as the *Flucht nacht vorn*, or the flight forward, as the troops advanced in panic to find shelter in Moscow. The appalling weather, the loss of manpower due to disease as well as combat, the inability to use mechanized forces, all produced a sense of deep depression among field commanders. At the end of November disaster appeared to be imminent with Soviet counter-attacks being launched against all three army groups. The OKH and the field commanders wanted to withdraw and regroup, but Hitler refused, and he had already issued his famous 'halt' order on 28 November. At the beginning of December Army Group Center was halted on the outskirts of Moscow, and within a few days was the subject of a violent Soviet counter-offensive which was to force it to retreat 200 miles. Hitler refused to accept the realities at the front where German units were decimated and frozen. Ironically, this ruthless policy probably helped to prevent a total collapse, and Hitler became convinced that the problem lay with the defeatism of the field commanders and pessimism at the OKH.

In December Hitler purged both the OKH and the field commanders of the *Ostheer*, removing doubters and those whom he regarded as unreliable, replacing them with robust and optimistic commanders. Rundstedt was replaced by Reichenau, Bock by Kluge, Leeb by Küchler, and many others were dismissed, including Guderian and Hoeppner at a lower level. On 19 December Hitler sacked Brauchitsch and assumed his appointment as C-in-C of the *Führerheer*, which meant in practice that he assumed the operational leadership of the *Ostheer*. Halder was retained with his staff to provide an operational executive for Hitler, whilst Jodl acted in a similar way for the OKW theaters. The remainder of Brauchitsch's responsibilities, such as organization, personnel, equipment and the *Ersatzheer* were transferred to Keitel. In the autumn of 1942 Hitler appointed his adjutant, Schmundt, to look after the *Personalamt*, and thus directly controled the selection and promotion of officers. The power of the general staff and the old officer corps had been broken by 1942. The *Führerheer* had been organized by Hitler in such a way as to leave it with no effective command and control, and it was thus a prey to the political and military ambitions of the *Luftwaffe*, *Kriegsmarine* and SS.

At the height of the crisis in the east, Japan had attacked the Americans, the British and the Dutch in the Far East on 7 December. Hitler welcomed this move and decided it was in Germany's interest to seize the initiative and he accordingly declared war on the USA on 11 December. Hitler was convinced that this would enable U-Boats to conduct unrestricted submarine warfare, and calculated that the USA would concentrate against Japan rather than Germany and Italy. This assumption combined with the German assessment that the US Army was small and insignificant was to prove dangerously inaccurate.

Although by the early winter months of 1942 the front had stabilized in Russia, the *Ostheer* was faced with shortages in manpower, weapons and equipment. Total German casualties by

Above: MG 34 machine gun crew on the alert.
Left: German soldiers inspect bogged-down Soviet T34 tanks. Inexperienced crews often mishandled these effective weapons in the early stages of the German invasion of the USSR, helping the Germans offset their poorer materiel.
Right: Winter warfare – tanks of the 11th Panzer Division move through a snow-bound Russian village.

the spring of 1942 amounted to 900,000, and due to battle and mechanical failure over 2300 armored vehicles had been lost, while half of all the horses which had started the campaign were dead. Shortages of weapons and equipment were easier to rectify than those of manpower, and despite the fact that by July 1942 the *Ostheer* had 29 more divisions than in June 1941, its strength had dropped by 360,000 soldiers. Hitler preferred to raise new divisions rather than make up the manpower deficiencies in the old ones. This gave an impressive but illusory order of battle. The OKH had asked that more men be released from reserved occupations on the home front, but this had been refused on political grounds, and the *Luftwaffe* and the *Kriegsmarine* were demanding a larger share of the available manpower.

In 1942, Germany was faced with fighting an attritional war with the *Wehrmacht* still organized, recruited and equipped for short, sharp campaigns, and with a war economy which was only partially mobilized. But neither Hitler nor the majority of German officers and soldiers believed that a fundamental change had occurred in the nature of the war, and Hitler was already planning a new offensive in 1942 using Army Group South in the Ukraine. Morale in the *Führerheer* was high, and many soldiers believed, partly as a result of propaganda, that the winter disasters had been due to the incompetence of certain senior officers rather than Hitler.

Hitler was optimistic in 1942, outlining a grandiose strategy which included a German offensive to clear the Ukraine and penetrate the Caucasus, where it would eventually meet the

German and Italian forces advancing from Egypt. As with so many of Hitler's plans, there were too many disjointed ideas and no clear aim. As far as the *Führerheer* was concerned, the Mediterranean and North African theaters were very much of secondary importance to the eastern theater. They were the OKW theaters, and local field commanders acted very much on their own initiative and responsibility.

Although Rommel and his tiny *Afrika Korps* operated brilliantly against the British, it was a minute force compared to the *Ostheer*. Rommel was regarded as an *arriviste* by many of his brother officers, and despite his subsequent reputation, was neither a devoted anti-Nazi nor a consistently brilliant field commander. Like Guderian, Model and Hoth, Rommel believed in leading from the front and although this had many advantages, at times it meant he was out of touch with his headquarters. Rommel was frequently undisciplined and prone to wildly fluctuating changes in mood. An admirer of Hitler, he received considerable attention and flattery from the Nazi press which he assiduously cultivated.

The summer offensive of the *Ostheer* began in May 1942 with a strengthened Army Group South consisting of 68 divisions, with the support of 50 Rumanian, Hungarian and Italian divisions. While Army Groups North and Center remained on the defensive, Army Group South began an offensive which by the end of June had destroyed the Soviet salient near Kharkov, capturing 200,000 Red army prisoners. Manstein's Eleventh Army had cleared the Crimea, and on 28 June Army Group Center advanced toward Voronezh, but failed to encircle the Red army forces along the Don. Disagreements between the field commanders and continual interference by Hitler, the *Feldherr*, meant that there was

considerable confusion over objectives. On 23 July, Hitler divided Army Group South into Army Group B in the north and Army Group A in the Caucasus.

Hitler became obsessed with capturing Stalingrad because of its political and propaganda significance. Paulus's Sixth Army, part of Army Group B, was drawn further eastward until it began a major street by street battle for Stalingrad. By this stage Army Groups B and A were overextended with long vulnerable lines of communication stretching back hundreds of miles across the steppe. German panzer strength was dissipated over a wide area, and inside Stalingrad was wasted fighting in built-up areas. The protection of both flanks of Paulus's Sixth Army along the Volga was the responsibility of Rumanian, Hungarian and Italian armies who lacked either the armor or the motivation to act as a flank guard. Halder had continued to present Hitler with gloomy reports, and finally, on 24 September 1942 he was sacked and replaced as chief of the general staff by Kurt Zeitzler, who was promoted hastily from major general to full general. Zeitzler achieved this rapid promotion because he had a reputation as an obedient optimist.

On 19 November the Red army launched a major offensive which smashed through the Rumanians and within two days had encircled the Sixth Army, part of the Fourth Panzer Army and two Rumanian divisions within the perimeter of Stalingrad. Both Hitler and the OKH were in a state of confusion, but when Göring promised that the German forces in Stalingrad could be supplied by the *Luftwaffe*, Hitler decided to order Paulus to hold on until a relief force arrived.

Hitler refused to withdraw Army Group A from the Caucasus to provide the nucleus for a relief force, preferring instead to cobble together a few divisions under Manstein calling the command 'Army Group Don.' The appalling weather and the determined resistance of the Red army made the advance of the

Below: German paratrooper uses a flame-thrower to flush out Red Army soldiers in a Russian village.

relieving force a slow business, and by the middle of December, Army Group Don was itself under pressure from Soviet attacks. Under orders not to attempt a breakout, the Sixth Army gradually weakened through hunger, disease and cold. The *Luftwaffe* was unable to supply anything like the daily requirements of the encircled force, and in attempting to do so lost large numbers of transport aircraft. By 31 December 1942 there was a 100-mile gap between the Sixth Army and the nearest German units. On 22 January 1943, Paulus asked Hitler's permission to begin surrender negotiations, but this was refused. Hitler had decided that if the Sixth Army could not be relieved, then like the ancient Teutons it should fight to the last man. On 31 January Hitler promoted Paulus to field marshal in the belief that he would be influenced by the fact that no field marshal had been captured since 1871. But within a few hours Paulus had surrendered, and Germany had lost an army of 280,000 men, 91,000 of whom became Soviet prisoners, and of these, less than 5000 would return to Germany after the war.

The disaster at Stalingrad was very nearly repeated on a larger scale against the rest of Army Group B. The Soviets launched a series of massive envelopment movements deep into the German rear which destroyed the Rumanian, Hungarian and Italian armies. The Soviet advance toward Rostov threatened to cut off Army Group A in the Caucasus, and it was only on 27 January that Hitler had agreed reluctantly to withdraw from this area. After capturing Rostov on 1 February the Soviets continued their westward advance capturing Kharkov on 16 February and pushing the Germans back to the Dniepr. The German defense position in the south was commanded by Manstein who managed to conduct

Right: General Kurt Zeitzler, Chief of the General Staff, 1942-44.
Below: General of Panzers Heinz Guderian visiting the Eastern Front, February 1943. Guderian succeeded Zeitzler as Chief of the General Staff.

a fighting withdrawal in the face of major Soviet attacks, and when the Red army finally came to a halt exhausted and short of transport, he organized a counter-stroke against the Soviet salient. By 15 March Army Group South had pushed the Red army back to the Donets and stabilized the front a misleading revival of fortune which inspired considerable false optimism.

The winter of 1942-43 had been disastrous for the *Führerheer*. Not only had it been defeated at Stalingrad and on the Don, but in North Africa the *Afrika Korps* had been beaten at El Alamein in October 1942 and had begun a retreat westward which would not end until it had reached Mareth in Tunisia. In November 1942 an Anglo-American force had landed in Algeria and Morocco, and as a consequence, German and Italian troops moved into Vichy France and reinforcements were sent to Tunisia. These scratch reinforcements were eventually joined by the *Afrika Korps*, and the field commanders, including Rommel, were pessimistic about the decision to hold Tunisia. But Hitler refused to consider withdrawing, and in May 1943 the allies destroyed the Axis force, and 95,000 German prisoners were taken. This disaster, coupled with that at Stalingrad, produced the German expression, 'Tunisgrad' to describe the double defeat.

After the defeat at Stalingrad, Hitler had agreed reluctantly to mobilizing Germany for 'total war.' But although he appointed Albert Speer as Minister of Armaments and War Production in 1942, little was really done to mobilize German resources effectively. Hitler was tired and irritable, and both contemptuous and suspicious of the general staff, preferring to rely upon ruthless, able field commanders like Model, Schörner and Kesselring. In theory, all power and responsibility for making decisions relating to politics, economics and military questions rested with Hitler as *Führer*. In practice, Hitler avoided making a final decision between competing interest groups and yet at the same time interfered in trivial detail. The rivalry between Jodl at the OKW and Zeitzler at the OKH aggravated the problems of decision making and the allocation of resources.

Above: Cheery German infantry cross a newly-built bridge in Russia, a picture taken for the German propaganda magazine *Signal.*

'Tunisgrad' had seen the destruction of some 30 German divisions, and for the *Ostheer,* there was a considerable shortage of teeth-arm troops. Hitler's growing mistrust of the *Führerheer* was revealed in his decision to allow the *Waffen* SS to expand. In 1939 the *Waffen* SS had been small and militarily insignificant, and had been permitted to serve alongside the *Führerheer* to give the SS a military ethos and respect which was felt necessary for them to conduct their police duties on the home front. A combination of Himmler's military ambitions and the fighting performance of certain *Waffen* SS divisions guaranteed Hitler's support. Himmler had been able to circumvent the restriction on recruitment of German nationals by recruiting eligible foreigners and ethnic Germans from the occupied territories. Hitler was impressed by the fighting performance of *Waffen* SS divisions such as the *Leibstandarte* and the *Totenkopf* on the Eastern front. These élite *Waffen* SS divisions appeared to be able to carry out difficult offensive and defensive operations which the *Führerheer* could no longer mount. Hitler was convinced this was because of the *Waffen* SS ideological training, their ferocious fighting spirit and their willingness to accept heavy casualties. So the *Waffen* SS was expanded, and the élite divisions were given panzers and received priority in the allocation of weapons and equipment. By September 1943 there were 15 *Waffen* SS divisions, seven of them designated 'panzer.'

Hitler had agreed also in the autumn of 1942 to allow the *Luftwaffe* to establish a field army which was controled and organized by the *Luftwaffe* high command and only came under the command of the OKH for operational purposes. By July 1943 this force consisted of two parachute divisions, a panzer division and 19 field divisions, apart from the *Luftwaffe* flak artillery units. So in 1943 there were three German field armies, the *Führerheer,* the *Waffen* SS and the *Luftwaffe* field army. Although the

Waffen SS appeared to challenge the *Führerheer*'s right to be the 'sole bearer of arms,' in reality this never happened, and most *Waffen* SS men were desperate to prove that they were, 'soldiers like any others.'

In February 1943, Guderian was recalled from the reserve and Hitler appointed him as Inspector-General of Panzer Troops, with the status of an independent army commander, responsible to Hitler personally, and not to the OKW or to the OKH. As Guderian's new command included all panzer, panzergrenadiers and anti-tank troops, but not assault gun troops who remained under the command of the artillery, he had in fact an army independent of the OKH and equal to that of the *Waffen* SS and *Luftwaffe.* Although Hitler may have hoped that Guderian would be able to organize the panzer troops in such a way as to allow him to repeat the successes of the first period of the war, in fact he merely created yet another rival organization and divorced the panzer arm from the rest of the *Führerheer.*

In July 1943 the *Führerheer* had 243 divisions; the *Waffen* SS 11 and the *Luftwaffe* 22. But this divisional strength was a facade as many of the *Führerheer*'s divisions had an imbalance between the administrative and combat soldiers, and the *Feldheer* was 616,000 men below establishment. This shortage of combat troops was partly compensated for by the gradual introduction of better weapons, including the Pz Mk V 'Panther' and the Pz Mk VI 'Tiger,' along with improved assault guns and tank destroyers.

Despite the new danger of an Anglo-American invasion of western Europe, Hitler and Zeitzler were determined to seize the initiative on the Eastern front. The aim was to destroy the offensive capability of the Red army and to restore the power and prestige of Germany. The sector chosen was the Soviet salient at Kursk which had remained after Manstein's successful counter-offensive. The planned offensive, *Citadel,* was to be undertaken by Army Groups Center and South, the latter commanded by Manstein. The Soviet salient would be attacked by Model's Ninth Army from the north and Hoth's Fourth Panzer Army and Group

Kempf from the south in a double envelopment which would destroy the Soviet forces within the salient. The start of the offensive was postponed frequently and Hitler accepted Model's request for a delay to enable new tanks and assault guns to be provided for the attacking units. It was not until 4 July that *Citadel* was launched, and by then the Soviets had been given sufficient time to turn the salient, which was 100 miles wide and 150 miles deep, into a defense in depth position, which contained 3300 tanks and 20,220 guns. Unfortunately for the Germans, the Soviets had reinforced their positions in the salient in preparation for their own offensive.

Despite the fact that the Germans deployed over 43 divisions against the Kursk salient, including 2200 tanks and 1000 assault guns, the offensive failed to achieve its objective. The Red army was not surprised, the German build-up was disrupted by partisan attacks, the *Luftwaffe* failed to achieve air superiority, and bad weather turned the battlefield into a quagmire. Instead of *Citadel* being a decisive envelopment battle, it turned into one of attrition which remorselessly destroyed the offensive capability of the *Ostheer*. On 25 July, Hitler decided to break off the attack because of German losses and as a result of Soviet counter-offensives launched in the rear of Army Groups Center and South. The Kursk battle became known as the 'death ride of the panzers,' as the *Ostheer* and the Red army slogged it out on 13 July on what was until recently the greatest tank battle in history. In *Citadel* the Germans lost about 500,000 casualties and over half the armored vehicles deployed for the offensive.

Just as the Kursk battle was reaching a climax on 10 July, the Anglo-Americans landed in Sicily presenting the *Führer* with a new crisis. As early as May 1943 Hitler had instructed the OKW to prepare contingency plans against an Anglo-American invasion of Italy and the collapse of the fascist regime. The German plans included preparations for the occupation of Italy and the neutralization of Italian forces in the Balkans. The allied invasion of Sicily did not affect seriously the German offensive at Kursk, as *Waffen* SS formations were not withdrawn until a decision had already been taken to break off the battle. On 25 July, Mussolini was overthrown and a new Italian government formed under Marshal Badoglio which pledged its continued loyalty to the Axis. But Hilter was in no doubt that the Italians would try and change sides, and over the next few months he began to move additional German divisions into Italy under the pretext of halting the allies in the south. The four scratch German divisions in Sicily fought a useful delaying action before being evacuated to the mainland on 17 August 1943.

When the Badoglio government signed a secret act of surrender on 3 September and the allies landed on the mainland, the Germans were ready to respond with the 15 divisions they had deployed in Italy. The Germans immediately disarmed the Italian army on the mainland, southern France and the Balkans, and at the same time checked the allied landing at Salerno. By quick and decisive action the Germans had stabilized a new front, and the allies were to be faced with a slow crawl up the Italian peninsula. Under Kesselring's command, the Germans were to conduct a brilliant defensive withdrawal making use of every natural feature and forcing the allies to fight attritional battles such as that at Cassino. But the collapse of Italy and the allied offensive in the Mediterranean forced Hitler to divert *Wehrmacht* units away from more important theaters such as Russia and France. By 1 June 1944 there were 27 German divisions in Italy and 25 in the Balkans.

Below left: Waffen SS tank crew looking confident and relaxed. The SS divisions were gradually given higher priority in equipment supplies.
Below: Infantry mortar position firing in support of an attack from a typical village on the Eastern Front.

The situation in Russia was critical for the *Führerheer* after the failure at Kursk in July 1943. The Red army began to launch a series of major offensives against all three army groups. The *Ostheer* did not have the manpower or weapons to hold the amount of territory occupied, and the logical solution would have been to have shortened the line to a new defensible position and conducted a defense in depth using mobile panzer forces to launch counter-attacks. But Hitler refused to yield any ground, arguing that this would mean giving up valuable economic areas of Russia, would encourage the Soviets, and discourage Germany's allies like Rumania and Hungary. Manstein argued that German troops should be withdrawn from France to reinforce the *Ostheer*, and that Army Group South should fall back behind the Dniepr, but Hitler rejected both these suggestions.

The combat strength of the *Ostheer* bore little relation to the designation of units, and many divisions only had an effective force of 1,000 men, and they might very well be responsible for holding a front of up to 12 miles. By September 1943 there were only 257 tanks and 220 assault guns available in the whole of Army Group South. The speed and violence of successive Soviet envelopments combined with the *Führer*'s reluctance to allow his field commanders to withdraw meant that eventually, although some German troops were able to break out from encirclement, invariably they had to abandon their heavy weapons and equipment.

Between July 1943 and May 1944, the *Ostheer* suffered a series of major defeats and was forced to withdraw from Russia after repeated Soviet offensives. Army Group South was pushed westward across the Dniepr, and the Crimea was isolated and eventually captured by the Red army in May 1944. By March 1944 Army Group South was beginning to disintegrate, and when Hube's First Panzer Army was encircled, an enraged Hitler blamed Manstein, who was dismissed and replaced by Model. The situation was equally dangerous for Army Group Center which found itself the target of Soviet envelopment offensives during the winter of 1943-44 which forced the front back to Vitebsk. For Army Group North, the position to the south threatened to

expose the right flank, and Küchler begged Hitler to permit a withdrawal to a new defensive position. This was rejected, and Küchler was replaced by Model, who was, however, eventually forced to withdraw to the line of the old Estonian-Soviet border.

During the winter of 1943-44 the *Ostheer* suffered a perceptible lowering of morale, with examples of desertion and panic-stricken flight by many formations, including the *Luftwaffe* field divisions. With shortages of food, equipment and clothing, units of the *Ostheer* resembled the old mercenary bands of the Thirty Years' War, held together by comradeship, the leadership of individual commanders and the fear of the enemy. In March 1944 Hitler issued a new version of his 'no withdrawal' strategy with an order defining 'fortified areas' and 'local strongpoints.' In future, any location could be described as a 'fortified area,' and the troops within it would have the duty to continue fighting even if cut off, thus forcing the enemy to divert forces from the main axis of their advance. With this 'breakwater strategy,' Hitler hoped to blunt the advance of the Red army. To ensure that his orders were carried out, Hitler promoted as field commanders such officers as Model and Schörner, who were personally loyal and determined and ruthless fighters who could stabilize the front. In May 1944 the *Ostheer* held a front of 1650 miles which extended from Lake Peipus on the Baltic, south via Vitebsk to the Pripet Marshes, and then west to Kovel, and again south along the Carpathians and across to Jassy, west of Odessa on the Black Sea.

The *Führerheer* in 1943 was remarkably different from that of 1939. Losses in manpower saw a reduction in the personnel establishment of an infantry division, so that by 1943 it was 10,000 compared with 18,000 in 1939. Although this decrease in personnel was compensated for partly by an increase in firepower, many designated 'divisions' were such in name only. The *kampfgruppe*, or battle group, became a common unit found on the *Führerheer*'s order of battle, denoting an ad hoc formation of all arms brought together for either a limited or more permanent period of time. There was a corresponding decrease in the number of 'army troops' such as artillery and pioneer units. The crisis in manpower was met by transferring *Luftwaffe* and

Kriegsmarine personnel into ground formations; recruiting men up to fifty years of age and the use of invalids — there was a division consisting of men with stomach disorders stationed in Holland; the replacement of men by women in support units; and finally, the widespread recruitment of ethnic Germans, Alsatians, Poles and Ruthenians, along with whole ethnic groups, such as the Cossacks, from Russia. Within a few months of the invasion of the Soviet Union, the *Ostheer* had formed *Ostbataillonen* for security duties, and before long there was a Cossack Corps which eventually came under SS control. Finally, many of the Russian formations were brought together to form 'the Russian Liberation Army' under the command of the captured Soviet General Andrei Vlasov. Nazi propaganda made much of the fact that many Europeans were serving in the *Führerheer* or the *Waffen SS*, taking part in the great crusade against Bolshevism. Faced with the realities of total war, even Himmler was prepared to make 'honorary aryans' out of former '*untermenschen*.'

Although German soldiers were issued with a variety of new patterns of equipment and clothing, including camouflage jackets and better webbing, the overall quality of uniforms and equipment was drastically reduced by 1944. The economy field uniform of 1944 consisted of a battle dress blouse, trousers and ankle boots. Increasingly, the combat performance of any German field unit could be assessed partly by the quality of its uniforms, weapons and equipment.

Left: Paulus signs the Soviet-sponsored 'Free Germany' appeal for the overthrow of Hitler.
Right: Field Marshal von Manstein, regarded by many as the ablest German general of the war.
Below: German 2cm quadruple anti-aircraft gun on Sicily before the Allied invasion in 1943

By the spring of 1944, the *Führerheer* was being attacked on an increasingly violent scale by partisans in the east, and by a variety of resistance groups in the west. The *Führerheer* not only had responsibility for rear area security along its own lines of communication, but from June 1940 had been responsible for the military administration of Belgium, northern France, Serbia and Greece. The *Führerheer* made a clear distinction between the west and the east in its attitude toward the civil population and its response to resistance. In Poland, Yugoslavia and Russia, the *Führerheer* was prepared to use reprisals and harsh methods to cope with resistance and partisan warfare, and at times there was little to distinguish between the responses of the *Führerheer* and the *SS*. But in the west the *Führerheer* was more restrained and preferred selective reprisals against the resistance and the cooperation of the local police.

From the very beginning, Hitler demanded a policy of drastic reprisals against any form of resistance in the occupied territories. Although some German commanders, like Stülpnagel in Paris and Falkenhausen in Brussels, were reluctant to take extreme measures as they believed this would merely provoke the local population, they had to comply with Hitler's orders. In both the west and east the *Führerheer* only allocated a few units for security duties, and these were manned by over-age reservists who had few heavy weapons and lacked motor transport. Along with the SS, the *Führerheer* recruited all kinds of scratch formations from among the local populations for security duties. In Russia they included Estonians, Lithuanians and Ukrainians, in Yugoslavia ethnic Germans and Croats.

Left: German paratroopers played a leading role in defense of Italy in 1943-44.
Below: Heavy artillery of the *Waffen* SS Division *Handschar* during anti-partisan operations in Yugoslavia in 1943.

Above: Machine gun section of the SS *Polizei* Division in France during the fighting in 1940.

In the west, resistance was organized on a relatively small scale until the formation of the Maquis bands in France in 1943, and even then, the Germans managed to retain control of their lines of communications and contain at a tolerable level attacks on their main installations until the winter of 1943-44. But in the east, there was widespread partisan warfare in Yugoslavia and Russia, which the few scattered security formations of the *Ostheer* and the SS had difficulty in containing. Large tracts of territory such as the Pripet Marshes in Russia, were outside German control. Increasingly, coordination for internal security became the responsibility of Himmler's SS, and even in Russia, an OKH theater, Hitler appointed SS *Obergruppenführer* Erich von dem Bach-Zelewski as Chief of Anti-Partisan Warfare in October 1942. The lack of coordination between the plethora of partisan and resistance groups, and their shortage of heavy weapons, meant that only rarely could they defeat the German security forces or divert front line troops to the rear. Even at the point of liberation the Germans were able to crush any national uprisings, which without external support, could not face the *Führerheer* and the SS. National uprisings in Poland and Slovakia in 1944 were brutally crushed, and the one in Paris was only saved by the disobedience of the German commander and the timely arrival of outside support from the allied armies. The spiral of terror and counter-terror between the partisans on one side and the *Führerheer* and the SS on the other produced a barbaric war, in which the *Führerheer* resorted increasingly to the measures of the SS.

From 1941 to 1943 the war in the east had dominated the attention of Hitler and the OKH, with the Mediterranean and the Balkans being mere sideshows. But Hitler was aware of the need to strengthen the defenses of western Europe against an allied invasion. As early as March 1942 he had ordered the preparation of major defensive positions which not only covered ports but also all potential landing sites and extended from north Norway to the Franco-Spanish border. What Nazi propaganda was to refer to grandiosely as the 'Atlantic Wall,' was in fact an unconnected series of fortified positions which needed to be covered by a large mobile panzer force with air support. The Germans had neither the resources nor the manpower to make the Atlantic Wall a continuous or effective fortification or to cover it with panzers and air power. Until 1943 the *Führerheer* in the west was being 'milked' continuously to provide replacements for the *Ostheer*, and what resources were available had to be spread along a front extending from Norway to Spain and into the Mediterranean.

Although the Channel coast seemed the most likely area for an allied invasion, Hitler was obsessed with the fear that the allies might launch a diversionary attack on Norway. By 1943 there were 300,000 *Wehrmacht* personnel in Norway and a vast diversion of scarce coastal batteries and mines away from the Channel coast. Hitler concluded that the Pas de Calais would be the main landing place for the allies. Its proximity to the British mainland and its strategic position in relation to Germany made it an obvious choice. Hitler imposed this assessment on the *Führerheer* which was accepted by the majority of field commanders and staff officers. The opinion of Hitler and the OKW was reinforced by the failure of German intelligence to penetrate the allied deception plans.

Over the period 1943-44 Hitler reinforced the west with personnel and equipment so that by May 1944, Rundstedt, the C-in-C West, had in his command 59 divisions, of which eight were panzer, two panzer grenadier, 23 static and six reserve training divisions. Although the panzer divisions were mobile and well armed with tanks such as the Panther and Tiger, many of the infantry divisions were short of personnel, weapons and transport. The élite panzer and infantry divisions compensated for their manpower shortages by an increase in firepower, with additional anti-armor weapons such as the *panzerfaust* and new mobile mortars, the *nebelwerfer*. But the west still had to compete with

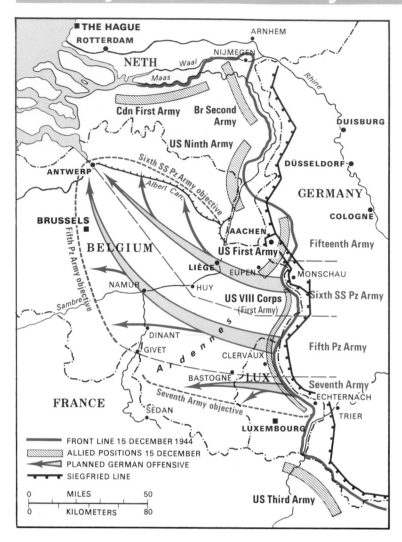

FRONT LINE 15 DECEMBER 1944
ALLIED POSITIONS 15 DECEMBER
PLANNED GERMAN OFFENSIVE
SIEGFRIED LINE

the east for reinforcements, and with no central mobile reserve, Hitler could only shuffle panzer divisions from one threatened front to another.

The German command structure and organization in the west was a complex edifice consisting of overlapping areas of responsibility. Rundstedt, the C-in-C West was only nominally in command, since he was unable to deploy divisions without Hitler's authority, and he had only limited control over *Luftwaffe*, *Kriegsmarine* and *Waffen* SS units. He had powerful independent subordinates like Rommel, who commanded Army Group B, and Schweppenberg who commanded Panzer Group West. There was a serious disagreement between Rommel and Rundstedt over how to defeat the allied invasion. Rundstedt favored drawing the allies inland and then destroying them with the panzer reserve, while Rommel, fearful of allied air superiority, wanted to destroy them on the beaches. Hitler was determined to retain strategic and even tactical control over the deployment of divisions in the west, so the majority of panzer divisions were kept in the OKW reserve scattered across northern France.

The Anglo-American landings in Normandy surprised the Germans who were poorly served by their intelligence organizations. Rommel was on leave, and the majority of German units were unprepared for the main allied invasion to be in Normandy. The defending divisions were overwhelmed by the allies, and the Germans failed to launch a quick, concerted panzer counterattack which probably would have pushed the allies into the sea. Hitler, who was not alone in his assessment that Normandy was a diversion from the main allied landing in the Pas de Calais, was reluctant to release the panzer reserve. Instead, German reinforcements were fed piecemeal into the battle under constant allied air attack and naval bombardment. Hitler refused to fight a flexible defense, and demanded that all ground should be held. This meant a 'patchwork cobbling' and the dissipation of strength

of the best German formations as they were deployed as *kampfgruppen* to plug the leaking defenses. On 2 July, Rundstedt was sacked as C-in-C West and replaced by Kluge.

Hitler and Zeitzler's attention was not only on Normandy in June 1944, but also on the Eastern front. On 22 June the Red army launched a massive offensive against Army Group Center which collapsed and retreated in disorder, losing 28 divisions and nearly 300,000 casualties. On 14 July a second Soviet offensive in the south forced the Germans to retreat 130 miles to the Polish and Slovak borders. Faced with twin disasters in the west and east, Hitler took emergency measures by raising divisions on the spot in Germany from soldiers on leave. All kinds of ad hoc formations were sent both west and east, and a string of field commanders were dismissed for supposed offenses such as 'disobeying orders' or for 'cowardice.'

On 20 July Hitler was very nearly killed at his headquarters at Rastenberg in East Prussia by a bomb planted by a Lieutenant Colonel von Stauffenberg, an officer on the staff of Fromm's *Ersatzheer*, who had direct access to the *Führer*. The 'Bomb Plot Conspiracy,' was largely organized by serving and retired members of the general staff. A few civilians were involved, but very few members of the *Luftwaffe* and the *Kriegsmarine*. The origins of the plot lay in the loose conspiracy that had begun among members of the general staff even before the war. Conspirators were to be found on the staff of Army Group Center, in the headquarters of the *Ersatzheer*, in Berlin, among the staff of the *Wehrkreise*, and the headquarters of the military administrations in Paris and Brussels. Retired officers included Beck, Witzleben and Hoeppner, but the success of the conspiracy depended on Stauffenberg's bomb killing Hitler and the *Führerheer* seizing power in Germany and the occupied territories.

When the bomb failed to kill Hitler, the plot was doomed as the majority of German soldiers and civilians accepted Hitler as *Führer* and head of state. In Berlin and other cities, the conspirators were able to activate *Führerheer* units by issuing the codeword, *Valkyrie*, by which government and Nazi Party buildings were cordoned off and SS and police officials arrested. But when it became obvious that Hitler was alive, the conspiracy collapsed, and the plotters were arrested by the very *Führerheer* units they had activated. Many generals knew of the plot, but had

Above left: The German plan for the 'Battle of the Bulge.'
Below: Rommel inspects a tank hunting unit in Normandy in the spring of 1944.

preferred to remain inactive until the outcome was known. Fromm was one such officer, and as soon as the conspiracy had collapsed he attempted to cover his tracks by ordering the execution of Stauffenberg and other conspirators.

A badly shaken Hitler was determined to take his revenge, and he ordered Himmler to begin an investigation into the conspiracy. For Hitler, the 'Bomb Plot' was the final act of disloyalty by the general staff. He dismissed Zeitzler, who was under suspicion, and replaced him as chief of the general staff with Guderian. Fromm was arrested and replaced by Himmler as C-in-C of the *Ersatzheer*, which meant that the SS became responsible for the training, discipline and administration of all new *Führerheer* formations. On 23 July, the traditional military salute was replaced by the *deutsche Gruss*, or Nazi salute. On 1 August the punishment of *Sippenhaft* was instituted, whereby the relatives of soldiers became responsible for their actions. Increased powers were given to the *Nationalsozialistische Führungsoffiziere*, NSFO, or National Socialist Leadership Officers, which meant that the Nazi Party attempted to establish a political watchdog within the *Führerheer*.

To prevent accused officers exercising their legal right to be tried by other officers, Hitler ordered that they should first be tried by military honor courts and dismissed the *Führerheer* so that they could then be dealt with by the People's Court. Keitel, Rundstedt and Guderian all lent their authority to this process, and over the subsequent six months a large number of serving and retired officers were tried by the People's Court, where they were ridiculed by the President, Roland Freisler, and usually sentenced to death. Generals such as Witzleben, Wagner, Hoeppner, Stieff and Fellgiebel were all executed for their part in the conspiracy. Already under suspicion and demoralized by events in Normandy, Kluge committed suicide. Rommel, who may have heard gossip about the conspiracy but who was never even a passive member, was forced to commit suicide on Hitler's orders. But Nazi propaganda was careful to distinguish between

Above: Lieutenant Colonel Claus von Stauffenberg.
Below: Field Marshal von Witzleben on trial after the Bomb Plot. As an additional humiliation those accused of participation in the Bomb Plot were given ill-fitting civilian clothes for their court appearances. Hitler later took great satisfaction in watching films of the subsequent executions.

the 'clique of unscrupulous reactionary officers' and the mass of 'loyal officers and soldiers.'

The military conspirators had taken the decision to kill Hitler out of a combination of moral considerations, in that he was a tyrant and had broken natural laws, and practical considerations in that he was leading Germany to defeat. But given the allied war aim of 'unconditional surrender,' the conspirators' intention, if they had succeeded, of negotiating Germany out of the war retaining the pre-1939 borders, was, to say the least, naive. The majority of German soldiers and civilians still retained faith in Hitler and regarded the conspirators as self-seeking traitors who had attempted to undermine national unity in the face of the threat from communism.

The 'Bomb Plot' had no discernible impact on the operational ability of the *Führerheer*. In Normandy, the Germans were conducting a rigid defense which the US Army was to break through on 25 July, punching a hole in the line at St Lô. Hitler refused to authorize any tactical withdrawals and so the panzer divisions of Army Group B were frittered away in local counter-attacks against the British at Caen, and against the Americans at Avranches. By 13 August the Americans had swept south and much of Army Group B was in danger of being encircled by the Anglo-Americans. The only escape route to the east was through a narrow gap around the town of Falaise.

Left: A *Waffen* SS NCO demonstrates the *panzerfaust*. The final version of this weapon had a range of 100 meters and was effective against virtually every Allied tank. The *panzerfaust* was probably the best infantry anti-tank of the war.
Below: SS police troops dug in at Arnhem awaiting further British air landings, September 1944.

Above: A German assault gun takes up a camouflaged position ready for the Ardennes offensive on the Western Front in December 1944.

Hitler refused to order a withdrawal, and eventually on 18 August, Model, who had succeeded Kluge as C-in-C West, ordered a breakout on his own initiative. Over 100,000 German troops had been confined within a pocket only 20 miles wide and 10 miles deep under repeated artillery bombardment and air attack. The remnants of élite panzer divisions and some small *Kampfgruppen* held open the jaws of the allied pincer to allow nearly half the trapped personnel to escape, but 10,000 were killed and 50,000 captured. At the height of the crisis in Normandy, the allies landed in southern France and soon overwhelmed the weak formations making up Army Group G. Between 18 August and 2 September the German retreat from France became a rout. From the debacle in Normandy, only the remnants of divisions with about 120 armored vehicles could be evacuated across the Seine. Scenes of panic and disorder were common among retreating German units harried by allied armored and air attacks and ambushed by an enraged French resistance. By 2 September the allies had reached the Belgian border and there were hardly any significant German formations between them and the German border. But as part of Hitler's 'breakwater strategy,' 160,000 soldiers had been left behind to defend the Atlantic and Channel ports from the Gironde estuary to Ostend in the hope that this would deny supply facilities and tie down large numbers of allied troops.

In the east, one disaster followed closely on another. The collapse of Army Group Center had unmasked the flank of Army Group North which was encircled by the Soviets against the Baltic coast. As the Soviets reached the vicinity of Warsaw at the beginning of August 1944, the Polish civil population rose up in arms to eject the Germans and liberate Warsaw before the Red

army arrived. But the Polish Home Army was too weak, and without the active support of the Red army, was forced to fight a hopeless battle against the Germans until they finally surrendered in October. The German operations had been controlled by the SS and not the *Führerheer*. On 23 August, Rumania left the Axis after secret negotiations with the Soviets and then declared war on Germany. By the end of the month the German forces in Rumania had been destroyed with the loss of 180,000 soldiers, and this collapse threatened the whole German position in the Balkans.

Guderian's appointment as chief of the general staff had made little appreciable difference because Hitler merely used him as a functionary to pass on orders. Faced with a continuous series of crises in both the west and east, Hitler began to resort to a game of musical chairs switching commanders like Model, Schörner and Friessner from one Army Group to another. Politically reliable and fanatical officers could expect promotion and rewards, while those who were suspected of being politically shaky or who questioned *Führer* orders were dismissed, or arrested, and in some cases executed.

Between June and September 1944, the *Führerheer* had lost a total of nearly two million men on all fronts, and in the whole of 1944 the equivalent of 106 divisions had been destroyed or disbanded. Long retreats and the encirclement battles in the west and east had resulted in the loss of many armored vehicles, heavy equipment, supply dumps and workshops. Although an increase in German war production had been able to replace many of these

Above: Albert Speer, Minister for Armaments consults with his *Fuhrer.*
Opposite: The Soviet forces close in on Berlin.

losses, with in some cases, improved weapons, such as the King Tiger tank and the Mk V assault gun, it had been achieved only at the cost of exhausting the remaining stocks of raw materials. Lost divisions were frequently replaced by under-strength and poorly armed *Volksgrenadier* divisions, first formed in July 1944 and controled by Himmler's *Ersatzheer.*

On 25 September 1944, Hitler ordered the establishment of the *Volkssturm*, or Home Guard, which was to be trained and equipped by Himmler's *Ersatzheer*, but controled by the Nazi Party. Only when deployed operationally would it come under the command of the *Führerheer.* The *Volkssturm* was a last-ditch attempt to mobilize the German people in defense of the Reich and the spirit of 1813 was evoked as a parallel by Nazi propaganda. Some old SA commanders saw it as Röhm's revenge of a people's militia which would replace the *Führerheer.*

After September 1944 the *Führerheer* consisted of a hotchpotch of assorted formations: once powerful panzer divisions like the *Grossdeutschland*, ad hoc *kampfgruppen, Volksgrenadier* divisions whose personnel consisted of over-age conscripts, detachments of the *Luftwaffe* and *Kriegsmarine* deployed as infantry, Hitler Youth boys and the First World War veterans of the *Volkssturm.* In theory, the *Waffen* SS had 38 divisions by the winter of 1945, but the majority of these were no stronger than a regiment and their personnel varied from the Bosnian Moslems in the 13th *Handschar* to the Frenchmen in the 33rd *Charlemagne.* Behind the lines, field commanders like Schörner, the 'strength through fear' general, and Himmler, in his capacity as *Reichsführer* SS and Chief of the German Police, Minister of the Interior and by the autumn of 1944, an army commander, established *fliegende Feld- und Standgerichte*, or flying field court martials, whose job it was to seek out deserters and shirkers and execute them by summary justice.

But the Germans were given a valuable respite in the first two weeks of September because in the west the allies had outrun their logistical supplies after liberating Belgium and appeared

divided over strategy, and in the east the Soviets paused to organize their resources. In the west, Hitler brought Rundstedt back from the reserve as C-in-C West where he found the Germans could only muster about eleven divisions and about 100 tanks against an imposing allied order of battle. The disorganized remnants of another 40 divisions had to be re-equipped and manned with new personnel. Within a remarkably short period of time the Germans reorganized their defenses in the west, sending whatever forces were available to Holland and by re-activating the moribund *Westwall.* The allied Operation *Market Garden*, begun on 17 September, was designed to seize the Dutch bridges over the Waal and Rhine by airborne forces who would establish a route for ground forces to outflank the Germans and reach the Ruhr. But although the Germans were surprised, they reacted quickly and cut-off the British airborne division at Arnhem. Although the allied ground forces eventually reached Arnhem, the operation had failed in its objective and the Germans had stabilized the front.

Hitler had no intention of allowing the initiative to pass into allied hands, and at the beginning of September had already begun to plan an offensive aimed at dividing the British and American armies and reaching the Channel coast. He hoped to repeat the success of the Ardennes breakthrough of May 1940. Both Rundstedt, and Model, who now commanded Army Group B, had reservations about this plan which involved the use of the *Führerheer*'s last strategic reserves of 16 divisions in two panzer armies. On 16 December the German Ardennes offensive achieved complete surprise and the weak American front-line forces were easily defeated. Poor visibility restricted allied air superiority, but within ten days the offensive had been halted. The Americans fought a determined defensive battle and reinforcements, combined with the lifting of visibility which meant allied air power could operate, stopped the Germans who were violently counter-attacked. Although the Americans had suffered 75,000 casualties, these could be replaced. The German losses of 100,000 men, 800 tanks and 1000 aircraft were irreplaceable.

By Christmas 1944 the *Führerheer* largely consisted of paper formations whose strength bore no relation to their official designation. Hitler's strategy was to hold the line everywhere and at the same time to hoard a few reserves to mount occasional offensives. Hitler hoped that the allies would fall out amongst themselves, and like Frederick the Great, he would be saved at the eleventh hour. Even Guderian's solution of moving a few divisions from west to east or transferring divisions from stagnant theaters like Norway would not have radically altered the situation. Reserves of petrol and ammunition were exhausted, and the offensive power of the *Führerheer* was reduced to the so-called *Panzerjagdtruppen*, or soldiers on bicycles armed with *panzerfausts.*

Between January and April 1945 the defenses of Germany were breached on all fronts and the *Führerheer* was beaten in the field and reduced to scattered formations. On 12 January the Red army began its winter offensive by attacking in East Prussia and Silesia and by invading Hungary. By February, the Red army was on the Oder and only 60 miles from Berlin. Although a number of so-called fortresses, such as Breslau, Poznan and Königsberg fought on behind the Soviet lines, the position in the east was hopeless. As the *Führerheer* retreated along the Pomeranian coast, hundreds of thousands of German refugees clung to it for protection against the vengeance of the Red army. In the west, the allies breached the *Westwall* and crossed the Rhine. On 11 March Hitler replaced Rundstedt as C-in-C West with Kesselring who was transferred from Italy.

On 28 March, Hitler had a violent argument with Guderian over strategy, and dismissed him as chief of the general staff, replacing him with Hans Krebs. Living in the *Führerbunker* in Berlin, Hitler, along with Keitel and Jodl, was completely cut off from the realities of the war and could not see that the *Wehrmacht* was disintegrating under the combined allied offen-

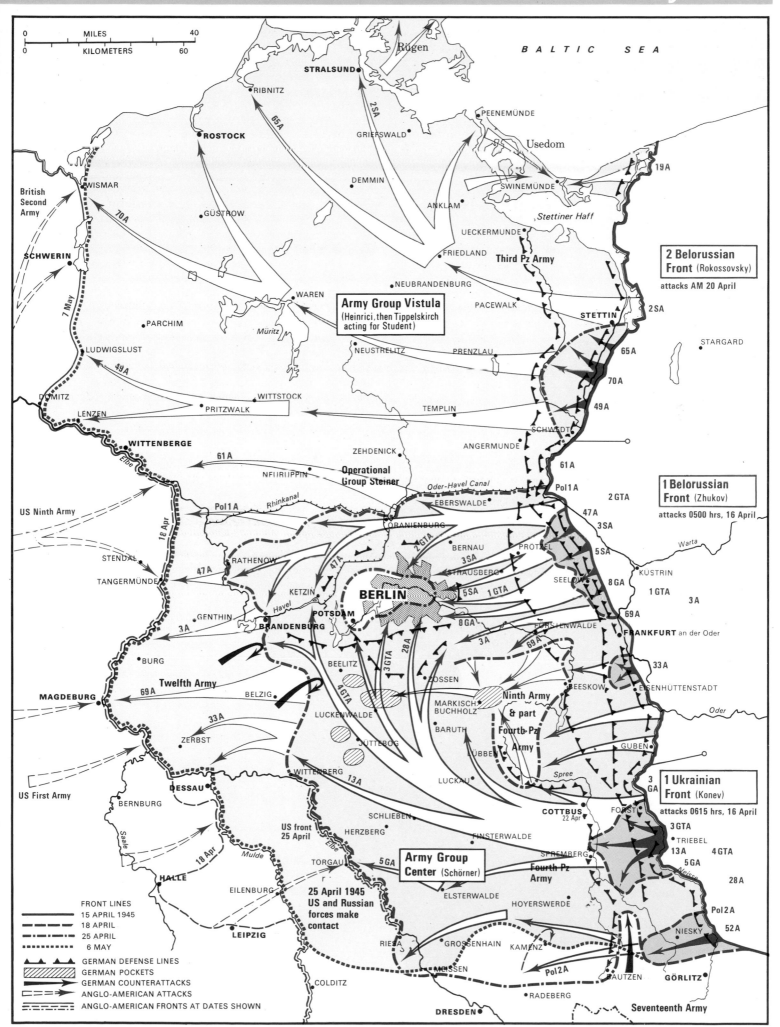

MILES
KILOMETERS

BALTIC SEA

Rügen

STRALSUND
• RIBNITZ
• ROSTOCK
British Second Army
WISMAR
SCHWERIN
• GÜSTROW
• PARCHIM
LUDWIGSLUST
DÖMITZ
LENZEN
WITTENBERGE
Elbe

2 SA
PEENEMÜNDE
GRIEFSWALD
Usedom
DEMMIN
SWINEMÜNDE
Stettiner Haff
ANKLAM
UECKERMÜNDE
FRIEDLAND
NEUBRANDENBURG
Third Pz Army
PACEWALK
STETTIN

19 A

2 Belorussian Front (Rokossovsky)
attacks AM 20 April

2 SA

STARGARD

NEUSTRELITZ
PRENZLAU
TEMPLIN
SCHWEDT
ANGERMÜNDE

65 A
70 A
49 A

WAREN
Müritz

Army Group Vistula
(Heinrici, then Tippelskirch acting for Student)

PRITZWALK
WITTSTOCK
ZEHDENICK

61 A
NEURUPPIN
Rhinkanal
Operational Group Steiner
Oder-Havel Canal
EBERSWALDE
ORANIENBURG

61 A
Pol1 A
2 GTA

Warta

1 Belorussian Front (Zhukov)
attacks 0500 hrs, 16 April

47 A
3 SA
5 SA
8 GA
69 A

KÜSTRIN

1 GTA
3 A

US Ninth Army
STENDAL
TANGERMÜNDE
RATHENOW
KETZIN
GENTHIN
BRANDENBURG
MAGDEBURG
BURG

18 Apr
47 A
3 A
69 A
Havel
POTSDAM
BERLIN
BERNAU
STRAUSBERG
PROTZEL
SEELOW
FÜRSTENWALDE
FRANKFURT an der Oder

2 GTA
3 SA
5 SA
1 GTA
8 GA
3 A
69 A
33 A

Twelfth Army
BELZIG
BEELITZ
3 GTA
4 GTA
LUCKENWALDE
JÜTERBOG
ZOSSEN
MARKISCH-BUCHHOLZ
BARUTH
LÜBBEN
BEESKOW
EISENHÜTTENSTADT
GUBEN
Oder
Spree

Ninth Army & part Fourth Pz Army

33 A
ZERBST
DESSAU
US First Army
BERNBURG
Saale
Mulde
HALLE
LEIPZIG
EILENBURG
WITTENBERG
13 A
LUCKAU
SCHLIEBEN
HERZBERG
FINSTERWALDE
COTTBUS
22 Apr
FORST

1 Ukrainian Front (Konev)
attacks 0615 hrs, 16 April

3 GTA
TRIEBEL
13 A
5 GA
4 GTA
28 A

US front 25 April
TORGAU
5 GA
Army Group Center (Schörner)
Fourth Pz Army
SPREMBERG
Neisse
Pol2 A
52 A

25 April 1945 US and Russian forces make contact
ELSTERWALDE
HOYERSWERDE
NIESKY

RIESA
GROSSENHAIN
KAMENZ
Pol2 A
BAUTZEN
GÖRLITZ
COLDITZ
MEISSEN
RADEBERG
DRESDEN

Seventeenth Army

FRONT LINES
———— 15 APRIL 1945
– – – 18 APRIL
–·–·– 25 APRIL
········ 6 MAY

▲▲▲ GERMAN DEFENSE LINES
▨▨ GERMAN POCKETS
➤ GERMAN COUNTERATTACKS
⇨ ANGLO-AMERICAN ATTACKS
═══ ANGLO-AMERICAN FRONTS AT DATES SHOWN

sives and the civilian population cowed under allied bombing. On 10 April, Model's Army Group B was encircled by the British in the Ruhr Pocket. Model avoided capture by committing suicide, but 300,000 German soldiers became prisoners. On 16 April the Red army began its offensive across the Oder, and after two days of bitter fighting broke through the German position and headed for Berlin which was soon encircled. The garrison of Berlin was a motley collection of *Wehrmacht* and *Volkssturm* units, and despite Hitler's frantic appeals for relief, there were no German forces in the vicinity even remotely capable of carrying out such an operation.

Given the allied demand for unconditional surrender and their fear of the Red army, the majority of *Wehrmacht* units desperately wanted to be captured by the Anglo-Americans. A number of senior German officers began to take independent action, and on 29 April the German forces surrendered in northern Italy. On the same day Hitler resolved to commit suicide, and in his last will and testament appointed Admiral Dönitz as President and C-in-C of the *Wehrmacht*, and Schörner as C-in-C of the *Führerheer*. Hitler committed suicide in Berlin on 30 April with the Red army only a few hundred yards away. On 2 May the German garrison in Berlin formally surrendered.

Dönitz established a temporary government at Flensburg on the Baltic and attempted to enter into negotiations with the

Anglo-Americans to gain time for more *Wehrmacht* units and German refugees to escape from the Red army. But the allies refused to allow any prevarication, and on 7 May, Jodl signed on Dönitz's behalf the instrument of unconditional surrender, an act which was repeated two days later by Keitel in Berlin. Throughout Europe, the *Wehrmacht* was disarmed and interned, and many officers and soldiers of the *Führerheer* found that they were listed by one or more of the allied powers as 'war criminals.'

During and after the Second World War, the combat performance of the *Führerheer* and the motivation of the German soldier have been the subject of much speculation. In the period 1939-41, the *Führerheer* achieved a series of spectacular victories against a coalition of enemies and attained a high degree of operational and logistical flexibility. From 1942-45 the *Führerheer* fought an increasingly attritional war against overwhelmingly powerful allied forces. The *Führerheer* suffered a series of major defeats in a variety of theaters and lost irreplaceable personnel and equipment. Both in victory and defeat, the German soldier appeared to be more effective than his opponents, and after 1943 continued to surprise them with his ability not only to fight doggedly in defense, but also to counter-attack vigorously at every opportunity. One explanation is that the German by temperament was a natural soldier and fighter and had had discipline and obedience instilled in him as a result of three hundred years of 'Prussian militarism.' Whilst accepting an element of truth in this subjective explanation, the real answer can be found in a more objective analysis.

From the time of the *Kaiserheer* the German military had

Below right: A German NCO moves through a defensive position ready to lay anti-tank mines.
Below: An infantryman emerges from a dugout.

unconditional surrender of Germany, the German soldier was more likely to fight on regardless, particularly against the Soviets. Unconditional surrender blurred the distinction between the Nazi and the anti-Nazi. The German soldier was also motivated by his concept of soldierly duty. This was not simply a question of blind obedience, but the fact that he learnt by heart as a recruit that it was his duty as a soldier to defend the Fatherland and the German people, that the highest soldierly virtue was courage which demanded hardness and determination, and that cowardice was disgraceful and hesitation unsoldierly. Many allied soldiers at the end of the war were puzzled when interrogating German prisoners who had been captured after a determined defense of a hopeless position, and were told that they had done so because 'it was their duty.'

The *Führerheer* developed a variety of methods to strengthen cohesion and prevent the breakdown of morale. Apart from maintaining an efficient military organization and attending to the physical wellbeing of soldiers, it used a wide range of propaganda techniques. During the First World War the OHL had organized propaganda to counter Bolshevik tendencies among the troops and to promote confidence in the political and military leadership. Before the Second World War, Hitler and the Nazi Party were keen to inculcate the necessary ideological motivation in the German soldier, and in 1939 the *Wehrmacht* established a Propaganda Branch whose task was to present the *Wehrmacht* to the German people, and later to the populations of the occupied territories and to bolster the morale of servicemen and counter enemy propaganda. Although the methods used were technically excellent with a wide range of newspapers, magazines and films, the value of the propaganda in maintaining morale was questionable, particularly after 1942, when it became divorced from

Left: Nazi propaganda poster showing a soldier urging civilians to work as hard as he fights for victory.
Below: Front cover of *Die Wehrmacht* magazine, March 1943, depicting German heroism at Stalingrad.

developed all their energies and resources toward the operational aspects of war. The army was developed as a fighting force with a special emphasis placed on cultivating the offensive whatever the circumstances. The army's doctrine, training and organization were all aimed at producing 'fighting power.' Consistently, throughout the Second World War, the *Führerheer* attempted to deploy the majority of its divisional manpower in the teeth arms, and it made sure that its best men were at the front. German divisions, in comparison to either American or British equivalents, had a much smaller staff and administrative component.

The quality of the German soldier deteriorated during the war as a result of casualties and the expansion of the *Führerheer*, so that the personnel included the young, the old, the invalided and conscripted ethnic Germans. Nevertheless, the *Führerheer* consistently produced a well trained soldier who was quickly absorbed into his unit as an effective fighting man. The leadership qualities of the German regimental officer and NCO were excellent, combining professional experience and a close camaraderie with their men.

The German soldier was motivated in a variety of ways during the Second World War. In general, the majority of soldiers were patriotic Germans who fought for their country, and their loyalty and devotion to Hitler was both as *Führer* and Supreme Commander. Even at the end of the war, soldiers still retained a vague belief in the *Führer*, while disliking many Nazi Party officials. The German soldier was also motivated by personal survival, in particular his membership of a close military community. Undoubtedly, membership of an élite regiment or division was important, but in common with soldiers in other armies, it was small group loyalty to the section or platoon that was the most dominant factor. After the allied decision in 1943 to seek the

Left: 'The Last Levy' — junior members of the Hitler Youth parade for military service in 1945.
Right: Hitler Youth and *Volkssturm* recruit waiting with *panzerfausts* for Soviet tanks in Berlin in 1945.

reality. Propaganda certainly helped to instill both a hatred and a fear of the enemy amongst German soldiers, particularly of the Russians, and later in the war the promise of 'retaliatory wonder weapons' may have temporarily raised morale.

Increasingly, Hitler demanded that the *Wehrmacht* adopt more positive ideological indoctrination, believing that this would maintain morale and prevent defeatism. In December 1943 the OKW had established the *Nationalsozialistische Führungs-offiziere*, NSFO, or National Socialist Leadership Officers, who were to propagate National Socialism and act as 'watchdogs' for the Party. Such ideological indoctrination had a minimal effect upon the morale of German soldiers, and as the majority of

NSFOs were young officers without combat experience, they were resented by most soldiers as being Party hacks with a safe job.

The *Führerheer* had instituted a generous system of rewards for motivating soldiers and maintaining morale. Pay was designed to give soldiers the maximum advantages, and with a variety of allowances, the German soldier was well paid in comparison to the conscripts of other armies. In theory, every German soldier was entitled to fourteen days leave a year, and almost until the end of the war, the Germans tried to maintain an efficient and fair system. Furthermore, it was at the discretion of field commanders to reward soldiers for some act of bravery with an immediate grant of special leave.

Before the war Hitler had instituted a new system of decorations and medals for the *Wehrmacht*. During the First World War there had been a limited number of decorations and medals available and separate categories existed for officers and soldiers. After 1939, Hitler revived the Iron Cross decoration which was graded from second and first class through the Knight's Cross, the Knight's Cross with Oak Leaves, then Swords, then Diamonds, and finally with Golden Oak Leaves, Swords and Diamonds. These decorations were cumulative, and in the case of the Knight's Cross were awarded ultimately on Hitler's personal authority. To supplement the Knight's Cross the German Cross in Silver and Gold was instituted as well as a War Merit Cross and a variety of combat and proficiency badges. Although there was a wide distribution of such decorations, medals and badges in the *Führerheer*, they were, nevertheless, an object of intense interest and competition among German soldiers.

In contrast to the system of rewards was the quite draconian system of military justice. Under the Nazi regime a new capital offence of 'undermining fighting morale' was added to the existing ones of treason, murder, desertion, attack on a superior in the field, and plunder. In contrast to the First World War when 48

Below: An SS firing squad prepares to shoot suspected deserters from the fighting on the Eastern Front.

Above: Pz Kw VI, the famous Tiger tank.
Above left: German soldier using a rangefinder from a camouflaged position.
Below left: A Panther tank turret dug in as a strongpoint in the streets of a German town.

soldiers had been executed under military justice, in the Second World War it was over 11,700, with 'undermining fighting morale' and desertion making up the majority of offences. Undoubtedly, such a system of military justice did deter some soldiers, but when the *Führerheer* was being encircled and routed in the period 1944-45, it frequently proved impossible to prevent desertion or absence without leave. The establishment of 'flying field court-martials' behind the lines acted as a deterrent to those who wished to retreat, and 'strength through fear' generals like Schörner were as happy summarily to execute colonels as they were cooks.

The Soviets had quite a lot of success persuading captured German soldiers to lend their names to various communist front organizations such as the *Nationalkomitee 'Freies Deutschland'* or the National Committee 'Free Germany.' Hitler was incensed that a number of captured senior officers, including Paulus, participated in this organization and broadcast anti-Nazi propaganda to Germany. German soldiers in captivity provided the Red army with invaluable military information, and select individuals were used to undertake subversive missions behind the German lines.

The final disintegration of the *Führerheer* came about only in the last few weeks of the war with the breakdown of the military infrastructure, the death of Hitler and the decision of Dönitz and the OKW to surrender. There was no 'stab-in-the-back' in 1945, the *Führerheer* had been beaten both strategically and tactically.

After the war, the majority of German generals explained the origins of the war and the defeat of Germany as a consequence of Hitler's mental instability and the fact that he was a military ignoramus. But for most of the time in which Hitler was *Führer* and Supreme Commander of the *Wehrmacht*, those same generals had accepted his leadership and decisions. Initially, the German military establishment had been contemptuous of Hitler's social background and the fact that he had only been a corporal in the First World War. But as his risky diplomacy, and later his policy of *Blitzfeldzug* succeeded, he became the *Feldherr*, and gradually abrogated the power and responsibility of the chief of the general staff. The fatal flaw in Hitler was his inability to view any subject in proportion, and his refusal to have a coordinated policy and governmental organization within Nazi Germany. Ultimately, all power was vested in him, and he was unable to cope with being both head of the government and *Feldherr*. There was no coordination within the *Wehrmacht*, and the OKW was little more than Hitler's secretariat. Disagreements and competition between the *Wehrmacht*, the Nazi Party, the SS and all the governmental departments meant that strategic decisions and the allocation of resources became a matter of chance.

Hitler reduced the power of the general staff and attempted to create a *Führerheer*. But it was the organization, doctrine, training and professionalism inherited from the *Kaiserheer* and the *Reichsheer* which gave the *Führerheer* its fighting power and flexibility in the Second World War. The ability to raise, train and deploy a variety of ad hoc formations in a remarkably short period of time confounded the opponents of the *Führerheer*. But this combination of technical military professionalism and fighting power could not compensate for the *Führerheer*'s lack of strategic vision and incestuous conflicts between members of the officer corps, which were legacies of the old Prussian general staff.

The Bundeswehr and the Nationale Volksarmee

History of The German Army

During the Second World War the *Führerheer*, including the *Waffen* SS, suffered total casualties of nearly 5,100,000, of whom 2,000,000 had been killed. At the Yalta Conference in February 1945, the allied powers decided that, 'It is our inflexible purpose to destroy German militarism and Nazism to ensure that Germany will never again be able to disturb the peace of the world. We are determined to disarm and disband all German armed forces, break up for all time the German General Staff that has repeatedly contrived the resurgence of German militarism, remove and destroy all German military equipment . . .' At the Potsdam Conference in August 1945 the allies set up the Allied Control Council which attempted to regulate affairs between the American, British, French and Soviet zones. The Allied Control Council issued directives for the liquidation of German militarism. All German military organizations were disbanded, the fostering of military traditions was forbidden, all weapons were impounded, military literature seized, and military monuments and museums removed.

At the same time the allies separately and collectively began to prosecute individual members of the *Wehrmacht* for war crimes. At the Nuremberg War Crimes Tribunal both Keitel and Jodl were found guilty and executed. The defense offered by German soldiers, SS men and Nazi Party officials was either that they had only been obeying superior orders, or that they were not responsible for the consequences of their subordinates' actions. Although the killing of civilians and prisoners of war was not something unique to the *Führerheer* during the Second World War, the war crimes trials revealed the active or passive involvement of German soldiers in many dreadful cases. According to the OKW statistics nearly 5,754,000 Red army soldiers were captured by the Germans during the Second World

War. At the end of the war only 1,053,000 were still prisoners, with 818,000 having been released to civilian or military status. This meant that 3,700,000 were missing, the overwhelming majority of whom had died of disease or hunger or been worked to death, or had been shot or otherwise exterminated. Most of these prisoners had been the responsibility of the *Führerheer*. Wherever possible, former members of the *Wehrmacht* tried to blame the SS, who became the 'alibi of a nation.'

Millions of German soldiers were prisoners of war and all they wanted to do was to return to Germany and attempt to find their homes and their families among the mass of displaced persons and in the rubble and ruins. The German people were hostile or indifferent to all things military. Very few German families had emerged from the war unscathed and released prisoners were desperate to remove their uniforms and try to resume a normal life. And yet within a decade of the allied decision to destroy German militarism and the negative reaction of the German people to the war, the foundations had been laid for two German armies, the West German *Bundeswehr* and the East German *Nationale Volksarmee*.

The development of two postwar German armies was a consequence of the emergence of two German states following the breakdown of the wartime alliance. Hostility between, on the one hand the western powers, America, Britain and France, and on the other hand the Soviet Union, centered upon the future of Germany, which involved questions of politics, ideology, economics and security. The Soviets were determined that Germany would never again be a political and military threat, and to that end they had no intention of permitting free elections in their zone which would have resulted in a non-communist victory. Within their zone they had used the old German Communist Party under Walter Ulbricht to establish a political machine for implementing Soviet policy. In 1946, the Social Democrat Party in the Soviet zone was persuaded to merge with the Communist Party to form the Socialist Unity Party, or SED, a change in name only, as the new party was dominated by the communists.

Previous page: 'Citizens in uniform' – *Bundeswehr* soldiers on exercise. The MG3 machine guns shown are a standard Bundeswehr weapon. The design of the MG3 is based on the wartime MG 42.
Below: Leopard I tank of the *Bundeswehr* on the firing range. The Leopard I carries a 105mm gun.

The Bundeswehr a ... e Volksarmee

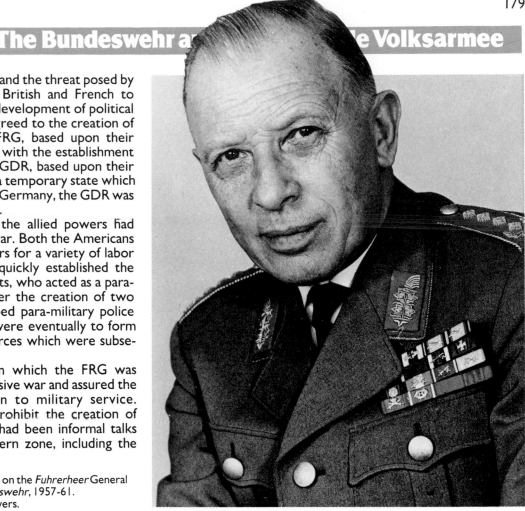

In the western zones, economic reality and the threat posed by the Soviets, persuaded the Americans, British and French to establish a unified zone and to allow the development of political parties. By 1949 the western allies had agreed to the creation of the Federal Republic of Germany, or FRG, based upon their former zones, and the Soviets countered with the establishment of the German Democratic Republic, or GDR, based upon their zone. While the FRG was always seen as a temporary state which one day would merge into a larger unified Germany, the GDR was established as *the* socialist German state.

The demilitarization of Germany by the allied powers had never been fully implemented after the war. Both the Americans and the British had used German prisoners for a variety of labor and guard duties, and the Soviets had quickly established the *Bereitschaften*, or special armed alert units, who acted as a para-military security force for the SED. After the creation of two Germanies in 1949, both states developed para-military police forces and Frontier Guard units which were eventually to form the basis for the new German armed forces which were subsequently to be created.

The *Grundgesetz*, or Basic Law, on which the FRG was founded, prohibited the waging of aggressive war and assured the basic right of conscientious objection to military service. However, this law did not explicitly prohibit the creation of armed forces. Even before 1949 there had been informal talks involving leading politicians in the western zone, including the

Right: General Adolf Heusinger, chief of operations on the *Fuhrerheer* General Staff, 1939-44, and Inspector-General of the *Bundeswehr*, 1957-61.
Below: Bundeswehr soldiers during NATO Maneuvers.

future first Chancellor of the FRG, Konrad Adenauer, concerning the possibility of some form of German rearmament. At the same time, following the breakdown of the Four Power Policy in 1948, certain groups among the western powers had suggested German participation in the collective defense effort of western Europe. Western concern had increased as the Soviets organized East German para-military police forces far in excess of the needs of internal security.

After the establishment of the North Atlantic Treaty Organ-ization, NATO, in April 1949, the Americans were anxious to see the establishment of West German armed forces, under NATO control, which could help to defend the FRG against a Soviet attack. The French were alarmed by this proposal, and instead, made a counter-proposal in October 1950 for a European Defense Community in which West German troop contingents would be employed as part of a larger European army. Ironically, this concept was eventually rejected in August 1954 by the French Assembly.

Left: 'Brothers in arms' – Soviet and East German (right) tank crewmen in a 1984 propaganda photograph.
Right: Bundeswehr mountain troops.

The Americans and the British then proposed a new solution within the existing NATO framework. In October 1954 the Americans, British and French signed the Paris Agreements terminating their occupation of West Germany, recognizing the FRG as a sovereign state, and inviting it to become a member of NATO on 8 May 1955. The FRG voluntarily agreed to build up an army and to place the combat-ready units directly under NATO command. Thus a solution had been found which satisfied NATO requirements for West German rearmament with the safeguards which many Europeans wished to insist upon against resurgent German militarism.

Concurrently with these developments, Adenauer had begun to prepare for West German rearmament. In the spring of 1950 he had appointed former General Gerhard von Schwerin as his military adviser who initially drew up plans for a 10,000 man force of Bundesgrenzschutz, or Federal Border Guard. In October 1950, Schwerin held a secret conference of former senior officers of the Führerheer, including Kielmansegg, Baudissin, Heusinger and Speidel. These officers concluded that future West German armed forces would have to combine political acceptability and technical proficiency.

On 27 October 1950, Adenauer appointed Theodor Blank, a member of the Bundestag, or Federal Parliament, as 'Commissioner of the Federal Government for all Questions Related to the Strengthening of the Allied Occupation Troops.' It was a cover name of sorts for a kind of shadow defense ministry, and so became known as the Dienstelle Blank, or the Blank Office. As a result of some rather incautious statements to the press, Schwerin was dismissed as Adenauer's military adviser, but other retired officers were absorbed into the Blank Office.

Over the next four years, these officers refined their ideas on military reform based on the premise that an adjustment of military values to democratic values and the principles of public order were more likely to promote rather than detract from military effectiveness. They wanted to change the 'Prussian drillbook' image of soldiering to overcome the widespread antimilitary sentiments amongst German youth which manifested themselves through the powerful ohne mich, or 'without me,' movement.

The new image of the German soldier was to be that of the Staatsbürger in uniform, or 'citizen in uniform.' In the words of the military reformers, 'the inner structure of the armed forces in a free society must be such that young soldiers can complete their military training without a fundamental break with their civilian environments.' They intended to achieve this objective through three reform measures. Firstly, complete subjection of military life to the principles governing the state, based on law and order with individual rights of the soldier to hold and express political opinions, the right of association, and legal protection against all military proceedings. Secondly, the democratization and demilitarization of the armed forces as far as possible with the relationship between soldiers and superiors to be based chiefly on the function, and therefore the military performance of individuals concerned. Finally, soldiers were to be educated toward independence and political activation of democracy against totalitarianism through the concept of innere führung, or inner leadership.

Following the FRG's admission to NATO in May 1954, the government began to prepare the necessary framework for the creation and organization of the new armed forces, to be called the Bundeswehr, or Federal Defense Force, which would consist of an army, navy and air force. The government had to move carefully as there was considerable opposition to rearmament.

Left: Bundeswehr soldiers begin an attack from a UH-1 transport helicopter.

International opinion was hostile, with the Soviets and their allies orchestrating a barrage of propaganda, claiming that the Bundeswehr was a revamped Wehrmacht, and that West Germans were being prepared as American cannon-fodder. Within the FRG the Social Democratic opposition was critical and there was considerable public disquiet. In 1955 a public opinion poll showed that only forty percent of West Germans were in favor of reconstituting armed forces.

Under the Paris Agreements of 1954 the FRG undertook to limit the size of the Bundeswehr to the maxima negotiated in the European Defense Treaty of May 1952, which was twelve divisions; to refrain from seeking to bring about the reunification of Germany or to alter the boundaries of the FRG by the use of force; and to refrain from the manufacture of atomic, biological and chemical weapons. Command of the Bundeswehr, which was assigned to NATO, was with the Supreme Allied Commander Europe, SACEUR. In 1956 the government, through the Bundestag, had to revise the constitution to provide legally for the basis of the Bundeswehr. The government was able to use Article 91, which permitted it to intervene in the affairs of the Lander for self defensive purposes, and Article 87, which allowed for frontier protection authorities to be raised, to provide the constitutional basis for the Bundeswehr.

The role of the new Bundeswehr was to be strictly limited and controled by the Bundestag, so that its internal and external defense functions would only commence after a State of Defense had been proclaimed after a vote in the Bundestag. Thus German law limited the role of the Bundeswehr to obeying the orders of a supranational commander, SACEUR, except when parliament authorized its employment on national territory for strictly defined purposes. Within the Bundeswehr, the Heer would make up 70 percent, the Luftwaffe 22 percent and the Marine 8 percent. Finally, the Bundeswehr would have no separate general staff.

Above: Bundeswehr trumpeters at a military tatoo. Some elements of pageantry have been retained by the *Bundeswehr*.

and dismissal of civil and military officers, the regulation of the system of ranks and design of uniforms, and the proclamation of a state of war. In peacetime, the Federal Minister of Defense was to be C-in-C of the *Bundeswehr*, but in wartime, this role would be assumed by the Chancellor.

The government was concerned also to define the *Bundeswehr*'s place in the state and the rights of the citizen in uniform. The Soldier's Law of 19 March 1956 laid down the serviceman's constitutional rights and responsibilities. In addition, a series of supplements were added to the Soldier's Law, including the Military Appeals Act, which allows the soldier to lodge complaints and appeals to the civil courts; the Military Penal Act which laid down that the soldier remains under the jurisdiction of civil courts; and the Law Pertaining to the Election of Soldiers' Representatives who were to function as spokesmen for subordinates and assistants to superiors. Finally, all members of the *Bundeswehr* had the right of direct, confidential appeal on matters of basic constitutional rights to the Parliamentary Defense Commissioner who was appointed by the President of the *Bundestag* after election by the *Bundestag* and who had powers to investigate such matters.

The government and the reformers hoped that through this legislation, which guaranteed parliamentary control of the *Bundeswehr* and extensive civil rights to servicemen combined with *innere führung*, they would exorcise the danger of the *Bundeswehr* becoming 'a state within a state,' and thus a threat to democracy.

Recruitment for the *Bundeswehr* was to be based on conscription under the Defense Duty Law of 21 July 1956. The military reformers had argued for a period of conscription lasting eighteen months, but for political reasons, Adenauer rejected their advice and a twelve month period was introduced, although later this was extended to eighteen months. Potential conscripts could register as conscientious objectors and appear before an examining board who would consider their sincerity. By introducing conscription, the government hoped to meet the political

Control of the *Bundeswehr* was to be divided between the executive and parliament. Parliament was to be responsible for defense legislation, the military budget, and, when necessary, the declaration of a state of war. Two investigatory agencies were to work for the *Bundestag*, the Defense Committee and the Defense Commissioner. The executive powers were to be divided, with the Federal President limited to the appointment

Right: A *Bundeswehr* Bo 105 helicopter armed with TOW guided antitank missiles in low-level flight.
Below: Bundeswehr Leopard II tank and personnel carriers on exercise.

Above: A Soviet soldier instructs an East German infantryman in the use of a light machine gun.

requirement of making the *Bundeswehr* a force of 'citizens in uniform' as well as the military requirement of maintaining twelve divisions.

A more serious problem for Adenauer and his military advisers was the question of where to find the necessary experienced soldiers to form the initial regular officer and NCO cadre. All of those available had served under Hitler and were thus a potential danger to parliamentary democracy and the ethos of the new *Bundeswehr*. The answer was provided through setting up special screening commissions consisting of veteran opponents to Nazism and 'politically clean' former *Wehrmacht* officers. The screening commissions demanded that every applicant for a *Bundeswehr* commission show 'irreproachable' behavior before, during and after the war. It was hoped that old Nazis and other undesirables would be filtered out, and by and large the commissions fulfilled their difficult task. Although the Soviets and East Germans claimed that the *Bundeswehr* was largely officered by Nazi 'retreads,' by the end of 1956, less than one percent, 566 men, were *Waffen* SS veterans.

On 12 November 1955, the first 101 soldiers of the *Bundeswehr* received their commissions, and on the 1 January 1956, the first training company of the *Bundeswehr* was organized. By the end of the year the *Bundeswehr* had expanded to 66,000 men, with 9572 volunteers from the *Bundesgrenzschutz*, and in 1960 the *Bundeswehr* had 270,000 soldiers.

The first two decades of the *Bundeswehr*'s development were fraught with political and military difficulties. Despite the fact that the FRG was fully integrated into NATO, some west European countries remained suspicious. As Franz Josef Strauss, Federal Defense Minister 1956-62, was to comment, 'The *Bundeswehr* is supposed to be strong enough to hold back the Russians, but not so strong as to frighten the Belgians.' Within the FRG there was continued opposition from within the Social Democrat Party, and the strength of the *ohne mich* movement was demonstrated by a rise in the number of conscripts registering as conscientious objectors. Some Germans rejected the *Bundeswehr* as a military joke, scoffing at the idea of 'citizens in uniform' and *innere führung*, believing that effective armed forces had to be based on the traditional virtues of discipline and obedience. The image and

independence of the *Bundeswehr* was also compromised by drab and functional uniforms, and the fact that, initially, its weapons, equipment and training were provided in their entirety by the United States.

Like the Federal Republic it serves, the *Bundeswehr* has been painfully aware of its historic roots. The heir of the *Führerheer*, the *Reichsheer* and the *Kaiserheer*, it purports to reject many German military traditions incompatible with parliamentary democracy, and in reality, these military traditions had been broken twice, in 1945 and 1918. The *Bundeswehr* has been unsure of its military traditions, and even such anti-Nazi acts as the participation of soldiers in the 'Bomb Plot' against Hitler have been controversial. In 1965 the Defense Ministry issued a memorandum entitled, '*Bundeswehr* and Tradition.' This document attempted to give some traditional meaning to German military service. It addressed concepts such as ideals of freedom, democracy and loyalty to fellow countrymen and the homeland. The flag, the Iron Cross, and other military symbols were placed in their historic perspective.

Although the old regiments, the flags and the customs had been eliminated, there were unofficial attempts to link the new units of the *Bundeswehr* with those from earlier military traditions. At one stage, the *Bundeswehr Panzeraufklarungbataillon 11* had become the *Traditionsträger* of the 17th Cavalry Regiment of the *Reichsheer*, which in turn had been the *Traditionsträger* of the 2nd Prussian Dragoons from Schwedt-am-Oder. Despite considerable opposition, there were limited expressions of traditional military ceremonies within the *Bundeswehr*. All recruits for the army are sworn into federal service and their regiment whilst holding an edge of the national colors, which is normally done before the regimental formation, and often at night by torchlight. But public reaction can still be hostile, and on 6 May 1980, anti-war demonstrators disrupted the Grand Tattoo held to celebrate both the swearing in of the annual intake of recruits and the 25th anniversary of the FRG's membership of NATO. The dilemma of traditions and the only means of resolution for the *Bundeswehr* was articulated in 1978 by General Harald Wust who said, 'There is no *Bundeswehr* tradition outside the tradition of the Federal Republic. There is however a military tradition of the *Bundeswehr* within the context of our national tradition. Both must be in basic agreement.'

In 1984 the army component of the *Bundeswehr* consisted of

Above: GDR border troops swearing allegiance on their regimental colors.
Right: East German Workers' Combat Group on parade in East Berlin.

335,000 men, of whom 181,000 were conscripts serving for fifteen months. The *Feldheer* consisted of three corps, of twelve divisions, with a Territorial army of 44,200. The army is integrated into the NATO command and control structure and is deployed within the FRG alongside national contingents from Belgium, Britain, Canada, France, the Netherlands and the USA. The army has no general staff, but officers are posted to staff appointments with field units, headquarters and the Ministry of Defense and to NATO. Today, the *Bundeswehr* is well armed and equipped with the products of the FRG's own armaments industry, including such items as the formidable *Leopard* main battle tank. The *Bundeswehr* now makes up the single largest component of NATO's ground forces on the Central Front. The *Bundeswehr* is committed to NATO's strategy of flexible response, which includes forward defense of alliance territory and combines deterrence with defense.

Military observers note that in field exercises the *Bundeswehr* appears efficient and effective, with all ranks displaying a high degree of professionalism. But there is some concern that while the officers are good technical leaders and man-managers they are not field commanders, and whilst the conscripts are proficient they lack enthusiasm. Furthermore, in the event of a conflict with the Warsaw Pact, the *Bundeswehr* would quickly find itself deployed against the other German army, the *Nationale Volksarmee*, NVA, or National People's Army.

The origins of the NVA can be found in the development of para-military police units within the Soviet zone, later the GDR. Ostensibly, the expansion of para-military police units and eventually the establishment of the NVA was to counter West German rearmament. In reality, they were organized to bolster the position of the SED, to guarantee internal security, and, as far as Ulbricht was concerned, to be the outward symbol of a separate, legitimate socialist German state.

From the very beginning, the Soviets had an ambivalent attitude towards East German rearmament. While wishing to secure a communist state in East Germany and mobilize its resources for Soviet defense interests, they were uneasy about any German rearmament, even under their strict control. In 1952 the para-military police units were organized as the *Kasernierte Volks-*

Above: NVA tank photographed returning to barracks after a parade in East Berlin.

polizei, or People's Barrack Police, and consisted of seven line divisions. So in January 1956, when the GDR's People's Chamber passed the Act on the Foundation of the National People's Army and the Ministry of National Defense, the organization was already in existence. The East Germans claimed that the establishment of the NVA was a spontaneous reaction to the formation of the *Bundeswehr*, but in fact a shadow army had already existed in the form of the 120,000 man *Kasernierte Volkspolizei.*

The Defense Law of 20 September 1961 laid down the basic civil obligation to undergo service in the NVA, in one or other of the arms or in the air defense organization. This prepared the way for the introduction of compulsory military service, which was enacted in the Conscription Bill of 24 January 1962. Whilst it is not possible to be a conscientious objector, it is possible to serve in the Construction Units as a form of substitute service. From its very foundation, the NVA was to be a 'people's army,' and a 'class army.' It was founded on the basis of communist ideology and the policies of the Soviet Union. Its role was to protect the 'socialist fatherland,' the 'socialist community of states,' 'peace' itself, and to ensure the 'victory of socialism round the globe.'

According to the Defense Law of the GDR, the defense of the state depends 'on the political power exercised by the working class under the leadership of its Marxist-Leninist Party in alliance with the class of collective farmers, with the intelligentsia and with other actively employed citizens.' But to speak purely of 'national defense,' is too narrow a concept as far as the GDR is concerned. The NVA is firmly controlled by the politburo of the Central Committee of the SED. Holders of most of the senior positions in the NVA are also members of the Central Committee, and its influence and power extends to military as well as political matters. Army General Heinz Hoffman, a veteran member of the German Communist Party, has been Minister of National Defense since 1960, and he is also Supreme Commander of the NVA. The SED also maintains a political organization at every level within the NVA which acts both as an invigilator and as a catalyst for socialism.

The basis of the NVA, and indeed the GDR, is the irrevocable alliance with the Soviet Union. According to the SED, the Red army liberated the German people from fascism, and the Group of Soviet Forces in Germany guarantees the protection of the German people from future fascist threats from the west. The Soviet armed forces were responsible for organizing, training and equipping, firstly the People's Barrack Police, and secondly the

NVA. The NVA has been firmly under Soviet control since 1956 and is integrated still further through the GDR's membership of the Warsaw Pact.

Initially, the SED had to overcome the extremes of reaction among the population of East Germany, from strong pacifism to reactionary nostalgia for German military traditions, and instead create a socialist military attitude. A considerable amount of basic pre-military training was undertaken through schools and clubs, and through links with the Combat Groups of the Working Class. Socialist military education in the GDR developed a system of 'hate-training' aimed at class enemies both at home and abroad.

The NVA has been characterized by a fundamentally different ethos and tradition from previous German armies and from that of the *Bundeswehr*. The SED was determined to break with the past and create a truly 'class army,' which would be foremost in the ranks of the world socialist movement. At first, there had been problems finding the right cadre to form the establishment of the People's Barrack Police and then the NVA. A certain number of old German Communist Party members were available, but the majority were recruited from former German prisoners of war, some of whom had been members of the Soviet sponsored 'Free Germany Committee.'

The traditional field-gray uniform of the German army, with a slightly redesigned helmet, was introduced to stress the 'national' character of the NVA. An important element in the creation of the NVA as a 'class army,' was *Traditionspflege*, or the cult of tradition. The strands in 'progressive military tradition' included the struggle of the German working class and its revolutionary party; the part played by German patriots and internationalists in other countries' national and social liberation movements; the impact of progressive forces on the history of the German people; the achievements of the NVA in the military safeguarding of the GDR's socialist construction, and the consolidation of 'brotherhood-in-arms' with the allied armed forces, especially the Soviet armed forces. The SED wanted to stress the revolutionary traditions in German history, including the Peasants' War of 1525, the 'People's War' of 1813, the Revolution of 1848, the November Revolution of 1918, the Communist Uprising in the Ruhr in 1920 and the German participation in the International Brigade during the Spanish Civil War.

The theme of German-Russian 'brotherhood-in-arms' is very prominent in the NVA's cult of tradition. Such important events emphasized include the Convention of Tauroggen in 1812 and the

Top right: East German soldiers on a river crossing exercise.
Right: Recruits to the NVA swearing allegiance to the colors.
Far right: NVA soldier operates a rangefinder from a camouflaged position.
Below: ZSU-23-4 anti-aircraft system in service with the NVA.

fraternization between German and Russian soldiers in 1917. But gradually, the NVA, reflecting a wider trend within the GDR, has taken up other themes from German history. Military reformers such as Scharnhorst, Gneisenau and Clausewitz are regarded as 'progressive' elements in German history. The cult of tradition within the NVA takes the form of the presentation of banners and oath-taking ceremonies; meetings with working class veterans; visits to historic sites and military museums and anniversary commemorations.

Since 1956, every NVA unit has had its own banner, and many units have been awarded cuff bands and titles of socialist heroes such as Karl Liebknecht or Friedrich Engels. Considerable emphasis has been placed on military ceremonial and discipline as this is believed to foster socialist military pride. Military parades and honor guards are an important part of NVA ceremonial, and the mounting of the guard has been re-established on the Unter den Linden in East Berlin. A permanent armed guard has been established at the *Neue Wache*, now the Memorial to the Victims of Fascism.

The NVA is organized into an army, navy and air force element. The army is 120,000 strong, of whom 71,500 are conscripts who serve for eighteen months. The field army of the NVA consists of two tank divisions and four motor rifle divisions. However, these

Left: Former Soviet Defense Minister Ustinov and NVA General Hoffman at Jena in 1983.
Right: East German leader Walter Ulbricht visits an army tank unit.
Below: Military parade in East Berlin in 1976 celebrating the NVA's twentieth anniversary.

divisions do not operate as a field army, but are deployed separately and are closely integrated with the Group of Soviet Forces Germany. Supplementing the NVA are some 82,500 paramilitary forces, consisting of frontier troops, People's Police Alert Units and the Workers' Militia. The NVA is organized, trained and equipped by the Soviet Union. The officer cadre of the NVA are nearly all SED party members and are seen as party functionaries and military technicians rather than traditional soldiers. Officers and NCOs make up nearly forty percent of the ground forces of the NVA, and as the majority are either active party members or regarded as politically reliable, this guarantees the class nature of the NVA. Unlike the *Bundeswehr*, the NVA depends upon firm political control and unquestioning obedience. Drill forms a very important part of the training of the NVA soldier.

Units of the NVA participated in the 'socialist fraternal assistance' given to Czechoslovakia in August 1968. Contingents from two NVA divisions joined other Warsaw Pact troops, but within a few days were restricted in their movements. The entry of NVA troops struck the Czechs and many other people as too reminiscent of the German occupation of 1938-39. Furthermore, many Czechs spoke German and argued with NVA soldiers thus presenting problems of morale and discipline. NVA personnel have also been involved in military cooperation with Third World countries. Initially, this formed part of a concerted effort on the part of the SED to gain international recognition for the GDR. But it also fitted in with the ideological belief that the NVA had a duty towards furthering international socialism. By 1977, 22 African and Middle East countries had received military aid from the GDR, with NVA personnel serving in Libya, Tanzania, Angola and Mozambique.

The political and military reliability and efficiency of the NVA is questionable. The NVA is carefully controled both by the Soviets and the SED and has reached a high degree of technical military proficiency. But its role within the Warsaw Pact is limited, and the enthusiasm of its conscript soldiers for a war in central Europe must be in doubt. Today, the *Bundeswehr* and the NVA represent different German states, different ideologies and different military traditions. However, both armies are the heirs of a German military tradition reaching back four centuries.

Index

Page numbers in italics refer to illustrations.

Absolute monarchy 11, 38, 41, 43
Adam, General Wilhelm 122
Adenauer, Konrad 180, 181, 182, 184
Afrika Korps 6, 140-41, 148, 156, 157
airborne troops 133, 143, 150, 168
aircraft 82, *85,* 118, 120, 147, *183*
Albedyll, General von 76
Alsace-Lorraine 69, 72, 74, 90, 106
American Civil War 82
American War of Independence 34
Anglo-Hanoverian army 34
annihilatory war 91-2, 107, 128, 132
Antonescu, General Ion *152*
Ardennes 74, 143, 145
  1944 offensive in 164 (map), *167,* 168
armaments industry 21, 72, 82, 107, 185
armored warfare 118, 131, 132-3, 145-6, 147, 159
Arnhem *166,* 168
artillery, role of 24, 29, 44, 65, 69, 75, 82, 94, 95,
  100, 118
attritional war 92, 97, 103, 107, 128, 135, 159, 170
Auerstadt, battle of *38,* 41, 42 (map)
Auftragstaktik 82, 90, 97
Austerlitz, battle of 38
Austria 10, 13, 26, 38, 46, 49, 52, 59, 60, 64-8, 73,
  74, 87, 90, 92, 132, 136
  Anschluss 136, 138
Austria-Hungary 64, 73
Austrian army 7, 10, 11, 28, 29, 32, 34, 46, 59, 60,
  66, 67-8, 72, 90, 92, 101, 104, 132, *137*

Baden 59, 67, 68
Badoglio, Marshal Pietro 159
Bach-Zelewski, SS *Obergruppenführer* Erich von
  dem 163
'Battle of the Bulge' 164 (map), *167,* 168
Baudissin, General Wolfgang 181
Bautzen, battle of 46
Bavaria 7, 11, 46, 67, 72, 105, 117, 120
  troops from 11, *20,* 49, 59, *62, 86*
Bavarian Succession, War of 11, 25
Bazaine, Marshal François Achille 69
Beck, General Ludwig 121, 122, 129, 131, 134, *134,*
  136, 164
Beer Hall Putsch *119,* 120, *120*
Behrenhorst Georg Heinrich von 38
Belgian army 90, 145, 185
Belgium 74, 75, 90, 108, 120, 152-5, 162
Benedek, General August 68
Bennigsen, General Levin August 48
Berlin *72, 78,* 109, *110-11, 116, 173*
  advance on in 1945 168, 169 (map), 170
Bernadotte, Marshal Charles John 48
Bethmann Hollweg, Theobald von 78, 92
Bismarck, Otto von 60, 65, 66, 68, 69, 72-3, 75, 77
Blank, Thoedor 181
Blaskowitz, General von 142
Blenheim, battle of 15
Blitzkrieg 132, 142, 147
Blomberg, General Werner von *121,* 122, 123,
  131, *132,* 134-6, 137
Blücher, Marshal Gebhard von *6,* 41, 43, *45,* 46,
  48-9
Bock, Field Marshal Fedor von *135,* 143, 145, 146,
  147, 150, 154
Bolsheviks, Bolshevism 101, 104-5, 106, 108, 161,
  171
Boxer Rebellion 84, *84, 86,* 87
Boyen, General Hermann von 43, 48, 52, *52,* 54, 59
Brandenburg, Brandenburg-Prussia 11, 13, 17, 24
Brauchitsch, Field Marshal Walther von 120, 136,
  136, 142, 143, 147, 154
Brest-Litovsk 101
Britain 41, 48, 75, 76, 108, 128, 135, 138, 143, 147,
  178-81
British army 34, 49, 72, 90, 92, 97, 101, 103, 104,
  142-6, 148, 150, 157, 158, 159, 164, 166, 170,
  185

Bronsart, General 77
Brüchmuller, Colonel Georg 103
Brüning, Heinrich 121
Brunswick, Dukes of *32,* 38, *38,* 41, *47*
Bulgaria 72, 104, 108, 149
Bulgarian army 72, 101, 150
Bülow, Baron Friedrich Wilhelm von 40
Bundeswehr 7, 176-83, 178, 181-2, 184-5, 186, 189

Cannae, battle of 73
Cantonal Règlement 21, 27, 38, 44
Caporetto, battles at 101, 103
Carlsbad Degrees 54
Cassano, battle of 15
cavalry, role of 29, 44, 69, 82, 118
'citizens in uniform' 181, 182, 184
Clausewitz, Karl von 7, 40, 44, 46, 48, 54-5, *55,* 72,
  90, 189
communications 52, 59, 68, 81, 108
communism, communists 104, 106, 108-10, 117,
  117-18, 120, 121, 122, 128, 138, 148, 149, 178
Confederation of the Rhine 38, 46, 49
Czechoslovakia 128, 132, 134, 135, 136, 137, 138,
  138-9, 189

Defense in depth 97, 101
Democratic Republic 179, 184, 185-6, 189
Denmark *51, 55,* 59, 60, 65-6, 144-5, 150
Derfflinger, Field Marshal von *8,* 13
Dietl, General 145
discipline, maintenance of 27, 33, 45, 84, 107, 118,
  165, 172
Dönitz, Admiral Karl 170, 175
Dreikaiserbund 73
Dreyse, Nikolaus von 59
drill 28-9, 33, 44, 84, 107
Dutch army 13, 145, 185

East Africa *84,* 108
East Prussia 27, 41, 43, 46, 74, 90, *91,* 138, 150, 168
Eben Emael fortress 143, 145
Ebert, Friedrich 108, 110, 111, 114, 117, *117,* 120
education and training 40, 52, 54, 82, 107
Eicke, General 146
El Alamein, battle 157
Engels, Friedrich 60, 189
envelopment plans 73-5, 90-91, 118, 132, 138, 142,
  159
Epp, General von *114*
Eugene, Prince 15

Falaise Gap 166-7
Falkenhausen, General 162
Falkenhayn, General Erich von 91, 92, 97, 101, *103*
Falkenhorst, General von 144
Federal Republic 179, 181, 184
Fehrbellin, battle of *8,* 13, *14*
Fellgiebel, General 165
Finland 152, *152*
Foch, Marshal Ferdinand 104
France 10, 13, 17, 43, 46, 48, 59, 64-5, 69, 72-4,
  90-92, 108, 120, 128, 134, 135, 136, 138, 150,
  167, 178-80
Franco-Prussian War 61 (map), 62, *64-9,* 69, 72, 77,
  82, 84
Franz Ferdinand, Archduke 90
Franz Joseph, Emperor 64
Frederick I, of Prussia 13, 15
Frederick II 20, 22-3, 24-5, *25-6,* 26-9, *30, 32,* 32-4,
  34-5, 38, 41, 73, 77, 84, 138, 168
Frederick Charles, Prince 66, 69
Frederick William, Elector 11, 13, *14, 15,* 29
Frederick William I 15, *16,* 17, *19,* 21, 24
Frederick William II 38
Frederick William III 38, 40, 41, 43, 44, 45, 46, 52,
  54, 55, 59
Frederick William IV 59, 60
Frederick William, Prince 60, 69
Freiburg, battle of *28*
Freikorps 109-10, 114, *115, 116,* 117-18, 123
Freisler, Roland 165
French army 7, 10, 11, 13, 33, 34, *36-7,* 38, 41, 43,
  46, 48-9, 64, 69, 90-92, 97, 101, 103, 104, 131,
  136, 142-7, 185

French Revolution 38, 40
Friessner, General 167
Fritsch, General Werner von 122, 129, 131, 134,
  135, 135-6, 137
Fromm, General Friedrich 138, 164, 165
Führerheer 108, 120, *126-7,* 131, *142-52, 154-5,*
  163, *164-8,* 170-72, *174-5,* 175, 178
  and armored warfare 132-3
  and rear area security 162-3
  expansion of 129, 131-3, 155, 171
  in Balkans 150, 159, 162, 167
  in Denmark and Norway 145
  in France 1940 *142-3,* 143-4, *144-5,* 145-7, 162
  in France/Germany 1944/5 *164,* 166
  in Poland 142, 143, *144*
  in Sicily/Italy 159
  OKH 131, 133, 137-8, 142, 143, 145, 147, 149,
    150, 152, 154-8 passim, 163
  operational doctrine 133, 171, 175
  organization 132, 133, 134, 137-8, 150, 158, 160,
    164, 168, 175
  Ostheer 149, 150, *150-51,* 152, 154-61, *155-6,*
    158-9, 167
Fuller, General John F C 131

General staff 59, 65-6, 72-3, 75, 76, 77, 81-2, 90, 92,
  103, 108, 110, 114, 118, 119, 178
  development of 7, 45, 48, 55, 57
  in *Führerheer* 137, 143, 154, 164, 165, 175
  organization 29, 52, 55, 57, 64, 69
  Weimar *Truppenamt* 117-18, 120, 129
Gessler, Dr Otto 117, 120
George William, Elector *10*
German national unity 59, 60
Gneisenau, General August von 43, 48-9, 52, *52,*
  57, 82, 189
Goebbels, Joseph 121
'goose step' 7, 84
Goring, *Reichsmarschall* Hermann 124, 129, 133,
  135, 136, 147, 156
Great Northern War 11
Greece 148, 150
Groener, General Wilhelm, 77, 104, *104,* 105-6,
  108-11 118, 120
Grolman, General Karl von 43, 48, 52, 54, 57
Grossgörschen, battle of 46
Grouchy, Marshal 49
Guderian, General Heinz 118, 131, 132-3, 142,
  143, 146, 152, 154, 156, *157,* 158, 165, 167, 168
Gumbinnen, battle of 90

Haig, FM Sir Douglas 101
Halder, Colonel General Franz *136,* 136-7, 138,
  143, 147, 149, 152, *152,* 154, 156
Hammerstein-Equord, General Kurt von 120, 121,
  122
Hannibal 73
Hanover 34, 41, 49, 52, 68, 84, 87
Hanoverian army/troops 34, 40, 49, 65, 84, 87
Harpe, General 131
Hasse, Major General Otto 117
Hegel, Georg Wilhelm 40, 55
Henry, Prince, of Prussia 27
Hereros *70-71,* 84
Heusinger, General Adolf *179,* 181
Heydrich, Reinhard 149
Heye, General Wilhelm 120
Himmler, Heinrich 124, 133, 135, 138, 149, 158,
  161, 165, 168
Hindenburg, Oskar von 120, 121
Hindenburg, FM Paul von 90, 92, 97, 101, 104, *104,*
  106, 107, 108, 110, 111, 120, *121,* 121-2, 124,
  124, 147
hired armies 11, 34
Hitler, Adolf *119, 121, 131-3, 137-9,* 143, 147, 152,
  172, 175
  rise of 120, 121-4
  and army expansion 129, 131-4, 136
  and Balkans 148-9, 150
  declares war on US 154
  and Poland 138, 142
  and North Africa 148, 157
  and Sicily/Italy 159
  and *Ostfront* 138, 148-9, 152, 154-9, 160, 163,
    164

and defense in the west 163-4, 166-7, 168
assassination attempt 164-6, 184
last days in Berlin 170
and OKH 145, 147, 154
and SS 133, 149-50, 158
and Wehrmacht 136, 142, 145, 165, 167, 175
beliefs 128-9, 132, 142
foreign policy 128, 134-5, 136, 137, 148
racial war 149-50
Hochkirk, battle of 32
Hochstadt, battle of *15*
Hoeppner, General Erich 131, 137, 154, 164, 165
Hoffman, Colonel 90, *104*
Hoffman, General Heinz 186, *188*
Hohenfriedberg, battle of 32, *33*, 34
Holland 74, 75, 145
Hoth, General H 131, 152, 156, 159
Hube, General H V 160
Hungarian army 150, 156, 157

Independent Socialists 104, 106, 109, 110, 117
industrial expansion 59, 77
infantry, role of 24, 28-9, 32, 44, 82, 118
Iron Cross award 46, 172, 184
irregular troops 28, 46, 69
Italian army 101, 148, 150, 156, 157
Italian War, 1859 65
Italy 64, 65, 92, 101, 103, 159, *162*

Japanese army 72
Jena, battle of *38-9*, 41, *41*, 42 (map)
Jews 128, 138, 142, 149
Jodl, General Alfred 136, 142, 143, 144, 147, 154, 157, 168, 170, 178
Joffre, Marshal J J 90
Jünger, Ernst 107, 119-20

Kahr, Gustav von 120
Kaiserheer 7, 69, *72*, 72-8, *74-5*, *77-8*, 81-2, *83*, 84, 87, *88-9*, 90-92, *91*, *93*, 94-5, *94-7*, 97, 100-101, 103-11, *103-11*, 117, 119, 120
doctrine 72-5, 81-2, 84, 87, 92, 94, 97, 100, 103, 107, 170-71, 175
general staff 72-3, 75, 76, 77, 81-2, 90-91, 97, 103, 107, 108, 110
officer corps 73, 76, 77, 78, 81, 90, 105-7, 118
OHL 90, 91, 92, 94, 97, 101, 103, 105, 107-10 *passim*, 171
organization 72, 81, 97, 103, 106-7, 175
recruitment 81, 87, 106, 118
Reserve Officers' Corps 78
Schutztruppen 70-71
uniform 72, *77*, 87, *87*, 95
weapons 72, 82, 107
1918 Offensive 103-4, 109 (map)
Kaisermanöver 77, 82, *83*
Kaisermarine 76, 82, 94, 108
Kaiserreich 7, 69, 72, 75, 78, 87, 105-6, 108, 114
Kameke, General Georg von 76-7
Kampfgruppen 160, 164, 167, 168
Kant, Immanuel 40
Kapp Putsch 114, 117
Keitel, Bodewin 136
Keitel, FM Wilhelm 136, 142, 143, 147, *152*, 154, 165, 168, 170, 178
Keith (general) 27
Kesselring, FM Albert 147, 157, 159, 168
Kielmansegg (general) 181
King's German Legion 46, 49, 87
Kleist, Ewald von 27
Kleist, FM Ewald von 131, 145, 146-7, 152
Kluck, General Alexander von 90
Kluge, FM Gunther von 147, 154, 164, 165, 167
Knesebeck, Karl von 40
Kolberg, defense of 43
Kolin, battle of 32
Könen, auditor-general 43
Königgratz, battle of *56*, *58*, 68
Krauseneck, Major General von 59
Krebs, General Hans 168
Kriegsakademie 45, 54, 77, 82, 110, 118
Kriegsmarine 131, 144, 145, 147, 150, 154, 155, 161, 164, 168
Kriegsspiel 57, *75*
Krupp company 72, 82

Küchler, General von 154, 160
Kunersdorf, battle of *22-3*
Kursk offensive 158-9, 160

Landespolizei 118, 129, 132
Landsturm 46, 60, 81
Landwehr 43, *44*, 46, 48, 52, 54, 57, 59, 60, 64, 74, 78, 81, 87, 132
Leeb, FM Wilhelm J 143, 147, 150, 154
Leipzig, battle of *45*, 48, 49
Lenin, V I 101
Leningrad 150, 152
Leopold, Prince, of Anhalt-Dessau 13, 15, *15*, *17*, 21, 24, 27
Lettow-Vorbeck, Colonel Paul von *107*, 108
Leuthen, battle 32, *32*, 33, 34, *35*
liberal democratic movement 52, 54, 59
Liddell Hart, B H 131
Liebknecht, Karl 110, 189
Ligny, battle of 48-9
List, FM Siegmund 145, 147
Lossow, General Otto von 120
Lottum, Karl von 43, 45
Louis XIV 11, 13
Louis Philippe 59
Ludendorff, General Erich 77, 90, 92, 95, 97, 100-101, 103, 104, *104*, 107, 120, 147
Luftwaffe 129, 131, 132, 133, 138, 142, 143, 144, 145, 147, 150, 154-60 *passim* 164, 168
Lüttwitz, General Walter von 114
Lutz, General Otto 131
Luxemburg, Rosa 110
Luxembourg 90

MacMahon, Marshal M E 69
Maginot Line 142, 147
Manstein, FM Erich von 120, 143, 156, 157, 158, 160, *161*
Manteuffel, Major Edwin von 60, 64
Marlborough, Duke of 15
Marx, Karl 60
Max, Prince, of Baden 104, 106
Mediterranean 148, 156, 159, 163
mercenaries 10, 11, 27, 38, 44, 160
Michaelis, Georg 92
Milch, FM Ernst 129, 147
militarism 7, 55, 84, 170, 178
Military Cabinet 55, 64, 68, 76-7
military law and punishment *16*, 17, 27, 41, 45, 59, 165, 172, 175
Military School of Officers 45
military tradition 84, 87, 118, 132, 134, 184, 186, 189
militia 40, 44, 118, 124; *see also Landwehr*
mobilization plans 48, 52, 59, 64-5, 69, 72, 75, 81, 90
Model, FM Walther 156-60 *passim*, 167, 168, 170
Mollendorf, Field Marshal 38, 41
Mollwitz, battle of 32, *32*
Moltke, FM Helmuth von 55, 60, *60*, 64-9, 72, 77, 81, 82, 118, 132
Moltke, General Helmuth von (the younger) 74-5, 76, 77, 90, 91, 147
Morse, Samuel 59
Moscow, advance on 149, 152, 153 (map), 154
Muffling, General von 55, 57, 59
Munich *119*, 120
Munich Settlement 137, 138, *139*
Murat, Marshal Joachim *38*, 41
Mussolini, Benito *133*, 159

Napoleon I 38, 41, 43, 44, 46, *48*, 48-9, 52, 57, 73
Napoleon III 64, 68, 69
national consciousness 33, 38, 46, 49, 54, *54*, 60, 66, 78
National Socialist Leadership Officers 172
Nationale Volksarmee 7, 178, *184-7*, 185-6, 189, *189*
Nazi party, Nazis 120-23, 128, 132, 136, 142, 150, 165, 168, 171, 172, 175, 178, 184
NCOs 27, 57, 87, 106, 107, 132, *170*, 171
Neurath, Konstantin 135
Nivelle, General Robert 101, 103
Normandy landings 164, 166-7
North Africa 148, *148*, 150, *151*, 156, 157-8

North Atlantic Treaty Organization 180-81, 184, 185
North German Confederation 68
Norway 144-5, 150, 163
Noske, Gustav 110, 111, 114, *117*

Occupation policies 108, 138, 142, 149-50, 162, 171
officer corps 21, 26-7, 33, 38, 41, 45, 52, 60
education and training 40, 52, 54
in *Führerheer* 129, 132, 154, 175
in *Kaiserheer* 73, 76, 77, 78, 87, 90, 105, 111, 119
in *Reichsheer* 114, 117, 118, 121, 124
Olmütz, Convention of 60
Operation *Barbarossa* 149, 150
Operation *Market Garden* 168
Oster, Colonel Hans 137

Papen, Franz von *121*, 121-2, 124
parachute troops 133, 143, 150, *150*, 158, *162*
paramilitary forces 118, 121, 129, 133, 179, 180, 185, 189
Paris 44, 48, 59, 69, *69*, 74, 90, *145*, 147, 162, 163
partisans 159, 162-3
Paulus, FM Friedrich von 131, 156-7, *160*, 175
Peter III, Tsar 33
Poland 10, 13, 38, 43, 59, 74, 92, 106, 108, 117, 118, 120, 128, 132, 134, 138, 142, 162, 163, 167
invasion of 142, 143, *144*
Pour le Mérite order 27
Prague *139*; battle of *27*, 32
Preussich-Eylau, battle of 43
Prittwitz, General 90
Prussia 7, 11, 13, 38, 41, 46, 48, 49, 52, 55, 59, 60, 64-8, 69, 72, 77-8
Prussian army 7, 13, 17, *20*, 21, 25, 26, 32-4, *34*, *39*, 46, *47*, 48-9, *51*, *56*, *58*, 59, 60, 65, 66-9, 72, 78, 84, 87
lange Kerle 16, *19*, 21
officer corps 21, 26-7, 33, 38, 41, 43
organization 27-8, 60, 64
personnel of *14*, 15, *15*, 26, *28*, *54*
recruitment *16*, 17, *19*, 21, 26, 27, 34, 38, 43, 48-9
reforms in 41, 43-6, 48, 54, 55, 57, 60, 64
uniform 21, *43*, 44, *53*, *54*, 65

Quatre Bras, battle of *47*, 48

Racial policies 128, 138, 149-50
Raeder, Admiral Erich 135
railroads 59, 60, 64, 65, 68, 69, 81, 90, 108
Ramillies, battle of 15
Ratisbon, battle of 46
recruitment *16*, 17, *19*, 21, 26, 27, 34, 38, 43, 81, 87, 106, 118, 129, 182, 184
Reichenau, FM Walther 122, 124, 147, 154
Reichsheer 110, 111, *112-13*, 114, *117*, 117-24, 122-4, 129, 131
apoliticism of 114, 120, 121
doctrine 118, 175
expansion of 129, 131, 132, 133, 134
Heeresleitung 114, 117, 131
oath of loyalty 124, *125*
officer corps 114, 117, 118, 121, 124
organization 114, 117, 118, 131
Truppenamt 117-18, 121, 129
Reichswehr 110, 114, 123, 124, 128, 129, 131
Reinhard, Colonel 114
Remarque, Erich Maria 118
Reserve Officers Corps 78
resistance groups 162-3, 167
Retzow, General von 27
revolutionary crisis 1848 *54*, 59-60, 186
rewards and decorations 172
Reyher, General von 60
Rezonville, battle of 69
Rhineland 120, 132, *134*, 134-5
road networks 52, 59, 68
Röhm, Captain Ernst 123-4, 168
Rohr, Captain Willy 100
Rommel, General Erwin 107, 146, 156, 157, 164, *164*, 165
Roon, General Albrecht *57*, 60, 69

Rossbach, battle of *25, 29, 32, 33,* 34
Royal Air Froce 147
Royal Navy 76, 108
Ruhr, occupation of 120
Rumania, Rumanians 101, 149, 156, 157, 167
Rundstedt, FM Karl Rudolf 143, 146, 147, 150, 154, 163, 164, 165, 168
Russia (Imperial) 10, 46, 49, 52, 64, 72-3, 75, 90, 92, 101, 103, 104, 110
Russian army 7, 41, 43, 46, 48, 72, 74, 75, 90, 92
Russo-Japanese War 82

SA *119, 120,* 121, 122, 123-4, 168
Saint-Privat, battle of 69
Sanders, General Liman von 108
Saxony 11, 38, 59, 120
    troops from 26, 32, 34, 41, 49, 65, 68, 72
Scharnhorst, General Gerhard von 40-41, *41,* 43-4, 45, 46, 48, 52, 57, 59, 82, 189
Schill, Major Ferdinand von 46
Schleicher, General Kurt von 120-22, *121,* 124
Schleswig-Holstein 59, 60, 65-6, 67
Schlieffen, General Alfred von *73,* 73-5, 77, 92, 118, 132
Schlieffen Plan 73-5, 90, 92 (map), 94, 108, 118
Schmidt, *panzer* officer 131
Schmundt, Hitler's adjutant 154
Schörner, FM Ferdinand 107, 157, 160, 167, 168, 170, 175
Schwarzenberg, Prince Karl Philipp 46
Schwedler, General 136
Schweppenberg, General 131, 164
Schwerin, Field Marshal 25, 27, *27*
Schwerin, General Gerhard von 181
Sedan, battle of 65 (map), *66,* 69
Seeckt, General Hans von 111, *111,* 114, 117-19, 120
Serbia 90, 92
Seven Years' War 25, 26, 32, 34
Seydlitz, Friedrich Wilhelm von *25,* 29
Silesia 26, 32, 82, 109, 118, 120, 138, 168
Silesian Wars 25, 26, 29, 32
Smolensk 149, 150
Social Democrats 108, 110, 111, 114, 121, 178, 181, 184
social exclusiveness 27, 77, 118, 132
socialism, socialists 77-8, 87, 104, 106, 108-10, 111, 117
Somme battles 92, 95, 97
South African (Boer) War 82
South West Africa *70-71,* 84
Soviet army 148, 149, 152, 178
    in 1941-2 150, 152, 154, 156-7
    in 1943-4 158-9, 160, 164
    in 1945 168, 170
Soviet Union 118-19, 120, 128, 138, 142, 144, 148, 149, 162-3, 178, 180, 181, 184, 185, 186, 189
    German training in 118, 120, 129, 131
    Non-Aggression Pact 138
Spain 46, 48
Spanish Succession, War of 13, 15
Spartacists 108-9, 110
Speer, Albert 157
Speidel, General Hans 181
Sperrle, FM Hugo 147
SS 124, *131,* 133, 138, 142, 149-50, 161, 162, 163, 163, 165, *166,* 167, *172,* 175, 178; *see also Waffen SS*
Stahlhelm organization 118, *123*
Stalin, Josef 142, 148, 152
Stalingrad 156-7, 158, *171*
standing armies, development of 10-11, 13, 17, 26, 44
Stauffenberg, Colonel Claus von 164-5, *165*
Stein, Heinrich Friedrich von 43
Steinmetz, General 69
Steuben, Friedrich Wilhelm von 34
Stieff, General Helmuth 165
Stosstruppen 100, 103, 107, 120
Strauss, Franz Josef 184
Stulpnägel, General Karl von 137, 162
Sweden 10, 13, 64
Swedish army 10, 11, 13, 29, 46, 48

Tanentzien, General 43
tanks 95, 118, 120, *124, 131,* 142, 145-7, 149, 150, 154, *155,* 158, 159, 160, 163
    types *126-7, 130,* 131, *142, 144,* 154, *154,* 163, 168, *174-5, 182,* 185, *186*
Tannenberg, battle of 90, 118
Tauroggen, Convention of *43,* 46, 186
telegraph system 52, 59, 68, 81
Thielmann, General 48
Thirty Years' War 10, 11, 13, 24, 160
Thoma, General 131
Tilsit, Peace of 43
Torgau, battle of *30*
trench warfare 94-5, *96, 100*
Traditionsträger 84, 118, 132, 184
transport 82, *97,* 118, 131, 132, 133, 142, 149, *149, 150*
Tschischwitz, General Erich von 131
Turin, battle of 15
Turkey 64, 72, 104
Turkish army 60, 72, 108, 114
two-front war, danger of 72-3

Ulbricht, Walter 178, 185, *189*
uniform 7, 21, 28, 33, 44, 72, *77,* 87, *87,* 95, 123, 132, 161
United States 72, 94, 103, 154, 178-81
United States army 154, 157, 158, 159, 164, 166, 168, 185
universal service 38, 40, 43-4, 46, 48
unrestricted submarine warfare 94, 108, 154
Ustinov, D F *188*

Valmy, battle of *36-7,* 38
Verdun, battle of 92
Versailles Treaty 110-11, 117, 123, 128, 129
Vienna, Congress of 52
Vietinghoff, General S 131
Vlasov, General Andrei 161
Volksgrenadier divisions 168
Volkssturm 168, 170

Waffen SS 131, 133, 144, 150, *150,* 158, 159, *159, 162,* 164, *166,* 168, 178, 184
Wagner, General Eduard 149, 165
Wagram, battle of 46
Waldersee, General Alfred von 73, *73,* 76
Wallenstein, Albrecht von 10, *11*
War of Liberation 46, 48, 84
Wars of Unification 55, 72, 78
Warsaw 142, 167
Washington, George 34
Waterloo, battle of *6,* 49, *49*
Wehrmacht 131, 132, 135, 155, 170, 171, 172
    OKW 136, 143, 144, 148, 150, 154, 156, 157, 159, 163, 164, 172, 175
Weichs, General 131
Weimar Republic 110, 111, 114, 117-24, 129
Wellington, Duke of *6,* 48, 49
Westphalia, Treaty of 13
William I 60, 64, 66, 69, 72, 76
William II 73, *74-5,* 76, 77, 82, *83,* 84, 90, 91, 92, 104, 105-6, 108
William, Prince 120
Wilson, Woodrow 104
Witzleben, FM von *137,* 147, 165, *165*
Witzleben, Major General Erwin von 55
World War I 90-111, 118, 119, 132, 147
World War II 108, 138, 142-75
Wrangel, General von 59, 65-6
Wurttemberg 11, 67, 68
    troops from *11, 21,* 34, 72
Wust, General Harald 184
Wylich, Karl Heinrich von 45

Yorck, von Wartenburg, General Hans *43,* 44, 46
Ypres battles 91, 101, 103
Yugoslavia 149, *149,* 150, 162, 163

Zeitzler, General Kurt 156, 157, *157,* 158, 164
Zieten, General Hans von *25, 29, 32*
Zorndorf, battle of 32, *34*

Acknowledgments

The author and publishers would like to thank David Eldred who designed this book and Ron Watson who compiled the index. The picture researcher was Wendy Sacks and the editor Donald Sommerville. The following agencies and individuals kindly supplied the illustrations on the pages noted.

AKG, Berlin: pages 11 (top), 18-19 (both), 22/3, 26 (top), 30/31, 34 (bottom), 50/51, 55 (top), 56 (top), 56/7, 58 (bottom), 68, 69, 94-5 (all three), 98/9, 102. Front jacket, top right, bottom right.
Bison Picture Library: pages 41, 119 (top), 129, 131 (top), 133 (bottom), 136 (top), 142-3 (all three), 150-51 (all four), 152 (both), 154, 156, 157 (top), 158-9 (all three), 162-3 (all three), 166 (top), 170 (both), 174 (top), 186 (bottom), 187 (all three). Front jacket, bottom right, center.
Anne S K Brown Military Collection, Brown University: pages 2-3, 34 (top), 62/3, 66/7.
Bundesarchiv: pages 7 (bottom), 73 (bottom), 78/9, 111 (top), 118 (right), 119 (bottom), 120, 121 (top), 133 (top), 139 (top left), 140/1, 144 (bottom), 145 (bottom), 147, 148 (bottom), 164 (bottom), 167, 168.
DPA: pages 180 (top), 184-5 (all three), 188-9 (all three).
SPC Dalziel: pages 7 (top), 186 (top).
Archiv Gerstenberg: pages 14 (top & bottom right), 16 (all three), 17 (top), 20 (all four), 21 (bottom), 25 (bottom), 27, 29, 32 (top left), 32/3, 33 (bottom), 35 (bottom), 38 (bottom), 40/41, 43 (both), 48, 49, 53, 54 (bottom), 55 (bottom), 58 (top), 61 (top), 64 (bottom), 70/1, 72, 73 (top), 74 (both), 75, 77 (top), 78 (top), 82, 83 (all three), 85 (bottom), 86 (both), 87 (top), 90, 92, 97 (both), 100, 103 (both), 104 (both), 105 (top), 107 (left), 110, 112/13, 114, 115, 116-17 (all three), 118 (left), 121 (bottom), 122 (both), 123 (both), 125, 132, 134 (top), 135 (top), 137 (bottom), 145 (top), 165 (both), 172 (both), 173. Front jacket, oval inset; back jacket.
Imperial War Museum: pages 81, 100/101, 106, 107 (right), 108/9, 124/5, 126/7, 128/9, 130, 131 (bottom), 134 (bottom), 139 (bottom), 148 (top), 161 (bottom), 166 (bottom).
MBB: page 183.
Mansell Collection: pages 15 (top right), 25 (top), 45 (top), 66, 93 (top), 105 (bottom).
MARS, Lincs: page 64 (top).
MARS/Bundesarchiv: pages 79, 80 (both).
National Army Museum: pages 4-5, 6, 46, 47 (top).
Maps © Richard Natkiel: pages 17 (bottom), 32 (bottom), 33 (top), 42, 47 (bottom), 61 (bottom), 65, 93 (bottom), 109, 146, 153, 164 (top), 169.
Peter Newark's Western Americana: pages 1, 10 (bottom), 11, 13 (both), 21 (top), 26 (bottom), 28 (top), 36/7, 38/9 (top), 45 (bottom), 60, 76 (top), 76/7, 85 (top), 91 (top), 96, 111 (bottom), 135 (bottom), 136 (bottom), 138, 139 (top right), 144 (top), 149, 155 (both), 171 (both), 175. Front jacket, top left..
Novosti Press Agency: pages 160, 174 (bottom).
Personality Pictures Library, Lincs: page 57.
Schloss Charlottenburg: pages 8/9, 24/5, 52 (top).
Rolf Steinberg: pages 12 (both), 14 (bottom left), 15 (top left & bottom), 35 (top), 39 (bottom), 44, 52 (bottom), 54 (top), 84 (both), 87 (bottom), 88/9, 91 (bottom). Front jacket, top center.
US National Archives: pages 156 (bottom). 161 (top).
West German MOD: pages 7 (middle), 176/7, 178, 179 (both), 180 (bottom), 181, 182 (both).